Karl Marx

AAKAR BOOKS CLASSICS

ON COLONIALISM

Karl Marx
Frederick Engels

On Colonialism
Karl Marx and Frederick Engels

First Aakar Edition 2016
Reprinted 2018

ISBN 978-93-5002-393-8

Published by
AAKAR BOOKS
28 E Pocket IV, Mayur Vihar Phase I
Delhi 110 091
aakarbooks@gmail.com
www.aakarbooks.com

Printed at
Sapra Brothers, Noida

CONTENTS

FROM MARX'S *CAPITAL*

LETTERS

PUBLISHERS' NOTE

In the articles collected in this volume Karl Marx and Frederick Engels deal with the history of colonialism, provide a strictly scientific, Marxist analysis of the economic causes behind the predatory colonial policy of the capitalist states, lay bare the links between colonialism and capitalism and expose the monstrous exploitation of the colonial peoples by Great Britain, France and other capitalist states. In articles on the national-liberation movement of the oppressed peoples they show the great historic significance of this movement and its prospects.

Most of these articles were written in the 1850s when mighty popular anti-colonialist movements developed in Asia.

In 1853 Marx wrote a series of articles on India for the progressive American newspaper *New-York Daily Tribune*.

Tearing the mask off "the profound hypocrisy and inherent barbarism of bourgeois civilisation", Marx showed in these articles that at all its stages British policy towards India was determined exclusively by the mercenary interests of the British ruling classes. "The British Rule in India", "The Government of India" and other articles give a stunning picture of how the colonialists oppressed and ruined the Indian people. "There cannot remain any doubt but that the misery inflicted by the British on Hindustan," Marx pointed out, "is of an infinitely more intensive kind than all Hindustan had to suffer before."

While dragging "peoples through blood and dirt, through misery and degradation", Marx wrote, the British bourgeoisie was, at the same time, forced to sow the seeds of capitalist industry in India. But "all the English bourgeoisie may be forced to do will neither emancipate nor materially mend the social condition of the mass of the people, depending not only on the development of the productive powers, but on their appropriation by the people". And he drew the conclusion that the only thing that could lead to the "regeneration of that great and interesting country" was its liberation from British oppression.

When a national revolt broke out in India against British rule in 1857, Marx and Engels followed the freedom struggle of the Indians with close attention and warm understanding. In a series of articles contributed to the *New-York Daily Tribune* they analysed the course of the uprising and showed its causes, its nation-wide character and its link with "a general disaffection exhibited against English supremacy on the part of the great Asiatic nations". Some of these articles are to be found in this volume.

Many articles are on China. Beginning with the first Opium War of 1839-42, British troops as well as those of France and the United States of America attacked China time and again with the purpose of enslaving her and turning her into a colony. "The British Quarrel with China", "English Ferocity in China", "The Opium Trade" and other articles were written by Marx when in 1856 the British started the second Opium War against China. The British merchant-smugglers, who grew rich from the criminal opium trade, and the avaricious British industrialists, for whom the sale of their goods in the vast Chinese market held out the promise of fabulous profits, were the capitalist oligarchy for the sake of whose interests British troops killed, looted and horribly tortured the peaceful population of China in 1839-42, 1856-58 and 1860. Marx and Engels showed in their articles that already then the foreign invaders were meeting with strong resistance from the Chinese people. The war fought by the Chinese against British invaders, Engels wrote, was "a war *pro aris et focis*, a popular war for the maintenance of Chinese nationality".

In his "Revolution in China and in Europe" Marx gave currency to the idea of a link between the revolutionary movement in Europe and the national liberation movement of the Asian peoples, an idea that Lenin subsequently used as the foundation for his theory on the alliance of the working class fighting for socialism in the capitalist countries with the working masses of the colonial and semi-colonial East.

A number of articles in the collection are devoted to Ireland. They show how centuries of British colonial rule reduced Ireland to extreme poverty and ruin. Marx and Engels ardently sympathised with and actively supported the Irish people's heroic struggle against British domination.

Also of special interest are articles about Algeria under the yoke of French colonialism. One article deals with the history of Afghanistan and her struggle against British armed forces, which repeatedly tried to destroy the independence of that small country but were invariably repelled by the Afghan people.

Chapters from Vols. I and III of Marx's *Capital*, in which he reviews colonialism, have been included in this book.

The concluding section contains letters written by Marx and Engels, in which they analyse many questions—timely also in our day—connected with the national liberation movement of the colonial and semi-colonial peoples.

History has fully borne out the forecast of Marx, Engels and Lenin that the downfall of the colonial system was inevitable. The socialist revolution in Russia and the world socialist system that emerged after the Second World War have given tremendous impetus to the national liberation movement in the colonies and semi-colonies. Conspicuous successes have been scored within a short period by the peoples of Asia, Africa and Latin America, who have embarked on a heroic struggle for freedom and independence. The majority of the colonial peoples have shaken off the chains of colonial slavery, formed independent states and taken the road of national rejuvenation and the eradication of the backwardness and poverty forced on them by colonial exploitation. A growing number of peoples, who have liberated themselves from the colonial yoke, are beginning to build socialist social relations.

The imperialist states, above all the United States of America, persist in their efforts to retard the development of liberated countries and bring their peoples back under the yoke of colonial dependence. For many years the United States waged war against the Vietnamese people. In the Middle East, encouraged by American imperialism and equipped with American weapons, the Israeli militarists, refusing to comply with the UN resolution requiring Israel to withdraw all troops from captured Arab territories, organise repeated attacks against the Arab states. The U.S. imperialists are waging a relentless battle against all progressive movements and support all the unpopular reactionary regimes in Latin America. The British imperialists organise inhuman reprisals against the Irish freedom fighters in Northern Ireland, and support the racist regimes in Southern Africa that have enslaved the indigenous population of that region and have deprived it of human rights.

But the rebuff to imperialist aggression is everywhere growing increasingly powerful, and there is no question that all the attempts of imperialism to turn the tide of history are bound to fail. The national liberation movement receives all-round support from the world socialist system and, above all, from the Soviet Union. As noted at the 24th Congress of the C.P.S.U. held in March-April 1971, "imperialism is being subjected to ever greater pressure by the forces which have sprung from the national liberation struggle. The main thing is that the struggle for national liberation in many countries has in practical terms begun to grow into a struggle against exploitative relations, both feudal and capitalist. Today, there are already quite a few countries which have taken the non-capitalist way of development, that is, the path of building a socialist society in the long term."

Karl Marx and Frederick Engels

MANIFESTO OF THE COMMUNIST PARTY

(Excerpts)

The discovery of America, the rounding of the Cape, opened up fresh ground for the rising bourgeoisie. The East-Indian and Chinese markets, the colonisation of America, trade with the colonies, the increase in the means of exchange and in commodities generally, gave to commerce, to navigation, to industry, an impulse never before known, and thereby, to the revolutionary element in the tottering feudal society, a rapid development.

The feudal system of industry, under which industrial production was monopolised by closed guilds, now no longer sufficed for the growing wants of the new markets. The manufacturing system took its place. The guild-masters were pushed on one side by the manufacturing middle class; division of labour between the different corporate guilds vanished in the face of division of labour in each single workshop.

Meantime the markets kept ever growing, the demand ever rising. Even manufacture no longer sufficed. Thereupon, steam and machinery revolutionised industrial production. The place of manufacture was taken by the giant, Modern Industry, the place of the industrial middle class, by industrial millionaires, the leaders of whole industrial armies, the modern bourgeois.

Modern industry has established the world market, for which the discovery of America paved the way. This market has given an immense development to commerce, to navigation, to communication by land. This development has, in its turn, reacted on the extension of industry;

and in proportion as industry, commerce, navigation, railways extended, in the same proportion the bourgeoisie developed, increased its capital, and pushed into the background every class handed down from the Middle Ages....

The need of a constantly expanding market for its products chases the bourgeoisie over the whole surface of the globe. It must nestle everywhere, settle everywhere, establish connexions everywhere.

The bourgeoisie has through its exploitation of the world market given a cosmopolitan character to production and consumption in every country. To the great chagrin of Reactionists, it has drawn from under the feet of industry the national ground on which it stood. All old-established national industries have been destroyed or are daily being destroyed. They are dislodged by new industries, whose introduction becomes a life and death question for all civilised nations, by industries that no longer work up indigenous raw material, but raw material drawn from the remotest zones; industries whose products are consumed, not only at home, but in every quarter of the globe. In place of the old wants, satisfied by the productions of the country, we find new wants, requiring for their satisfaction the products of distant lands and climes. In place of the old local and national seclusion and self-sufficiency, we have intercourse in every direction, universal interdependence of nations. And as in material, so also in intellectual production. The intellectual creations of individual nations become common property. National one-sidedness and narrow-mindedness become more and more impossible, and from the numerous national and local literatures, there arises a world literature.

The bourgeoisie, by the rapid improvement of all instruments of production, by the immensely facilitated means of communication, draws all, even the most barbarian, nations into civilisation. The cheap prices of its commodities are the heavy artillery with which it batters down all Chinese walls, with which it forces the barbarians' intensely obstinate hatred of foreigners to capitulate. It compels all nations, on pain of extinction, to adopt the bourgeois mode of production; it compels them to introduce what it calls civilisation into their midst, *i.e.*, to become bourgeois themselves. In one word, it creates a world after its own image.

The bourgeoisie has subjected the country to the rule of the towns. It has created enormous cities, has greatly increased the urban population as compared with the rural, and has thus rescued a considerable part of the population from the idiocy of rural life. Just as it has made the country dependent on the towns, so it has made barbarian and semi-barbarian countries dependent on the civilised ones, nations of peasants on nations of bourgeois, the East on the West....

Written in December
1847-January 1848

First published in German
in pamphlet form in
February 1848, London

Printed according to the
English translation put out
by F. Engels in London in
1888

ARTICLES WRITTEN IN 1850-1888

Karl Marx and Frederick Engels

FIRST INTERNATIONAL REVIEW
(Excerpt)

In conclusion, another typical oddity from China, brought by Gützlaff, the well-known German missionary. The slowly but surely increasing over-population in that country had long made local social conditions very oppressive for the big majority of the nation. Then came the English and won free trade for themselves by dint of force in five ports. Thousands of British and American ships sailed to China, and soon the country was flooded with cheap British and American machine-made goods. Chinese industry, reposing as it did on hand labour, succumbed to the competition of the machine. The imperturbable Celestial Empire went through a social crisis. The taxes ceased coming in, the State was on the brink of bankruptcy, the population was pauperized *en masse*, revolts broke out, the people went out of hand, mishandled and killed the Emperor's mandarins and the Fohist bonzes. The country is on the verge of perdition, and is even threatened by a violent revolution. But what is still worse, people have appeared among the rebellious plebs who point to the poverty of some and the wealth of others, who demand a different distribution of property—and even the complete abolition of private property. When Herr Gützlaff returned among civilized people and Europeans after an absence of twenty years he heard talk of socialism and asked what it was. After he was given an explanation he exclaimed with alarm: "Is there anywhere that I can escape that pernicious teaching? The very same thing has been preached for some time by many people of the mob in China!"

Chinese socialism may stand in the same relation to the European variety as Chinese philosophy stands to the Hegelian. Yet it is a gratifying fact that the bales of calico of the English bourgeoisie have in eight years brought the oldest and most imperturbable empire on earth to the threshold of a social upheaval, one that will in any case hold most significant consequences for civilisation. When in their imminent flight across Asia our European reactionaries will ultimately arrive at the Wall of China, at the gates that lead to the stronghold of arch-reaction and arch-conservatism, who knows if they will not find there the inscription:

République Chinoise,
Liberté, Egalité, Fraternité.

London, January 31, 1850

Published in the *Neue Rheinische Zeitung. Politisch-ökonomische Revue*, No. 2, 1850

Printed according to the text of the magazine

Translated from the German

Karl Marx

REVOLUTION IN CHINA AND IN EUROPE[1]

A most profound yet fantastic speculator on the principles which govern the movements of Humanity,[2] was wont to extol as one of the ruling secrets of nature, what he called the law of the contact of extremes. The homely proverb that "extremes meet" was, in his view, a grand and potent truth in every sphere of life; an axiom with which the philosopher could as little dispense as the astronomer with the laws of Kepler or the great discovery of Newton.

Whether the "contact of extremes" be such a universal principle or not, a striking illustration of it may be seen in the effect the Chinese revolution[3] seems likely to exercise upon the civilized world. It may seem a very strange, and a very paradoxical assertion that the next uprising of the people of Europe, and their next movement for republican freedom and economy of government, may depend more probably on what is now passing in the Celestial Empire,—the very opposite of Europe,—than on any other political cause that now exists,—more even than on the menaces of Russia and the consequent likelihood of a general European war. But yet it is no paradox, as all may understand by attentively considering the circumstances of the case.

Whatever be the social causes, and whatever religious, dynastic, or national shape they may assume, that have brought about the chronic rebellions subsisting in China for about ten years past, and now gathered together in one formidable revolution, the occasion of this outbreak has unquestionably been afforded by the English cannon forcing upon China that soporific drug called opium.[4] Before the

British arms the authority of the Manchu dynasty[5] fell to pieces; the superstitious faith in the eternity of the Celestial Empire broke down; the barbarous and hermetic isolation from the civilized world was infringed; and an opening was made for that intercourse which has since proceeded so rapidly under the golden attractions of California and Australia. At the same time the silver coin of the Empire, its lifeblood, began to be drained away to the British East Indies.

Up to 1830, the balance of trade being continually in favour of the Chinese, there existed an uninterrupted importation of silver from India, Britain and the United States into China. Since 1833, and especially since 1840, the export of silver from China to India has become almost exhausting for the Celestial Empire. Hence the strong decrees of the Emperor against the opium trade, responded to by still stronger resistance to his measures. Besides this immediate economical consequence, the bribery connected with opium smuggling has entirely demoralized the Chinese state officers in the southern provinces. Just as the Emperor was wont to be considered the father of all China, so his officers were looked upon as sustaining the paternal relation to their respective districts. But this patriarchal authority, the only moral link embracing the vast machinery of the State, has gradually been corroded by the corruption of those officers, who have made great gains by conniving at opium smuggling. This has occurred principally in the same southern provinces where the rebellion commenced. It is almost needless to observe that, in the same measure in which opium has obtained the sovereignty over the Chinese, the Emperor and his staff of pedantic mandarins have become dispossessed of their own sovereignty. It would seem as though history had first to make this whole people drunk before it could rouse them out of their hereditary stupidity.

Though scarcely existing in former times, the import of English cottons, and to a small extent of English woollens, has rapidly risen since 1833, the epoch when the monopoly of trade with China was transferred from the East India Company[6] to private commerce, and on a much greater scale since 1840, the epoch when other nations, and especially our own, also obtained a share in the Chinese trade.

This introduction of foreign manufactures has had a similar effect on the native industry to that which it formerly had on Asia Minor, Persia and India. In China the spinners and weavers have suffered greatly under this foreign competition, and the community has become unsettled in proportion.

The tribute to be paid to England after the unfortunate war of 1840, the great unproductive consumption of opium, the drain of the precious metals by this trade, the destructive influence of foreign competition on native manufactures, the demoralized condition of the public administration, produced two things: the old taxation became more burdensome and harassing, and new taxation was added to the old. Thus in a decree of the Emperor,* dated Peking, Jan. 5, 1853, we find orders given to the viceroys and governors of the southern provinces of Wuchang and Hanyang to remit and defer the payment of taxes, and especially not in any case to exact more than the regular amount; for otherwise, says the decree, "how will the poor people be able to bear it?"

> "And thus, perhaps," continues the Emperor, "will my people, in a period of general hardship and distress, be exempted from the evils of being pursued and worried by the tax-gatherer."

Such language as this, and such concessions we remember to have heard from Austria, the China of Germany, in 1848.

All these dissolving agencies acting together on the finances, the morals, the industry, and political structure of China, received their full development under the English cannon in 1840, which broke down the authority of the Emperor, and forced the Celestial Empire into contact with the terrestrial world. Complete isolation was the prime condition of the preservation of old China. That isolation having come to a violent end by the medium of England, dissolution must follow as surely as that of any mummy carefully preserved in a hermetically sealed coffin, whenever it is brought into contact with the open air. Now, England having brought about the revolution of China, the question is how that revolution will in time react

---

* Hsien Feng.—*Ed.*

on England, and through England on Europe. This question is not difficult of solution.

The attention of our readers has often been called to the unparalleled growth of British manufactures since 1850. Amid the most surprising prosperity, it has not been difficult to point out the clear symptoms of an approaching industrial crisis. Notwithstanding California and Australia,[7] notwithstanding the immense and unprecedented emigration, there must ever, without any particular accident, in due time arrive a moment when the extension of the markets is unable to keep pace with the extension of British manufactures, and this disproportion must bring about a new crisis with the same certainty as it has done in the past. But, if one of the great markets suddenly becomes contracted, the arrival of the crisis is necessarily accelerated thereby. Now, the Chinese rebellion must, for the time being, have precisely this effect upon England. The necessity for opening new markets, or for extending the old ones, was one of the principal causes of the reduction of the British tea-duties, as, with an increased importation of tea, an increased exportation of manufactures to China was expected to take place. Now, the value of the annual exports from the United Kingdom to China amounted, before the repeal in 1833 of the trading monopoly possessed by the East India Company, to only £ 600,000; in 1836, it reached the sum of £ 1,326,388; in 1845, it had risen to £ 2,394,827; in 1852, it amounted to about £ 3,000,000. The quantity of tea imported from China did not exceed, in 1793, 16,167,331 lbs.; but in 1845, it amounted to 50,714,657 lbs.; in 1846, to 57,584-561 lbs.; it is now above 60,000,000 lbs.

The tea crop of the last season will not prove short, as shown already by the export lists from Shanghai, of 2,000,000 lbs. above the preceding year. This excess is to be accounted for by two circumstances. On one hand, the state of the market at the close of 1851 was much depressed, and the large surplus stock left has been thrown into the export of 1852. On the other hand, the recent accounts of the altered British legislation with regard to imports of tea, reaching China, have brought forward all the available teas to a ready market, at greatly enhanced prices. But with respect to the coming crop, the case stands very differently.

This is shown by the following extracts from the correspondence of a large tea-firm in London:

"In Shanghai the terror is extreme. Gold has advanced upward of 25 per cent, *being eagerly sought for hoarding*; silver has so far disappeared that *none could be obtained* to pay the China dues on the British vessels requiring port clearance; and in consequence of which Mr. Alcock has consented to become responsible to the Chinese authorities for the payment of these dues, on receipt of East India Company's bills, or other approved securities. *The scarcity of the precious metals* is one of the most unfavourable features, when viewed in reference to the immediate future of commerce, as this abstraction occurs precisely at that period when their use is most needed, to enable the tea and silk buyers to go into the interior and effect their purchases, for which a *large portion of bullion is paid in advance, to enable the producers to carry on their operations*.... At this period of the year it is usual to begin making arrangements for the new teas, whereas at present nothing is talked of but the means of protecting person and property, all transactions being at a stand.... If the means are not applied to secure the leaves in April and May, the early crop, which includes all the finer descriptions, both of black and green teas, will be as much lost as unreaped wheat at Christmas."

Now the means for securing the tea leaves, will certainly not be given by the English, American or French squadrons stationed in the Chinese seas, but these may easily, by their interference, produce such complications, as to cut off all transactions between the tea-producing interior and the tea-exporting sea ports. Thus, for the present crop, a rise in the prices must be expected—speculation has already commenced in London—and for the crop to come a large deficit is as good as certain. Nor is this all. The Chinese, ready though they may be, as are all people in periods of revolutionary convulsion, to sell off to the foreigner all the bulky commodities they have on hand, will, as the Orientals are used to do in the apprehension of great changes, set to hoarding, not taking much in return for their tea and silk, except hard money. England has accordingly to expect a rise in the price of one of her chief articles of consumption, a drain of bullion, and a great contraction of an important market for her cotton and woollen goods. Even *The Economist*,[8] that optimist conjuror of all things menacing the tranquil minds of the mercantile community, is compelled to use language like this:

"We must not flatter ourselves with finding as extensive a market for our exports to China as hitherto.... It is more probable that our export trade to China should suffer, and that there should be a diminished demand for the produce of Manchester and Glasgow."

It must not be forgotten that rise in the price of so indispensable an article as tea, and the contraction of so important a market as China, will coincide with a deficient harvest in Western Europe, and, therefore, with rising prices of meat, corn, and all other agricultural produce. Hence contracted markets for manufactures, because every rise in the prices of the first necessaries of life is counterbalanced, at home and abroad, by a corresponding reduction in the demand for manufactures. From every part of Great Britain complaints have been received on the backward state of most of the crops. *The Economist* says on this subject:

"In the South of England not only will there be left much land unsown, until too late for a crop of any sort, but much of the sown land will prove to be foul, or otherwise in a bad state for corn-growing. On the wet or poor soils destined for wheat, signs that mischief is going on are apparent. The time for planting mangel-wurzel may now be said to have passed away, and very little has been planted, while the time for preparing land for the turnip is rapidly going by, without any adequate preparation for this important crop having been accomplished.... Oat-sowing has been much interfered with by the snow and rain. Few oats were sown early, and late sown oats seldom produce a large crop.... In many districts losses among the breeding flocks have been considerable."

The price of other farm-produce than corn is from 20 to 30, and even 50 per cent higher than last year. On the Continent, corn has risen comparatively more than in England. Rye has risen in Belgium and Holland full 100 per cent. Wheat and other grains are following suit.

Under these circumstances, as the greater part of the regular commercial circle has already been run through by British trade, it may safely be augured that the Chinese revolution will throw the spark into the overloaded mine of the present industrial system and cause the explosion of the long-prepared general crisis, which, spreading abroad, will be closely followed by political revolutions on the Continent. It would be a curious spectacle, that of China sending disorder into the Western World while the Western powers, by English, French and American war-steamers, are conveying "order" to Shanghai, Nanking, and the mouths of the Great Canal. Do these order-mongering powers, which would attempt to support the wavering Manchu dynasty, forget that the hatred against foreigners and their exclusion from the Empire, once the mere result of China's geographical and ethnographical situation, have become a political system only since the conquest of the country by the race of the Manchu Tartars? There can be no doubt that the turbulent dissensions among the European nations who, at the later end of the 17th century, rivalled each other in the trade with China, lent a mighty aid to the exclusive policy adopted by the Manchus. But more than this was done by the fear of the new dynasty, lest the foreigners might favour the discontent existing among a large proportion of the Chinese during the first half century or thereabouts of their subjection to the Tartars. From these considerations, foreigners were then prohibited from all communication with the Chinese, except through Canton, a town at a great distance from Peking and the tea districts, and their commerce restricted to intercourse with the Hong merchants, licensed by the Government expressly for the foreign trade, in order to keep the rest of its subjects from all connection with the odious strangers. In any case an interference on the part of the Western governments at this time can only serve to render the revolution more violent, and protract the stagnation of trade.

At the same time it is to be observed with regard to India, that the British Government of that country depends for full one-seventh of its revenue on the sale of opium to the Chinese, while a considerable proportion of the Indian demand for British manufactures depends on the production of that opium in India. The Chinese, it is true, are no more likely to renounce the use of opium than are the Germans to forswear tobacco. But as the new Emperor is understood to be favourable to the culture of the poppy and the preparation of opium in China itself, it is evident that a death-blow is very likely to be struck at once at the business of opium-raising in India, the Indian revenue, and the commercial resources of Hindustan. Though this blow would not immediately be felt by the interests concerned, it would operate effectually in due time, and would come in to intensify and prolong the universal financial crisis whose horoscope we have cast above.

Since the commencement of the 18th century there has been no serious revolution in Europe which had not been preceded by a commercial and financial crisis. This applies no less to the revolution of 1789 than to that of 1848. It is true, not only that we every day behold more threatening symptoms of conflict between the ruling powers and their subjects, between the State and society, between the various classes; but also the conflict of the existing powers among each other gradually reaching that height where the sword must be drawn, and the *ultima ratio* of princes be recurred to. In the European capitals, every day brings dispatches big with universal war, vanishing under the dispatches of the following day, bearing the assurance of peace for a week or so. We may be sure, nevertheless, that to whatever height the conflict between the European powers may rise, however threatening the aspect of the diplomatic horizon may appear, whatever movements may be attempted by some enthusiastic fraction in this or that country, the rage of princes and the fury of the people are alike enervated by the breath of prosperity. Neither wars nor revolutions are likely to pull Europe by the ears, unless in consequence of a general commercial and industrial crisis, the signal of which has, as usual, to be given by England, the representative of European industry in the market of the world.

It is unnecessary to dwell on the political consequences such a crisis must produce in these times, with the unprecedented extension of factories in England, with the utter dissolution of her official parties, with the whole State machinery of France transformed into one immense swindling and stock-jobbing concern, with Austria on the eve of bankruptcy, with wrongs everywhere accumulated to be revenged by the people, with the conflicting interests of the reactionary powers themselves, and with the Russian dream of conquest once more revealed to the world.

Written on May 20, 1853

Published in the
New-York Daily Tribune,
No. 3794, June 14, 1853

Printed according to the text of the newspaper

Karl Marx

INDIA[9]

The Charter of the East India Company expires in 1854. Lord John Russell has given notice in the House of Commons, that the Government will be enabled to state, through Sir Charles Wood, their views respecting the future government of India, on the 3d of June. A hint has been thrown out in some ministerial papers, in support of the already credited public rumour, that the Coalition[10] have found the means of reducing even this colossal Indian question to almost Lilliputian dimensions. *The Observer*[11] prepares the mind of the English people to undergo a new disenchantment.

"Much less," we read in that confidential journal of Aberdeen, "than is generally supposed will remain to be done in the new organization for the government of our Eastern Empire."

Much less even than is supposed, will have to be done by my lords Russell and Aberdeen.

The leading features of the proposed change appear to consist in two very small items. Firstly, the Board of Directors[12] will be "refreshed" by some additional members, appointed directly by the Crown, and even this new blood will be infused "sparingly at first." The cure of the old directorial system is thus meant to be applied, so that the portion of blood now infused with "great caution" will have ample time to come to a standstill before another second infusion will be proceeded upon. Secondly, the union of Judge and of Exciseman in one and the same person, will be put an end to, and the judges shall be educated men. Does it not seem, on hearing such propositions, as if one were transported back into that earliest period of the Middle Ages, when the feudal lords began to be replaced as judges, by lawyers who were required, at any rate, to have a knowledge of reading and writing?

The "Sir Charles Wood" who, as President of the Board of Control,[13] will bring forward this sensible piece of reform, is the same timber who, under the late Whig Administration, displayed such eminent capacities of mind, that the Coalition were at a dreadful loss what to do with him, till they hit upon the idea of making him over to India. Richard the Third offered a kingdom for a horse;—the Coalition offers an ass for a kingdom. Indeed, if the present official idiocy of an oligarchical government be the expression of what England *can* do now, the time of England's ruling the world must have passed away.

On former occasions we have seen that the Coalition had invariably some fitting reason for postponing every, even the smaller measure. Now, with respect to India their postponing propensities *are* supported by the public opinion of two worlds. The people of England and the people of India simultaneously demand the postponement of all the legislation on Indian affairs, until the voice of the natives shall have been heard, the necessary materials collected, the pending inquiries completed. Petitions have already reached Downing St., from the three Presidencies,[14] deprecating precipitate legislation. The Manchester School have formed an "Indian Society,"[15] which they will put immediately into motion, to get up public meetings in the metropolis and throughout the country, for the purpose of opposing any legislation on the subject for this session. Besides, two Parliamentary Committees are now sitting with a view to report respecting the state of affairs in the Indian Government. But this time the Coalition Ministry is inexorable. It will not wait for the publication of any Committee's advice. It wants to legislate instantly and directly for 150 millions of people, and to legislate for 20 years at once. Sir Charles Wood is anxious to establish his claim as the modern Manu. Whence, of a sudden, this precipitate legislative rush of our "cautious" political valetudinarians?

They want to renew the old Indian Charter for a period of 20 years. They avail themselves of the eternal pretext of reform. Why? The English oligarchy have a presentiment of the approaching end of their days of glory, and they have a very justifiable desire to conclude such a treaty with English legislation, that even in the case of England's escaping soon from their weak and rapacious hands, they shall still retain for themselves and their associates the privilege of plundering India for the space of 20 years.

Written on May 24, 1853

Published in the
New-York Daily Tribune,
No. 3790, June 9, 1853

Printed according to the text
of the newspaper

Karl Marx

SIR CHARLES WOOD'S EAST INDIAN REFORMS[16]

The last India Bill of 1783 proved fatal to the Coalition Cabinet of Mr. Fox and Lord North. The new India Bill of 1853 is likely to prove fatal for the Coalition Cabinet of Mr. Gladstone and Lord John Russell. But if the former were thrown overboard, because of their attempt to abolish the Courts of Directors and of Proprietors, the latter are threatened with a similar fate for the opposite reason. On June 3, Sir Charles Wood moved for leave to bring in a bill to provide for the Government of India. Sir Charles commenced by excusing the anomalous length of the speech he was about to deliver, by the "magnitude of the subject," and "the 150,000,000 of souls he had to deal with." For every 30,000,000 of his fellow-subjects, Sir Charles could do no less than sacrifice one hour's breath. But why this precipitate legislation on that "great subject," while you postpone it "for even the most trifling matters?" Because the Charter of the East India Company expires on the 30th April, 1854. But why not pass a temporary continuance bill, reserving to future discussion more permanent legislation? Because it cannot be expected that we shall ever find again "such an opportunity of dealing quietly with this vast and important question"—i.e., of burking it in a Parliamentary way. Besides, we are fully informed on the matter, the Directors of the East India Company express the opinion that it is necessary to legislate in the course of the present session, and the Governor-General of India, Lord Dalhousie, summons the Government by an express letter by all means to conclude our legislation at once. But the most striking argument wherewith Sir Charles justifies his immediate legislation, is that, prepared as he may appear to speak of a world of questions, "not comprised in the bill he proposed to bring in,"

> the "*measure* which he has to submit is, so far as legislation goes, *comprised in a very small compass.*"

After this introduction Sir Charles delivered himself of an apology for the administration of India for the last twenty years. "We must look at India with somewhat of an Indian eye"—which Indian eye seems to have the particular gift of seeing everything bright on the part of England and everything black on the side of India.

> "In India you have a race of people slow of change, bound up by religious prejudices and antiquated customs. There are, in fact, all obstacles to rapid progress." (Perhaps there is a Whig Coalition party in India.)
>
> "The points," said Sir Charles Wood, "upon which the greatest stress has been laid, and which are the heads of the complaints contained in the petitions presented to the Committee, relate to the administration of justice, the want of public works, and the tenure of land."

With regard to the public works the Government *intends* to undertake some of "the greatest magnitude and importance." With regard to the tenure of lands, Sir Charles proves very successfully that its three existing forms—the *Zemindari*, the *Ryotwari*,[17] and the *Village* systems*—are only so many forms of fiscal *exploitation* in the hands of the Company, none of which could well be made general, nor deserved to be made so. An idea of establishing another form, of an altogether opposite character, does not in the least preoccupy the mind of Sir Charles.

> "With regard to the *administration of justice*," continues he, "the complaints relate principally to the inconvenience arising from the technicalities of English law, to the alleged incompetency of English judges, and to the corruption of the native officers and judges."

And now, in order to prove the hard labour of providing for the administration of justice in India, Sir Charles relates that already, as early as 1833, a Law Commission

---

* See this collection, pp. 39-41.—*Ed.*

was appointed in India. But in what manner did this Commission act, according to Sir Charles Wood's own testimony? The first and last result of the labours of that Commission was a *penal code*, prepared under the auspices of Mr. Macaulay. This code was sent to the various local authorities in India, which sent it back to Calcutta, from which it was sent to England, to be again returned from England to India. In India, Mr. Macaulay having been replaced as legislative counsel by Mr. Bethune, the code was totally altered, and on this plea the Governor-General,* not being then of opinion "that delay is a source of weakness and danger," sent it back to England, and from England it was returned to the Governor-General, with authority to pass the code in whatever shape he thought best. But now, Mr. Bethune having died, the Governor-General thought best to submit the code to a third English lawyer, and to a lawyer who knew nothing about the habits and customs of the Hindus, reserving himself the right of afterward rejecting a code concocted by wholly incompetent authority. Such have been the adventures of that yet unborn code. As to the technical absurdities of the law in India, Sir Charles takes his stand on the no less absurd technicalities of the English law procedure itself; but while affirming the perfect incorruptibilty of the English judges in India, he nevertheless is ready to sacrifice them by an alteration in the manner of nominating them. The general progress of India is demonstrated by a comparison of the present state of Delhi with that under the invasion of Kuli Khan. The salt-tax is justified by the arguments of the most renowned political economists, all of whom have advised taxation to be laid on some article of first necessity. But Sir Charles does not add what those same economists would have said, on finding that in the two years from 1849-50, and 1851-52, there had been a decrease in the consumption of salt, of 60,000 tuns, a loss of revenue to the amount of £415,000, the total salt revenue amounting to £2,000,000.

The measures proposed by Sir Charles, and "comprised in a very small compass," are:

---

* Dalhousie.—*Ed.*

1. The Court of Directors to consist of eighteen instead of twenty-four members, twelve to be elected by the Proprietors, and six by the Crown.

2. The revenue of Directors to be raised from £ 300 to £ 500 a year, the Chairman to receive £ 1,000.

3. All the ordinary appointments in the civil service, and all the scientific in the military service of India, to be thrown open to public competition, leaving to the Directors the nomination to the Cadetships in the Cavalry-of-the-Line.

4. The Governor-Generalship to be separated from the Governorship of Bengal, and power to be given to the Supreme Government to constitute a new Presidency in the districts on the Indus.

5. And lastly, the whole of this measure only to continue until the Parliament shall provide otherwise.

The speech and measure of Sir Charles Wood was subjected to a very strong and satirical criticism by Mr. Bright, whose picture of India ruined by the fiscal exertions of the Company and Government did not, of course, receive the supplement of India ruined by Manchester and Free Trade. As to last night's speech of an old East-Indiaman, Sir J. Hogg, Director or ex-Director of the Company, I really suspect that I have met with it already in 1701, 1730, 1743, 1769, 1772, 1781, 1783, 1784, 1793, 1813, etc., and am induced, by way of answer to his directorial panegyric, to quote merely a few facts from the annual Indian accounts published, I believe, under his own superintendence.

Total Net Revenues of India:

1849-50	£20,275,831	Loss of revenue within three years, £348,792
1850-51	20,249,932	
1851-52	19,927,039	

Total Charges:

1849-50	£16,687,382	Increase of expenditure within three years, £1,214,284
1850-51	17,170,707	
1851-52	17,901,666	

Land-Tax:

Bengal oscillated in last four years from	£3,500,000 to £3,560,000
North West oscillated in last four years from	£4,870,000 to £4,900,000
Madras oscillated in last four years from	£3,640,000 to £3,470,000
Bombay oscillated in last four years from	£2,240,000 to £2,300,000

	Gross Revenue in 1851-52	Expenditure On Public Works in 1851-52
Bengal	£10,000,000	£87,800
Madras	5,000,000	20,000
Bombay	4,800,000	58,500
Total	£19,800,000	£166 300

Out of £ 19,800,000 not £ 166,300 have been expended on roads, canals, bridges and other works of public necessity.

Written on June 7, 1853

Published in the *New-York Daily Tribune*, No. 3801, June 22, 1853

Printed according to the text of the newspaper

Karl Marx

THE BRITISH RULE IN INDIA

London, Friday, June 10, 1853

Telegraphic dispatches from Vienna announce that the pacific solution of the Turkish, Sardinian and Swiss questions is regarded there as a certainty.

Last night the debate on India was continued in the House of Commons in the usual dull manner. Mr. Blackett charged statements of Sir Charles Wood and Sir J. Hogg with bearing the stamp of optimist falsehood. A lot of Ministerial and Directorial advocates rebuked the charge as well as they could, and the inevitable Mr. Hume summed up by calling on Ministers to withdraw their bill. Debate adjourned.

Hindustan is an Italy of Asiatic dimensions, the Himalayas for the Alps, the Plains of Bengal for the Plains of Lombardy, the Deccan for the Apennines, and the Isle of Ceylon for the Island of Sicily. The same rich variety in the products of the soil, and the same dismemberment in the political configuration. Just as Italy has, from time to time, been compressed by the conqueror's sword into different national masses, so do we find Hindustan, when not under the pressure of the Mohammedan, or the Mogul, or the Briton, dissolved into as many independent and conflicting States as it numbered towns, or even villages. Yet, in a social point of view, Hindustan is not the Italy, but the Ireland of the East. And this strange combination of Italy and of Ireland, of a world of voluptuousness and of a world of woes, is anticipated in the ancient traditions of the religion of Hindustan. That religion is at once a religion of sensualist exuberance, and a religion of self-torturing asceticism; a religion of the Lingam and of the Juggernaut;[18] the religion of the Monk, and of the Bayadere.

I share not the opinion of those who believe in a golden age of Hindustan, without recurring, however, like Sir Charles Wood, for the confirmation of my view, to the authority of Kuli Khan.* But take, for example, the times of Aurungzeb; or the epoch, when the Mogul appeared in the North, and the Portuguese in the South; or the age of Mohammedan invasion, and of the Heptarchy in Southern India;[19] or, if you will, go still more back to antiquity, take the mythological chronology of the Brahmin himself,[20] who places the commencement of Indian misery in an epoch even more remote than the Christian creation of the world.

There cannot, however, remain any doubt but that the misery inflicted by the British on Hindustan is of an essentially different and infinitely more intensive kind than all Hindustan had to suffer before. I do not allude to European despotism, planted upon Asiatic despotism, by the British East India Company, forming a more monstrous combination than any of the divine monsters startling us in the Temple of Salsette.[21] This is no distinctive feature of British colonial rule, but only an imitation of the Dutch, and so much so that in order to characterize the working of the British East India Company, it is sufficient to literally repeat what Sir Stamford Raffles, the *English* Governor of Java, said of the old Dutch East India Company.

"The Dutch Company, actuated solely by the spirit of gain, and viewing their subjects with less regard or consideration than a West India planter formerly viewed a gang upon his estate, because the latter had paid the purchase money of human property, which the other had not, employed all the existing machinery of despotism to squeeze from the people their utmost mite of contribution, the last dregs of their labour, and thus aggravated the evils of a capricious and semi-barbarous Government, by working it with all the practised ingenuity of politicians, and all the monopolizing selfishness of traders."

All the civil wars, invasions, revolutions, conquests, famines, strangely complex, rapid and destructive as the succes-

---

* See this collection, p. 32.—*Ed.*

sive action in Hindustan may appear, did not go deeper than its surface. England had broken down the entire framework of Indian society, without any symptoms of reconstitution yet appearing. This loss of his old world, with no gain of a new one, imparts a particular kind of melancholy to the present misery of the Hindu, and separates Hindustan, ruled by Britain, from all its ancient traditions, and from the whole of its past history.

There have been in Asia, generally, from immemorial times, but three departments of Government: that of Finance, or the plunder of the interior; that of War, or the plunder of the exterior; and finally, the department of Public Works. Climate and territorial conditions, especially the vast tracts of desert, extending from the Sahara, through Arabia, Persia, India and Tartary, to the most elevated Asiatic highlands, constituted artificial irrigation by canals and waterworks the basis of Oriental agriculture. As in Egypt and India, inundations are used for fertilizing the soil of Mesopotamia, Persia, etc.; advantage is taken of a high level for feeding irrigative canals. This prime necessity of an economical and common use of water, which, in the Occident, drove private enterprise to voluntary association, as in Flanders and Italy, necessitated, in the Orient where civilization was too low and the territorial extent too vast to call into life voluntary association, the interference of the centralizing power of Government. Hence an economical function devolved upon all Asiatic Governments, the function of providing public works. This artificial fertilization of the soil, dependent on a Central Government, and immediately decaying with the neglect of irrigation and drainage, explains the otherwise strange fact that we now find whole territories barren and desert that were once brilliantly cultivated, as Palmyra, Petra, the ruins in Yemen, and large provinces of Egypt, Persia and Hindustan; it also explains how a single war of devastation has been able to depopulate a country for centuries, and to strip it of all its civilization.

Now, the British in East India accepted from their predecessors the departments of finance and of war, but they have neglected entirely that of public works. Hence the deterioration of an agriculture which is not capable of being conducted on the British principle of free competition, of *laissez-faire* and *laissez-aller*.[22] But in Asiatic empires we are quite accustomed to see agriculture deteriorating under one government and reviving again under some other government. There the harvests correspond to good or bad governments, as they change in Europe with good or bad seasons. Thus the oppression and neglect of agriculture, bad as it is, could not be looked upon as the final blow dealt to Indian society by the British intruder, had it not been attended by a circumstance of quite different importance, a novelty in the annals of the whole Asiatic world. However changing the political aspect of India's past must appear, its social condition has remained unaltered since its remotest antiquity, until the first decennium of the 19th century. The hand-loom and the spinning-wheel, producing their regular myriads of spinners and weavers, were the pivots of the structure of that society. From immemorial times, Europe received the admirable textures of Indian labour, sending in return for them her precious metals, and furnishing thereby his material to the goldsmith, that indispensable member of Indian society, whose love of finery is so great that even the lowest class, those who go about nearly naked, have commonly a pair of golden earrings and a gold ornament of some kind hung round their necks. Rings on the fingers and toes have also been common. Women as well as children frequently wore massive bracelets and anklets of gold or silver, and statuettes of divinities in gold and silver were met with in the households. It was the British intruder who broke up the Indian hand-loom and destroyed the spinning-wheel. England began with driving the Indian cottons from the European market; it then introduced twist into Hindustan and in the end inundated the very mother country of cotton with cottons. From 1818 to 1836 the export of twist from Great Britain to India rose in the proportion of 1 to 5,200. In 1824 the export of British muslins to India hardly amounted to 1,000,000 yards, while in 1837 it surpassed 64,000,000 yards. But at the same time the population of Dacca decreased from 150,000 inhabitants to 20,000. This decline of Indian towns celebrated for their fabrics was by no means the worst consequence. British steam and science uprooted, over the whole surface of Hindustan, the union between agriculture and manufacturing industry.

These two circumstances—the Hindu, on the one hand, leaving, like all Oriental peoples, to the Central Government the care of the great public works, the prime condition of his agriculture and commerce, dispersed, on the other hand, over the surface of the country, and agglomerated in small centres by the domestic union of agricultural and manufacturing pursuits—these two circumstances had brought about, since the remotest times, a social system of particular features—the so-called *village system*, which gave to each of these small unions their independent organization and distinct life. The peculiar character of this system may be judged from the following description, contained in an old official report of the British House of Commons on Indian affairs:

"A village, geographically considered, is a tract of country comprising some hundred or thousand acres of arable and waste lands; politically viewed it resembles a corporation or township. Its proper establishment of officers and servants consists of the following descriptions: The *potail*, or head inhabitant, who has generally the superintendence of the affairs of the village, settles the disputes of the inhabitants, attends to the police, and performs the duty of collecting the revenue within his village, a duty which his personal influence and minute acquaintance with the situation and concerns of the people render him the best qualified for this charge. The *kurnum* keeps the accounts of cultivation, and registers everything connected with it. The *tallier* and the *totie*, the duty of the former of which consists in gaining information of crimes and offences, and in escorting and protecting persons travelling from one village to another; the province of the latter appearing to be more immediately confined to the village, consisting, among other duties, in guarding the crops and assisting in measuring them. The *boundaryman*, who preserves the limits of the village, or gives evidence respecting them in cases of dispute. The superintendent of tanks and watercourses distributes the water for the purposes of agriculture. The Brahmin, who performs the village worship. The schoolmaster, who is seen teaching the children in a village to read and write in the sand. The calendar-Brahmin, or astrologer, etc. These officers and servants generally constitute the establishment of a village; but in some parts of the country it is of less extent; some of the duties and functions above described being united in the same person; in others it exceeds the above-named number of individuals. Under this simple form of municipal government, the inhabitants of the country have lived from time immemorial. The boundaries of the villages have been but seldom altered; and though the villages themselves have been sometimes injured, and even desolated by war, famine or disease, the same name, the same limits, the same interests, and even the same families, have continued for ages. The inhabitants gave themselves no trouble about the breaking up and divisions of kingdoms; while the village remains entire, they care not to what power it is transferred, or to what sovereign it devolves; its internal economy remains unchanged. The potail is still the head inhabitant, and still acts as the petty judge or magistrate, and collector or renter of the village."

These small stereotype forms of social organism have been to the greater part dissolved, and are disappearing, not so much through the brutal interference of the British tax-gatherer and the British soldier, as to the working of English steam and English free trade. Those family-communities were based on domestic industry, in that peculiar combination of hand-weaving, hand-spinning and hand-tilling agriculture which gave them self-supporting power. English interference having placed the spinner in Lancashire and the weaver in Bengal, or sweeping away both Hindu spinner and weaver, dissolved these small semi-barbarian, semi-civilized communities, by blowing up their economical basis, and thus produced the greatest, and, to speak the truth, the only *social* revolution ever heard of in Asia.

Now, sickening as it must be to human feeling to witness those myriads of industrious patriarchal and inoffensive social organizations disorganized and dissolved into their units, thrown into a sea of woes, and their individual members losing at the same time their ancient form of civilization and their hereditary means of subsistence, we must not forget that these idyllic village communities, inoffensive though they may appear, had always been the solid foundation of Oriental despotism, that they restrained the human mind within the smallest possible compass, making it the unresisting tool of superstition, enslaving it beneath traditional rules, depriving it of all grandeur and historical energies. We must not forget the barbarian egotism which, concentrating on some miserable patch of land, had quietly witnessed the ruin of empires, the perpetration of unspeakable cruelties, the massacre of the population of large towns, with no other consideration bestowed upon them than on natural events, itself the helpless prey of any aggressor who deigned to notice it at all. We must not forget that this undignified, stagnatory, and vegetative life, that this passive sort of existence evoked on the other part, in contradistinction, wild, aimless, unbounded forces of destruction, and rendered murder itself a religious rite in Hindustan. We must not forget that these little communities were contaminated by distinctions of caste and by slavery, that they subjugated man to external circumstances instead of elevating man to be the sovereign of circumstances, that they transformed a self-developing social state into never changing natural destiny, and thus brought about a brutalizing worship of nature, exhibiting its degradation in the fact that man, the sovereign of nature, fell down on his knees in adoration of Hanuman, the monkey, and Sabbala, the cow.

England, it is true, in causing a social revolution in Hindustan, was actuated only by the vilest interests, and was stupid in her manner of enforcing them. But that is not the question. The question is, can mankind fulfil its destiny without a fundamental revolution in the social state of Asia? If not, whatever may have been the crimes of England she was the unconscious tool of history in bringing about that revolution.

Then, whatever bitterness the spectacle of the crumbling of an ancient world may have for our personal feelings, we have the right, in point of history, to exclaim with Goethe:

"Sollte diese Qual uns quälen
Da sie unsre Lust vermehrt,
Hat nicht Myriaden Seelen
*Timur's Herrschaft aufgezehrt?"**

Published in the
New-York Daily Tribune,
No. 3804, June 25, 1853

Printed according to the text
of the newspaper

* *"Should this torture then torment us*
Since it brings us greater pleasure?
Were not through the rule of Timur
Souls devoured without measure?"
From Goethe's *West-östlicher Divan. An Suleika.—Ed.*

Karl Marx

INDIA[23]

On the 13th inst. Lord Stanley gave notice to the House of Commons that on the second reading of the India Bill (23d inst.) he would bring in the following resolution:

> "That in the opinion of this House further information is necessary to enable Parliament to legislate with advantage for the permanent government of India, and that at this late period of the session, it is inexpedient to proceed into a measure, which, while it disturbs existing arrangements, cannot be regarded as a final settlement."

But in April, 1854, the Charter of the East India Company will expire, and something accordingly must be done in one way or the other. The Government wanted to legislate permanently; that is, to renew the Charter for twenty years more. The Manchester School wanted to postpone all legislation, by prolonging the Charter at the utmost for one year. The Government said that permanent legislation was necessary for the "best" of India. The Manchester men replied that it was impossible for want of information. The "best" of India, and the want of information, are alike false pretences. The governing oligarchy desired, before a Reformed House should meet, to secure at the cost of India, their own "best" for twenty years to come. The Manchester men desired no legislation at all in the unreformed Parliament, where their views had no chance of success. Now, the Coalition Cabinet, through Sir Charles Wood, has, in contradiction to its former statements, but in conformity with its habitual system of shifting difficulties, brought in something that looked like legislation; but it dared not, on the other hand, to propose the renewal of the Charter for any definite period, but presented a "settlement", which it left to Parliament to unsettle whenever that body should determine to do so. If the Ministerial propositions were adopted, the East India Company would obtain no renewal, but only a suspension of life. In all other respects, the Ministerial project but apparently alters the Constitution of the Indian Government, the only serious novelty to be introduced being the addition of some new Governors, although a long experience has proved that the parts of East India administered by simple Commissioners, go on much better than those blessed with the costly luxury of Governors and Councils. The Whig invention of alleviating exhausted countries by burdening them with new sinecures for the paupers of aristocracy, reminds one of the old Russell administration, when the Whigs were suddenly struck with the state of spiritual destitution, in which the Indians and Mohammedans of the East were living, and determined upon relieving them by the importation of some *new Bishops,* the Tories, in the plenitude of their power, having never thought more than one to be necessary. That resolution having been agreed upon, Sir John Hobhouse, the then Whig President of the Board of Control, discovered immediately afterwards, that he had a relative admirably suited for a Bishopric, who was forthwith appointed to one of the new sees. "In cases of this kind," remarks an English writer, "where the fit is so exact, it is really hardly possible to say, whether the shoe was made for the foot, or the foot for the shoe." Thus with regard to the Charles Wood invention, it would be very difficult to say, whether the new Governors are made for Indian provinces, or Indian provinces for the new Governors.

Be this as it may, the Coalition Cabinet believed it had met all clamours by leaving to Parliament the power of altering its proposed act at all times. Unfortunately in steps Lord Stanley, the Tory, with his resolution which was loudly cheered by the "Radical" Opposition, when it was announced. Lord Stanley's resolution is, nevertheless, self-contradictory. On one hand, he rejects the Ministerial proposition, because the House requires more information for permanent legislation. On the other hand, he rejects it, because it is no permanent legislation, but alters existing arrangements, without pretending to finality. The Conservative view is, of course, opposed to the bill, because it involves a change of some kind. The Radical view is opposed to it, because it involves no real change at all. Lord Stanley, in these coalescent times has found a formula in which the opposite views are combined together against the Ministerial view of the subject. The Coalition Ministry affects a virtuous indignation against such tactics, and *The Chronicle*, its organ, exclaims:

"Viewed as a party move the proposed motion for delay is in a high degree factious and discreditable.... This motion is brought forward solely because some supporters of the Ministry are pledged to separate in this particular question from those with whom they usually act."

The anxiety of Ministers seems indeed to be serious. *The Chronicle* of today, again recurring to the subject, says:

"The division on Lord Stanley's motion will probably be decisive of the fate of the India Bill; it is therefore of the *utmost importance* that those who feel the *importance* of early legislation, should use every exertion to strengthen the Government."

On the other hand, we read in *The Times* of today:

"The fate of the Government India Bill has been more respectively delineated.... The danger of the Government lies in the entire conforming of Lord Stanley's objections with the conclusions of public opinion. Every syllable of this amendment tells with deadly effect against the Ministry."

I shall expose in a subsequent letter* the bearing of the Indian question on the different parties in Great Britain, and the benefit the poor Hindu may reap from this quarrelling of the aristocracy, the moneyocracy and the millocracy about his amelioration.

Written on June 17, 1853

Published in the *New-York Daily Tribune*, No. 3809, July 1, 1853

Printed according to the text of the newspaper

* See this collection, pp. 45-53—*Ed.*

Karl Marx

THE EAST INDIA COMPANY—ITS HISTORY AND RESULTS

London, Friday, June 24, 1853

The debate on Lord Stanley's motion to postpone legislation for India, has been deferred until this evening. For the first time since 1783 the Indian question has become a ministerial one in England. Why is this?

The true commencement of the East India Company cannot be dated from a more remote epoch than the year 1702, when the different societies, claiming the monopoly of the East India trade, united together in one single Company. Till then the very existence of the original East India Company was repeatedly endangered, once suspended for years under the protectorate of Cromwell, and once threatened with utter dissolution by Parliamentary interference under the reign of William III. It was under the ascendancy of that Dutch Prince when the Whigs became the farmers of the revenues of the British Empire, when the Bank of England sprung into life, when the protective system was firmly established in England, and the balance of power in Europe was definitively settled, that the existence of an East India Company was recognized by Parliament. That era of apparent liberty was in reality the era of monopolies not created by Royal grants, as in the times of Elizabeth and Charles I, but authorized and nationalized by the sanction of Parliament. This epoch in the history of England bears, in fact, an extreme likeness to the epoch of Louis Philippe in France, the old landed aristocracy having been defeated, and the bourgeoisie not being able to take its place except under the banner of moneyocracy, or the "*haute finance.*" The East India Company excluded the common people from the commerce with India, at the same time that the House of Commons excluded them from Parliamentary representation. In this as well as in other instances, we find the first decisive victory of the *bourgeoisie* over the feudal aristocracy coinciding with the most pronounced reaction against the people, a phenomenon which has driven more than one popular writer, like Cobbett, to look for popular liberty rather in the past than in the future.

The union between the Constitutional Monarchy and the monopolizing moneyed interest, between the Company of East India and the "glorious" revolution of 1688[24] was fostered by the same force by which the liberal interests and a liberal dynasty have at all times and in all countries met and combined, by the force of corruption, that first and last moving power of Constitutional Monarchy, the guardian angel of William III and the fatal demon of Louis Philippe. So early as 1693, it appeared from Parliamentary inquiries, that the annual expenditure of the East India Company, under the head of "gifts" to men in power, which had rarely amounted to above £1,200 before the revolution, reached the sum of £90,000. The Duke of Leeds was impeached for a bribe of £5,000, and the virtuous King himself convicted of having received £10,000. Besides these direct briberies, rival Companies were thrown out by tempting Government with loans of enormous sums at the lowest interest, and by buying off rival Directors.

The power the East India Company had obtained by bribing the Government, as did also the Bank of England, it was forced to maintain by bribing again, as did the Bank of England. At every epoch when its monopoly was expiring, it could only effect a renewal of its Charter by offering fresh loans and by fresh presents made to the Government.

The events of the Seven Years' War[25] transformed the East India Company from a commercial into a military and territorial power. It was then that the foundation was laid of the present British Empire in the East. Then East India stock rose to £263, and dividends were then paid at the rate of $12^1/_2$ per cent. But then there appeared a new enemy of the Company, no longer in the shape of rival societies, but in the shape of rival ministers and of a rival people. It was alleged that the Company's territory had been conquered by the aid of British fleets and British armies, and that no British subjects could hold territorial sovereignties independent of the Crown. The ministers of the day and the people of the day claimed their share in the "wonderful treasures" imagined to have been won by the last conquests. The Company only saved its existence by an agreement made in 1767 that it should annually pay £400,000 into the National Exchequer.

But the East India Company, instead of fulfilling its agreement, got into financial difficulties, and, instead of paying a tribute to the English people, appealed to Parliament for pecuniary aid. Serious alterations in the Charter were the consequence of this step. The Company's affairs failing to improve, notwithstanding their new condition, and the English nation having simultaneously lost their colonies in North America, the necessity of elsewhere regaining some great Colonial Empire became more and more universally felt. The illustrious Fox thought the opportune moment had arrived, in 1783, for bringing forward his famous India bill, which proposed to abolish the Courts of Directors and Proprietors, and to vest the whole Indian Government in the hands of seven Commissioners appointed by Parliament. By the personal influence of the imbecile King* over the House of Lords, the bill of Mr. Fox was defeated, and made the instrument of breaking down the then Coalition Government of Fox and Lord North, and of placing the famous Pitt at the head of the Government. Pitt carried in 1784 a bill through both Houses, which directed the establishment of the Board of Control, consisting of six members of the Privy Council, who were

"to check, superintend and control all acts, operations and concerns which in any wise related to the civil and military Government, or revenues of the territories and possessions of the East India Company."

On this head, Mill, the historian, says:

"In passing that law two objects were pursued. To avoid the imputation of what was represented as the heinous object of Mr. Fox's bill,

---

* George III.—*Ed.*

it was necessary that the principal part of the power should *appear* to remain in the hands of the Directors. For ministerial advantage it was necessary that it should in *reality* be all taken away. Mr. Pitt's bill professed to differ from that of his rival, chiefly in this very point, that while the one destroyed the power of the Directors, the other left it almost entire. Under the act of Mr. Fox the powers of the ministers would have been avowedly held. Under the act of Mr. Pitt, they were held in secret and by fraud. The bill of Fox transferred the power of the Company to Commissioners appointed by Parliament. The bill of Mr. Pitt transferred it to Commissioners appointed by the King."

The years of 1783 and 1784 were thus the first, and till now the only years, for the Indian question to become a ministerial one. The bill of Mr. Pitt having been carried, the Charter of the East India Company was renewed, and the Indian question set aside for twenty years. But in 1813 the Anti-Jacobin war, and in 1833 the newly introduced Reform Bill[26] superseded all other political questions.

This, then, is the first reason of the Indian question's having failed to become a great political question, since and before 1784; that before that time the East India Company had first to conquer existence and importance; that after that time the oligarchy absorbed all of its power which it could assume without incurring responsibility; and that afterwards the English people in general were at the very epochs of the renewal of the Charter, in 1813 and in 1833, absorbed by other questions of overbearing interest.

We will now take a different view. The East India Company commenced by attempting merely to establish factories for their agents, and places of deposit for their goods. In order to protect them they erected several forts. Although they had, even as early as 1689, conceived the establishment of a dominion in India, and of making territorial revenue one of their sources of emolument, yet, down to 1744, they had acquired but a few unimportant districts around Bombay, Madras, and Calcutta. The war which subsequently broke out in the Carnatic had the effect of rendering them after various struggles, virtual sovereigns of that part of India. Much more considerable results arose from the war in Bengal and the victories of Clive. These results were the real occupation of Bengal, Bihar, and Orissa. At the end of the 18th century, and in the first years of the present one, there supervened the wars with Tippoo Sahib, and in consequence of them a great advance of power, and an immense extension of the subsidiary system.[27] In the second decennium of the 19th century the first convenient frontier, that of India within the desert, had at length been conquered. It was not till then that the British Empire in the East reached those parts of Asia, which had been, at all times, the seat of every great central power in India. But the most vulnerable points of the Empire, from which it had been overrun as often as old conquerors were expelled by new ones, the barriers of the Western frontier, were not in the hands of the British. During the period from 1838 to 1849, in the Sikh and Afghan wars, British rule subjected to definitive possession the ethnographical, political, and military frontiers of the East Indian Continent, by the compulsory annexation of the Punjab and of Scinde.[28] These were possessions indispensable to repulse any invading force issuing from Central Asia, and indispensable against Russia advancing to the frontiers of Persia. During this last decennium there have been added to the British Indian territory 167,000 square miles, with a population of 8,572,630 souls. As to the interior, all the native States now became surrounded by British possessions, subjected to British *suzeraineté* under various forms, and cut off from the sea-coast, with the sole exception of Gujarat and Scinde. As to its exterior, India was now finished. It is only since 1849, that the one great Anglo-Indian Empire has existed.

Thus the British Government has been fighting, under the Company's name, for two centuries, till at last the natural limits of India were reached. We understand now, why during all this time all parties in England have connived in silence, even those which had resolved to become the loudest with their hypocritical peace-cant, after the *arrondissement* of the one Indian Empire should have been completed. Firstly, of course, they had to get it, in order to subject it afterward to their sharp philanthropy. From this view we understand the altered position of the Indian question in the present year, 1853, compared with all former periods of Charter renewal.

Again, let us take a different view. We shall still better understand the peculiar crisis in Indian legislation, on reviewing the course of British commercial intercourse with India through its different phases.

At the commencement of the East India Company's operations, under the reign of Elizabeth, the Company was permitted, for the purpose of profitably carrying on its trade with India, to export an annual value of £30,000 in silver, gold, and foreign coin. This was an infraction against all the prejudices of the age, and Thomas Mun was forced to lay down in *A Discourse of Trade, from England unto the East-Indies,* the foundation of the "mercantile system," admitting that the precious metals were the only real wealth a country could possess, but contending at the same time that their exportation might be safely allowed, provided the *balance of payments* was in favour of the exporting nation. In this sense, he contended that the commodities imported from East India were chiefly re-exported to other countries, from which a much greater quantity of bullion was obtained than had been required to pay for them in India. In the same spirit, Sir Josiah Child wrote *A Treatise Wherein Is Demonstrated I. That the East India Trade Is the Most National of all Foreign Trades.* By-and-by the partisans of the East India Company grew more audacious, and it may be noticed as a curiosity, in this strange Indian history, that the Indian monopolists were the first preachers of Free Trade in England.

Parliamentary intervention, with regard to the East India Company, was again claimed, not by the commercial, but by the industrial class, at the latter end of the 17th century, and during the greater part of the 18th, when the importation of East Indian cotton and silk stuffs was declared to ruin the poor British manufacturers, an opinion put forward in John Pollexfen's *England and East-India Inconsistent in Their Manufactures,* London, 1697, a title strangely verified a century and a half later, but in a very different sense. Parliament did then interfere. By the Act 11 and 12 William III, Cap. 10, it was enacted that the wearing of wrought silks and of printed or dyed calicoes from India, Persia and China should be prohibited, and a penalty of £200 imposed on all persons having or selling the same. Similar laws were enacted under George I, II and III, in consequence of the repeated lamentations of the afterwards so "enlightened" British manufacturers. And thus, during the greater part of the 18th century, Indian manufactures were generally imported into England in order to be sold on the Continent, and to remain excluded from the English market itself.

Besides this Parliamentary interference with East India, solicited by the greedy home manufacturer, efforts were made at every epoch of the renewal of the Charter, by the merchants of London, Liverpool and Bristol, to break down the commercial monopoly of the Company, and to participate in that commerce, estimated to be a true mine of gold. In consequence of these efforts, a provision was made in the Act of 1773 prolonging the Company's Charter till March 1, 1814 by which private British individuals were authorized to export from, and the Company's Indian servants permitted to import into, England almost all sorts of commodities. But this concession was surrounded with conditions annihilating its effects, in respect to the exports to British India by private merchants. In 1813 the Company was unable to further withstand the pressure of general commerce, and except the monopoly of the Chinese trade, the trade to India was opened, under certain conditions, to private competition. At the renewal of the Charter in 1833, these last restrictions were at length superseded, the Company forbidden to carry on any trade at all—their commercial character destroyed, and their privilege of excluding British subjects from the Indian territories withdrawn.

Meanwhile the East Indian trade had undergone very serious revolutions, altogether altering the position of the different class interests in England with regard to it. During the whole course of the 18th century the treasures transported from India to England were gained much less by comparatively insignificant commerce, than by the direct exploitation of that country, and by the colossal fortunes there extorted and transmitted to England. After the opening of the trade in 1813 the commerce with India more than trebled in a very short time. But this was not all. The whole character of the trade was changed. Till 1813 India had been chiefly an exporting country, while it now became an importing one; and in such a quick progression, that already in 1823 the rate of exchange, which had generally been 2/6 per rupee, sunk down to 2/ per rupee. India, the great workshop of cotton manufacture for the world, since immemorial times, became now inundated with English twists and cotton stuffs. After its own produce had been excluded from England, or only admitted on the most cruel terms, British manufactures were poured into it at a small and merely nominal duty, to the ruin of the native cotton fabrics once so celebrated. In 1780 the value of British produce and manufactures amounted only to £386,152, the bullion exported during the same year to £ 15,041, the total value of exports during 1780 being £12,648,616, so that the Indian trade amounted to only $^1/_{32}$ of the entire foreign trade. In 1850 the total exports to India from Great Britain and Ireland were £8,024,000, of which cotton goods alone amounted to £5,220,000, so that it reached more than $^1/_8$ of the whole export, and more than $^1/_4$ of the foreign cotton trade. But, the cotton manufacture also employed now $^1/_8$ of the population of Britain, and contributed $^1/_{12}$ of the whole national revenue. After each commercial crisis the East Indian trade grew of more paramount importance for the British cotton manufacturers, and the East Indian Continent became actually their best market. At the same rate at which the cotton manufactures became of vital interest for the whole social frame of Great Britain, East India became of vital interest for the British cotton manufacture.

Till then the interests of the moneyocracy which had converted India into its landed estates, of the oligarchy who had conquered it by their armies, and of the millocracy who had inundated it with their fabrics, had gone hand in hand. But the more the industrial interest became dependent on the Indian market, the more it felt the necessity of creating fresh productive powers in India, after having ruined her native industry. You cannot continue to inundate a country with your manufactures, unless you enable it to give you some produce in return. The industrial interest found that their trade declined instead of increasing. For the four years ending with 1846, the imports to India from Great Britain were to the amount of 261 million rupees; for the four years ending 1850 they were only 253 millions, while the exports for the former period, 274 millions of rupees, and for the latter period, 254 millions. They found out that the power of consuming their goods was contracted in India to the lowest possible point, that the consumption of their manufactures by the British West Indies was of the value of about 14s. per head of the population per annum, by Chile of 9s. 3d., by Brazil of 6s. 5d., by Cuba of 6s. 2d., by Peru of 5s. 7d., by Central America of 10d., while it amounted in India only to about 9d. Then came the short cotton crop in the United States, which caused them a loss of £11,000,000 in 1850, and they were exasperated at depending on America, instead of deriving a sufficiency of raw cotton from the East Indies. Besides, they found that in all attempts to apply capital to India they met with impediments and chicanery on the part of the Indian authorities. Thus India became the battle-field in the contest of the industrial interest on the one side, and of the moneyocracy and oligarchy on the other. The manufacturers, conscious of their ascendency in England, ask now for the annihilation of these antagonistic powers in India, for the destruction of the whole ancient fabric of Indian Government, and for the final eclipse of the East India Company.

And now to the fourth and last point of view, from which the Indian question must be judged. Since 1784 Indian finances have got more and more deeply into difficulty. There exists now a national debt of 50 million pounds, a continual decrease in the resources of the revenue, and a corresponding increase in the expenditure, dubiously balanced by the gambling income of the opium tax, now threatened with extinction by the Chinese beginning themselves to cultivate the poppy, and aggravated by the expenses to be anticipated from the senseless Burmese war.[29]

"As the case stands," says Mr. Dickinson, "as it would ruin England to lose her Empire in India, it is stretching our own finances with ruin, to be obliged to keep it."

I have shown thus, how the Indian question has become for the first time since 1783, an English question, and a ministerial question.

Published in the
New-York Daily Tribune,
No. 3816, July 11, 1853

Printed according to the text
of the newspaper

Karl Marx

THE INDIAN QUESTION—IRISH TENANT RIGHT

London, June 28, 1853

The debate on Lord Stanley's motion with respect to India commenced on the 23d, continued on the 24th, and adjourned to the 27th inst., has not been brought to a close. When that shall at length have arrived, I intend to resume my observations on the Indian question.

As the Coalition Ministry depends on the support of the Irish party, and as all the other parties composing the House of Commons so nicely balance each other that the Irish may at any moment turn the scales which way they please, some concessions are at last about to be made to the Irish tenants. The "Leasing Powers (Ireland) Bill", which passed the House of Commons on Friday last, contains a provision that for the improvements made on the soil and separable from the soil, the tenant shall have at the termination of his lease, a compensation in money, the incoming tenant being at liberty to take them at the valuation, while with respect to improvements in the soil, compensation for them shall be arranged by contract between the landlord and the tenant.

A tenant having incorporated his capital, in one form or another, in the land, and having thus effected an improvement of the soil, either directly by irrigation, drainage, manure, or indirectly by construction of buildings for agricultural purposes, in steps the landlord with demand for increased rent. If the tenant concedes, he has to pay the interest for his own money to the landlord. If he resists, he will be very unceremoniously ejected, and supplanted by a new tenant, the latter being enabled to pay a higher rent by the very expenses incurred by his predecessors, until he also, in his turn, has become an improver of the land, and is replaced in the same way, or put on worse terms. In this easy way a class of absentee landlords has been enabled to pocket, not merely the labour, but also the capital, of whole generations, each generation of Irish peasants sinking a grade lower in the social scale, exactly in proportion to the exertions and sacrifices made for the raising of their condition and that of their families. If the tenant was industrious and enterprising, he became taxed in consequence of his very industry and enterprise. If, on the contrary, he grew inert and negligent, he was reproached with the "aboriginal faults of the Celtic race." He had, accordingly, no other alternative left but to become a pauper—to pauperize himself by industry, or to pauperize by negligence. In order to oppose this state of things, "Tenant Right" was proclaimed in Ireland—a right of the tenant, not in the soil but in the improvements of the soil effected at his cost and charges. Let us see in what manner *The Times*, in its Saturday's leader, attempts to break down this Irish "Tenant Right":

> "There are two general systems of farm occupation. Either a tenant may take a lease of the land for a fixed number of years, or his holding may be terminable at any time upon certain notice. In the first of these events, it would be obviously his course to adjust and apportion his outlay so that all, or nearly all, the benefit would find its way to him before the expiration of his term. In the second case it seems equally obvious that he should not run the risk of the investment without a proper assurance of return."

Where the landlords have to deal with a class of large capitalists who may, as they please, invest their stock in commerce, in manufactures or in farming, there can be no doubt but that these capitalist farmers, whether they take long leases or no time leases at all, know how to secure the "proper" return of their outlays. But with regard to Ireland the supposition is quite fictitious. On the one side you have there a small class of land monopolists, on the other, a very large class of tenants with very petty fortunes, which they have no chance to invest in different ways, no other field of production opening to them, except the soil. They are, therefore, forced to become tenants at will. Being once tenants at will, they naturally run the risk of losing their revenue, provided they do not invest their small capital. Investing it, in order to secure their revenue, they run the risk of losing their capital, also.

"Perhaps," continues *The Times*, "it may be said, that in any case a tenantry could hardly expire without something being left upon the ground, in some shape or another, representing the tenant's own property, and that for this compensation should be forthcoming. There is some truth in the remark, but the demand thus created ought, under proper conditions of society, to be easily adjusted between landlord and tenant, as it might, at any rate, be provided for in the original contract. We say that the conditions of society should regulate these arrangements, because we believe that no Parliamentary enactment can be effectually substituted for such an agency."

Indeed, under "proper conditions of society," we should want no more Parliamentary interference with the Irish land-tenant, as we should not want, under "proper conditions of society," the interference of the soldier, of the policeman, and of the hangman. Legislature, magistracy, and armed force, are all of them but the offspring of improper conditions of society, preventing those arrangements among men which would make useless the compulsory intervention of a third supreme power. Has, perhaps, *The Times* been converted into a social revolutionist? Does it want a *social* revolution, reorganizing the "conditions of society," and the "arrangements" emanating from them, instead of "Parliamentary enactments"? England has subverted the conditions of Irish society. At first it confiscated the land, then it suppressed the industry by "Parliamentary enactments," and lastly, it broke the active energy by armed force. And thus England created those abominable "conditions of society" which enable a small *caste* of rapacious lordlings to dictate to the Irish people the terms on which they shall be allowed to hold the land and to live upon it. Too weak yet for revolutionizing those "social conditions," the people appeal to Parliament, demanding at least their mitigation and regulation. But "No," says *The Times;* if you don't live under proper conditions of society, Parliament can't mend that. And if the Irish people, on the advice of *The Times,* tried tomorrow to mend their conditions of society, *The Times* would be the first to appeal to bayonets, and to pour out sanguinary denunciations of the "aboriginal faults of the Celtic race," wanting the Anglo-Saxon taste for pacific progress and legal amelioration.

"If a landlord," says *The Times*, "deliberately injures one tenant, he will find it so much the harder to get another, and whereas his occupation consists in letting land, he will find his land all the more difficult to let."

The case stands rather differently in Ireland. The more a landlord injures one tenant, the easier he will find it to cppress another. The tenant who comes in, is the means of injuring the ejected one, and the ejected one is the means of keeping down the new occupant. That, in due course of time, the landlord, beside injuring the tenant, will injure himself and ruin himself, is not only a probability, but the very fact, in Ireland—a fact affording, however, a very precarious source of comfort to the ruined tenant.

"The relations between the landlord and tenant are those between two traders," says *The Times*.

This is precisely the *petitio principii* which pervades the whole leader of *The Times*. The needy Irish tenant belongs to the soil, while the soil belongs to the English lord. As well you might call the relation between the robber who presents his pistol, and the traveller who presents his purse, a relation between two traders.

"But," says *The Times*, "in point of fact, the relation between Irish landlords and tenants will soon be reformed by an agency more potent than that of legislation. The property of Ireland is fast passing into new hands, and, if the present rate of emigration continues, its cultivation must undergo the same transfer."

Here, at least, *The Times* has the truth. British Parliament does not interfere at a moment when the worked out old system is terminating in the common ruin, both of the thrifty landlord and the needy tenant, the former being knocked down by the hammer of the *Encumbered Estates* Commission, and the latter expelled by compulsory emigration. This reminds us of the old Sultan of Morocco. Whenever there was a case pending between two parties, he knew of no more "potent agency" for settling their controversy, than by killing both parties.

"Nothing could tend," concludes *The Times* with regard to Tenant Right, "to greater confusion than such a *communistic distribution of ownership*. The only person with any right in the land, is the landlord."

The Times seems to have been the sleeping Epimenides of the past half century, and never to have heard of the hot controversy going on during all that time upon the claims of the landlord, not among social reformers and Communists, but among the very political economists of the British middle class. Ricardo, the creator of modern political economy in Great Britain, did not controvert the "right" of the landlords, as he was quite convinced that their claims were based upon fact, and not on right, and that political economy in general had nothing to do with questions of right; but he attacked the land-monopoly in a more unassuming, yet more scientific, and therefore more dangerous manner. He proved that private proprietorship in land, as distinguished from the respective claims of the labourer, and of the farmer, was a relation quite superfluous in, and incoherent with the whole framework of modern production; that the economical expression of that relationship and the rent of land, might, with great advantage, be appropriated by the State; and finally that the interest of the landlord was opposed to the interest of all other classes of modern society. It would be tedious to enumerate all the conclusions drawn from these premises by the Ricardo School against the landed monopoly. For my end, it will suffice to quote three of the most recent economical authorities of Great Britain.

The London Economist, whose chief editor, Mr. J. Wilson, is not only a Free Trade oracle, but a Whig one, too, and not only a Whig, but also an inevitable Treasury-appendage in every Whig or composite ministry, has contended in different articles that exactly speaking there can exist no title authorizing any individual, or any number of individuals, to claim the exclusive proprietorship in the soil of a nation.

Mr. Newman, in his "Lectures on Political Economy," London, 1851, professedly written for the purpose of refuting socialism, tells us:

"No man has, or can have, a natural right to *land*, except so long as he occupies it in person. His right is to the use, and to the use only. All other right is the creation of artificial law" (or Parliamentary enactments as *The Times* would call it).... "If, at any time, land becomes needed to *live upon*, the right of private possessors to withhold it comes to an end."

This is exactly the case in Ireland, and Mr. Newman expressly confirms the claims of the Irish tenantry, and in lectures held before the most select audiences of the British aristocracy.

In conclusion let me quote some passages from Mr. Herbert Spencer's work, "Social Statics," London, 1851, also, purporting to be a complete refutation of communism, and acknowledged as the most elaborate development of the Free Trade doctrines[30] of modern England.

"No one may use the earth in such a way as to prevent the rest from similarly using it. Equity, therefore, does not permit property in land, or the rest would live on the earth by sufferance only. The landless men might equitably be expelled from the earth altogether.... It can never be pretended, that the existing titles to such property are legitimate. Should anyone think so let him look in the Chronicles. The original deeds were written with the sword, rather than with the pen. Not lawyers but soldiers were the conveyancers: blows were the current coin given in payment; and for seals blood was used in preference to wax. Could valid claims be thus constituted? Hardly. And if not, what becomes of the pretensions of all subsequent holders of estates so obtained? Does sale or bequest generate a right where it did not previously exist?... If one act of transfer can give no title, can many?... At what rate per annum do invalid claims become valid?... The right of mankind at large to the earth's surface is still valid. all deeds, customs and laws notwithstanding. It is impossible to discover any mode in which land can become private property.... We daily deny landlordism by our legislation. Is a canal, a railway, or a turnpike road to be made? We do not scruple to seize just as many acres as may be requisite. We do not wait for consent.... The change required would simply be a change of landlords.... Instead of being in the possession of individuals, the country would be held by the great corporate body—society. Instead of leasing his acres from an isolated proprietor, the farmer would lease them from the nation. Instead of paying his rent to the agent of Sir John, or His Grace, he will pay to an agent, or deputy-agent of the community. Stewards would be public officials instead of private ones, and tenantry the only land tenure.... Pushed to its ultimate consequences, a claim to exclusive possession of the soil involves land-owning despotism."

Thus, from the very point of view of modern English political economists, it is not the usurping English landlord but the Irish tenants and labourers, who have the only right in the soil of their native country, and *The Times,* in opposing the demands of the Irish people, places itself into direct antagonism to British middle-class science.

Published in the
New-York Daily Tribune,
No. 3816, July 11, 1853

Printed according to the text
of the newspaper

Karl Marx

THE GOVERNMENT OF INDIA[31]

The House of Commons, in order to do justice to the colossal dimensions of the subject, has been spinning out its Indian debate to an unusual length and breadth, although that debate has failed altogether in depth and greatness of interest. The division leaving Ministers a majority of 322 against 142, is in inverse ratio to the discussion. During the discussion all was thistles for the Ministry, and Sir Charles Wood was the ass officially put to the task of feeding upon them. In the division all is roses, and Sir Charles Wood receives the crown of another *Manu*. The same men who negatived the plan of the Ministry by their arguments, affirmed it by their votes. None of its supporters dared to apologize for the bill itself; on the contrary, all apologized for their supporting the bill, the ones because it was an infinitesimal part of a measure in the right direction, the others because it was no measure at all. The former pretend that they will now mend it in Committee; the latter say that they will strip it of all the fancy Reform flowers it parades in.

The Ministry maintained the field by more than one half of the Tory opposition running away, and a great portion of the remainder deserting with Herries and Inglis into the Aberdeen camp, while of the 142 opposite votes 100 belonged to the Disraeli fraction, and 42 to the Manchester School, backed by some Irish discontents and some inexpressibles. The opposition within the opposition has once more saved the Ministry.

Mr. Halliday, one of the officials of the East India Company, when examined before a Committee of Inquiry, stated:

"That the Charter giving a twenty years' lease to the East India Company was considered by the natives of India as *farming them out.*"

This time at least, the Charter has not been renewed for a definite period, but is revocable at will by Parliament. The Company, therefore, will come down from the respectable situation of hereditary farmers, to the precarious condition of tenants at will. This is so much gain for the natives. The Coalition Ministry has succeeded in transforming the Indian Government, like all other questions, into an open question. The House of Commons, on the other hand, has given itself a new testimonial of poverty, in confessing by the same division, its impotency for legislating, and its unwillingness to delay legislating.

Since the days of Aristotle the world has been inundated with a frightful quantity of dissertations, ingenious or absurd, as it might happen, on that question: Who shall be the governing power? But for the first time in the annals of history, the Senate of a people ruling over another people numbering 156 millions of human beings and spreading over a surface of 1,368,113 square miles, have put their heads together in solemn and public congregation, in order to answer the irregular question: Who among us is the actual governing power over that foreign people of 150 millions of souls? There was no Oedipus in the British Senate capable of extricating this riddle. The whole debate exclusively twined around it, as although a division took place, no definition of the Indian Government was arrived at.

That there is in India a permanent financial deficit, a regular over-supply of wars, and no supply at all of public works, an abominable system of taxation, and a no less abominable state of justice and law, that these five items constitute, as it were, the five points of the East Indian Charter, was settled beyond all doubt in the debates of 1853, as it had been in the debates of 1833, and in the debates of 1813, as in all former debates on India. The only thing never found out, was the party responsible for all this.

There exists, unquestionably, a Governor-General of India, holding the supreme power, but that Governor is governed in his turn by a home government. Who is that home government? Is it the Indian Minister, disguised under the modest title of President of the Board of Control, or is it the twenty-four Directors of the East India Company? On the threshold of the Indian religion we find a divine trinity, and thus we find a profane trinity on the threshold of the Indian Government.

Leaving, for a while, the Governor-General altogether one side, the question at issue resolves itself into that of the *double government,* in which form it is familiar to the English mind. The Ministers in their bill, and the House in its division, cling to this dualism.

When the Company of English merchant adventurers, who conquered India to make money out of it, began to enlarge their factories into an empire, when their competition with the Dutch and French private merchants assumed the character of national rivalry, then, of course, the British Government commenced meddling with the affairs of the East India Company, and the double government of India sprung up in fact if not in name. Pitt's act of 1784, by entering into a compromise with the Company, by subjecting it to the superintendence of the Board of Control, and by making the Board of Control an appendage to the Ministry, accepted, regulated and settled that double government arisen from circumstances in name as well as in fact.

The act of 1833 strengthened the Board of Control, changed the proprietors of the East India Company into mere mortgagees of the East India revenues, ordered the Company to sell off its stock, dissolved its commercial existence, transformed it, as far as it existed politically, into a mere trustee of the Crown, and did thus with the East India Company, what the Company had been in the habit of doing with the East Indian Princes. After having superseded them, it continued, for a while, still to govern in their name. So far, the East India Company has, since 1833, no longer existed but in name and on sufferance. While thus on one hand, there seems to be no difficulty in getting rid of the Company altogether, it is, on the other hand, very indifferent whether the English nation rules over India under the personal name of Queen Victoria, or under the traditional firm of an anonymous society. The whole question, therefore, appears to turn about a technicality of very questionable importance. Still, the thing is not quite so plain.

It is to be remarked, in the first instance, that the Ministerial Board of Control, residing in Cannon Row, is as much a fiction as the East India Company, supposed to reside in Leadenhall St. The members composing the Board of Control are a mere cloak for the supreme rule of the President of the Board. The President is himself but a subordinate though independent member of the Imperial Ministry. In India it seems to be assumed that if a man is fit for nothing it is best to make him a judge, and get rid of him. In Great Britain, when a party comes into office and finds itself encumbered with a tenth-rate "statesman," it is considered best to make him President of the Board of Control, successor of the Great Mogul, and in that way to get rid of him—*teste Carolo Wood.*

The letter of the law entrusts the Board of Control, which is but another name for its President, with

> "full power and authority to superintend, direct, and control all acts, operations and concerns of the East India Company which in any wise relate to or concern the Government or revenues of the Indian territories."

Directors are prohibited

> "from issuing any orders, instructions, dispatches, official letters, or communications whatever relating to India, or to the Government thereof, until the same shall have been sanctioned by the Board."

Directors are ordered to

> "prepare instructions or orders upon any subject whatever at fourteen days' notice from the Board, or else to transmit the orders of the Board on the subject of India."

The board is authorized to inspect all correspondence and dispatches to and from India, and the proceedings of the Courts of Proprietors and Directors. Lastly, the Court of Directors has to appoint a Secret Committee, consisting of their Chairman, their Deputy Chairman and their senior member, who are sworn to secrecy, and through whom, in all political and military matters, the President of the

Board may transmit his personal orders to India, while the Committee acts as a mere channel of his communications. The orders respecting the Afghan and Burmese wars, and as to the occupation of Scinde were transmitted through this Secret Committee, without the Court of Directors being any more informed of them than the general public or Parliament. So far, therefore, the President of the Board of Control would appear to be the real Mogul, and, under all circumstances, he retains an unlimited power for doing mischief, as, for instance, for causing the most ruinous wars, all the while being hidden under the name of the irresponsible Court of Directors. On the other hand, the Court of Directors is not without real power. As they generally exercise the initiative in administrative measures, as they form, when compared with the Board of Control, a more permanent and steady body, with traditional rules for action and a certain knowledge of details, the whole of the ordinary internal administration necessarily falls to their share. They appoint, too, under sanction of the Crown, the Supreme Government of India, the Governor-General and his Councils; possessing, besides, the unrestricted power to recall the highest servants, and even the Governor-General, as they did under Sir Robert Peel, with Lord Ellenborough. But this is still not their most important privilege. Receiving only £300 per annum, they are really paid in patronage, distributing all the writerships and cadetships, from whose number the Governor-General of India and the Provincial Governors are obliged to fill up all the higher places withheld from the natives. When the number of appointments for the year is ascertained, the whole are divided into 28 equal parts—of which two are allotted to the Chairman and Deputy Chairman, two to the President of the Board of Control, and one to each of the Directors. The annual value of each share of patronage seldom falls short of £14,000.

"All nominations," says Mr. Campbell, "are now, as it were, the private property of individuals, being divided among the Directors, and each disposing of his share as he thinks fit."

Now, it is evident that the spirit of the Court of Directors must pervade the whole of the Indian Upper Administration, trained, as it is, at schools of Addiscombe and Haileybury, and appointed, as it is, by their patronage. It is no less evident that this Court of Directors, who have to distribute, year after year, appointments of the value of nearly £400,000 among the upper classes of Great Britain, will find little or no check from the public opinion directed by those very classes. What the spirit of the Court of Directors is, I will show in a following letter on the actual state of India. For the present it may suffice to say that Mr. Macaulay, in the course of the pending debates, defended the Court by the particular plea, that it was impotent to effect all the evils it might intend, so much so, that all improvements had been effected in opposition to it, and against it by individual Governors who had acted on their own responsibility. Thus with regard to the suppression on the Suttee,[32] the abolition of the abominable transit duties, and the emancipation of the East Indian press.

The President of the Board of Control accordingly involves India in ruinous wars under cover of the Court of Directors, while the Court of Directors corrupt the Indian Administration under the cloak of the Board of Control.

On looking deeper into the framework of this anomalous government we find at its bottom a third power, more supreme than either the Board or the Court, more irresponsible, and more concealed from and guarded against the superintendence of public opinion. The transient President of the Board depends on the permanent clerks of his establishment in Cannon Row, and for those clerks India exists not in India, but in Leadenhall St.[33] Now, who is the master at Leadenhall St.?

Two thousand persons, elderly ladies and valetudinarian gentlemen, possessing Indian stock, having no other interest in India except to be paid their dividends out of Indian revenue, elect twenty-four Directors, whose only qualification is the holding of £1,000 stock. Merchants, bankers, and directors of companies incur great trouble in order to get into the Court for the interest of their private concerns.

"A banker," said Mr. Bright, "in the City of London commands 300 votes of the East India Company, whose word for the election of Directors is almost absolute law."

Hence the Court of Directors is nothing but a *succursal* to the English moneyocracy. The so-elected Court forms, in its turn, besides the above-mentioned Secret Committee, three other Committees, which are 1) Political and Military, 2) Finance and Home, 3) Revenue, Judicial and Legislative. These Committees are every year appointed by rotation, so that a *financier* is one year on the Judicial and the next year on the Military Committee, and no one has any chance of a continued supervision over a particular department. The mode of election having brought in men utterly unfit for their duties, the system of rotation gives to whatever fitness they might perchance retain, the final blow. Who, then, govern in fact under the name of the Direction? A large staff of irresponsible secretaries, examiners, and clerks at the India House, of whom, as Mr. Campbell observes, in his *Scheme for the Government of India,* only one individual has ever been in India, and he only by accident. Apart from the trade in patronage, it is therefore a mere fiction to speak of the politics, the principles, and the system of the Court of Directors. The real Court of Directors and the real Home Government, etc., of India are the permanent and irresponsible *bureaucracy,* "the creatures of the desk and the creatures of favour" residing in Leadenhall St. We have thus a Corporation ruling over an immense empire, not formed, as in Venice, by eminent patricians, but by old obstinate clerks, and the like odd fellows.

No wonder, then, that there exists no government by which so much is written and so little done, as the Government of India. When the East India Company was only a commercial association, they, of course, requested a most detailed report on every item from the managers of their Indian factories, as is done by every trading concern. When the factories grew into an empire, the commercial items into shiploads of correspondence and documents, the Leadenhall clerks went on in their system, which made the Directors and the Board their dependents; and they succeeded in transforming the Indian Government into one immense writing machine. Lord Broughton stated in his evidence before the Official Salaries Committee, that with one single dispatch 45,000 pages of collection were sent.

In order to give you some idea of the time-killing manner in which business is transacted at the India House, I will quote a passage from Mr. Dickinson.

"When a dispatch arrives from India, it is referred, in the first instance, to the Examiners' Department, to which it belongs; after which the chairs* confer with the official in charge of that department, and settle with him the tenor of a reply, and transmit a draught of this reply to the Indian Minister,[34] in what is technically called P.C., i.e., previous communication. The chairs, in this preliminary state of P.C. depend mainly on the clerks. Such is this dependence that even in a discussion in the Court of Proprietors, after previous notice, it is pitiable to see the Chairman referring to a secretary who sits by his side, and keeps on whispering and prompting and chaffing him as if he were a mere puppet, and the Minister at the other end of the system is in the same predicament. In this stage of P.C., if there is a difference of opinion on the draught it is discussed, and almost invariably settled in friendly communication between the Minister and the Chair; finally the draught is returned by the Minister, either adopted or altered; and then it is submitted to the Committee of Directors superintending the department to which it belongs, with all papers bearing on the case, to be considered and discussed, and adopted or altered, and afterward it is exposed to the same process in the aggregate Court, and then goes, for the first time, as an official communication to the Minister, after which it undergoes the same process in the opposite direction."

"When a measure is discussed in India," says Mr. Campbell, "the announcement that it has been referred to the Court of Directors, is regarded as an indefinite postponement."

The close and abject spirit of this bureaucracy deserves to be stigmatized in the celebrated words of Burke:

"This tribe of vulgar politicians are the lowest of our species. There is no trade so vile and mechanical as government in their hands. Virtue is not their habit. They are out of themselves in any course of conduct recommended only by conscience and glory. A large, liberal and prospective view of the interests of States passes with them for romance; and the principles that recommend it, for the wanderings of a disordered imagination. The calculators compute them out of their senses. The jesters and buffoons shame them out of everything grand and elevated. Littleness in object and in means to them appears soundness and sobriety."

The clerical establishments of Leadenhall St. and Cannon Row cost the Indian people the trifle of £160,000 annually. The oligarchy involves India in wars, in order to find employment for their younger sons; the moneyocracy

* This refers to the Chairman and Deputy Chairman of the Court of Directors of the East India Company.—*Ed.*

consigns it to the highest bidder; and a subordinate bureaucracy paralyze its administration and perpetuate its abuses as the vital condition of their own perpetuation.

Sir Charles Wood's bill alters nothing in the existing system. It enlarges the power of the Ministry, without adding to its responsibility.

Written on July 5, 1853

Published in the *New-York Daily Tribune*, No. 3824, July 20, 1853

Printed according to the text of the newspaper

Karl Marx

THE EAST INDIA QUESTION[35]

The clauses of the India Bill are passing one by one, the debate scarcely offering any remarkable features, except the inconsistency of the so-called India Reformers. There is, for instance, my Lord Jocelyn, M. P., who has made a kind of political livelihood by his periodical denunciation of Indian wrongs, and of the maladministration of the East India Company. What do you think his amendment amounted to? To give the East India Company a lease for 10 years. Happily, it compromised no one but himself. There is another professional "Reformer," Mr. Jos. Hume, who, during his long parliamentary life, has succeeded in transforming opposition itself into a particular manner of supporting the Ministry. He proposed not to reduce the number of East India Directors from 24 to 18. The only amendment of common sense, yet agreed to, was that of Mr. Bright, exempting Directors nominated by the Government from the qualification in East India Stock, imposed upon the Directors elected by the Court of Proprietors. Go through the pamphlets published by the East Indian Reform Association,[36] and you will feel a similar sensation as when, hearing of one great act of accusation against Bonaparte, devised in common by Legitimists, Orleanists, Blue and Red Republicans, and even disappointed Bonapartists. Their only merit until now has been to draw public attention to Indian affairs in general, and further they cannot go in their present form of eclectic opposition. For instance, while they attack the doings of the English aristocracy in

India, they protest against the destruction of the Indian aristocracy of native princes.

After the British intruders had once put their feet on India, and made up their mind to hold it, there remained no alternative but to break the power of the native princes by force or by intrigue. Placed with regard to them in similar circumstances as the ancient Romans with regard to their allies, they followed in the track of Roman politics. "It was," says an English writer, "a system of fattening allies, as we fatten oxen, till they were worthy of being devoured." After having won over their allies in the way of ancient Rome, the East India Company executed them in the modern manner of Change Alley.[37] In order to discharge the engagements they had entered into with the Company, the native princes were forced to borrow enormous sums from Englishmen at usurious interest. When their embarrassment had reached the highest pitch, the creditor got inexorable, "the screw was turned" and the princes were compelled either to concede their territories amicably to the Company, or to begin war; to become pensioners on their usurpers in one case, or to be deposed as traitors in the other. At this moment the native States occupy an area of 699,961 square miles, with a population of 52,941,263 souls, being, however, no longer the allies, but only the dependents of the British Government, upon multifarious conditions, and under the various forms of the subsidiary and of the protective systems. These systems have in common the relinquishment, by the native States of the right of self-defence, of maintaining diplomatic relations, and of settling the disputes among themselves without the interference of the Governor-General. All of them have to pay a tribute, either in hard cash, or in a contingent of armed forces, commanded by British officers. The final absorption or annexation of these native States is at present eagerly controverted between the reformers who denounce it as a crime, and the men of business who excuse it as a necessity.

In my opinion the question itself is altogether improperly put. As to the native *States* they virtually ceased to exist from the moment they became subsidiary to or protected by the Company. If you divide the revenue of a country between two governments, you are sure to cripple the resources of the one and the administration of both. Under the present system the native States succumb under the double incubus of their native Administration and the tributes and inordinate military establishments imposed upon them by the Company. The conditions under which they are allowed to retain their apparent independence are at the same time the conditions of a permanent decay, and of an utter inability of improvement. Organic weakness is the constitutional law of their existence, as of all existences living upon sufferance. It is, therefore, not the native *States*, but the native *Princes* and Courts about whose maintenance the question revolves. Now, is it not a strange thing that the same men who denounce "the barbarous splendours of the Crown and aristocracy of England" are shedding tears at the downfall of India Nabobs, Rajahs, and Jagirdars,[38] the great majority of whom possess not even the prestige of antiquity, being generally usurpers of very recent date, set up by English intrigue! There exists in the whole world no despotism more ridiculous, absurd, and childish than that of those Shahzamans and Shahriars of the *Arabian Nights*. The Duke of Wellington, Sir J. Malcolm, Sir Henry Russell, Lord Ellenborough, General Briggs, and other authorities, have pronounced in favour of the *status quo*; but on what grounds? Because the native troops under English rule want employment in the petty warfares with their own countrymen, in order to prevent them from turning their strength against their own European masters. Because the existence of independent States gives occasional employment to the English troops. Because the hereditary princes are the most servile tools of English despotism, and check the rise of those bold military adventurers with whom India has and ever will abound. Because the independent territories afford a refuge to all discontented and enterprising native spirits. Leaving aside all these arguments, which state in so many words that the native princes are the strongholds of the present abominable English system and the greatest obstacles to Indian progress, I come to Sir Thomas Munro and Lord Elphinstone, who were at least men of superior genius, and of real sympathy for the Indian people. They think that without a native aristocracy there can be no energy in any other class of the community, and that the subversion of that aristocracy will not raise but debase a whole people. They may be right as long as the natives, under direct English rule, are systematically excluded from all superior offices, military and civil. Where there can be no great men by their own exertion, there must be great men by birth, to leave to a conquered people some greatness of their own. That exclusion, however, of the native people from the English territory, has been effected only by the maintenance of the hereditary princes in the so-called independent territories. And one of these two concessions had to be made to the native army, on whose strength all British rule in India depends. I think we may trust the assertion of Mr. Campbell, that the native Indian aristocracy are the least enabled to fill higher offices; that for all fresh requirements it is necessary to create a fresh class; and that "from the acuteness and aptness to learn of the inferior classes, this can be done in India as it can be done in no other country."

The native princes themselves are fast disappearing by the extinction of their houses; but, since the commencement of this century, the British Government has observed the policy of allowing them to make *heirs by adoption*, or of filling up their vacant seats with puppets of English creation. The great Governor-General, Lord Dalhousie, was the first to protest openly against this system. Were not the natural course of things artificially resisted, there would be wanted neither wars nor expenses to do away with the native princes.

As to the *pensioned princes*, the £2,468,969 assigned to them by the British Government on the Indian revenue is a most heavy charge upon a people living on rice, and deprived of the first necessaries of life. If they are good for anything, it is for exhibiting Royalty in its lowest stage of degradation and ridicule. Take, for instance, the Great Mogul,* the descendant of Timur Tamerlane.[39] He is allowed £120,000 a year. His authority does not extend beyond the walls of his palace, within which the Royal idiotic race, left

* Bahadur Shah II.—*Ed.*

to itself, propagates as freely as rabbits. Even the police of Delhi is held by Englishmen above his control. There he sits on his throne, a little shrivelled yellow old man, trimmed in a theatrical dress, embroidered with gold, much like that of the dancing girls of Hindustan. On certain state occasions, the tinsel-covered puppet issues forth to gladden the hearts of the loyal. On his days of reception strangers have to pay a fee, in the form of guineas, as to any other *saltimbanque* exhibiting himself in public; while he, in his turn, presents them with turbans, diamonds, etc. On looking nearer at them, they find that the Royal diamonds are, like so many pieces of ordinary glass, grossly painted and imitating as roughly as possible the precious stones, and jointed so wretchedly, that they break in the hand like gingerbread.

The English money-lenders, combined with the English aristocracy, understand, we must own, the art of degrading Royalty, reducing it to the nullity of constitutionalism at home, and to the seclusion of etiquette abroad. And now, here are the radicals, exasperated at this spectacle.

Written on July 12, 1853

Published in the *New-York Daily Tribune*, No. 3828, July 25, 1853

Printed according to the text of the newspaper

Karl Marx

WAR IN BURMA[40]

London, Friday, July 15, 1853

By the latest overland mail from India, intelligence has been received that the Burmese ambassadors have rejected the treaty proposed by General Godwin. The General afforded them 24 hours more for reflection, but the Burmese departed within 10 hours. A third edition of the interminable Burmese war[41] appears to be inevitable.

Of all the warlike expeditions of the British in the East, none have ever been undertaken on less warranted grounds than those against Burma. There was no possible danger of invasion from that side, as there was from the North-West, Bengal being separated from Burma by a range of mountains, across which troops cannot be marched. To go to war with Burma the Indian Government is obliged to go to sea. To speak of maritime aggressions on the part of the Burmese is as ridiculous, as the idea of their coast-junks fronting the Company's war steamers would be preposterous. The pretension that the Yankees had strong annexation propensities applied to Pegu, is borne out by no facts. No argument, therefore, remains behind, but the want of employment for a needy aristocracy, the necessity of creating, as an English writer says, "a regular quality-workhouse, or Hampton Court[42] in the East." The first Burmese war (1824-26), entered into under the Quixotic administration of Lord Amherst, although it lasted little more than two years, added thirteen millions to the Indian debt. The maintenance of the Eastern settlements at Singapore, Penang and Malacca, exclusive of the pay of troops, causes an annual excess of expenditure over income amounting to £100,000. The territory taken from the Burmese in 1826 costs as much more. The territory of Pegu is still more ruinous. Now, why is it that England shrinks from the most necessary war in Europe, as now against Russia, while she tumbles, year after year, into the most reckless wars in Asia? The national debt has made her a trembler in Europe—the charges of the Asiatic wars are thrown on the shoulders of the Hindus. But we may expect from the now impending extinction of the opium revenue of Bengal, combined with the expenses of another Burmese war, that they will produce such a crisis in the Indian exchequer, as will cause a more thorough reform of the Indian Empire than all the speeches and tracts of the Parliamentary Reformers in England.

Published in the
New-York Daily Tribune,
No. 3833, July 30, 1853

Printed according to the text
of the newspaper

Karl Marx

INDIA[43]

The progress of the India bill through the Committee has little interest. It is significant, that all amendments are thrown out now by the Coalition coalescing with the Tories against their own allies of the Manchester School.

The actual state of India may be illustrated by a few facts. The Home Establishment absorbs 3 per cent of the net revenue, and the annual interest for Home Debt and Dividends 14 per cent—together 17 per cent. If we deduct these annual remittances from India to England, the *military charges* amount to about two-thirds of the whole expenditure available for India, or to 66 per cent, while the charges for *public works* do not amount to more than 2³/₄ per cent of the general revenue, or for Bengal 1 per cent, Agra 7³/₄, Punjab ¹/₈, Madras ¹/₂, and Bombay 1 per cent of their respective revenues. These figures are the official ones of the Company itself.

On the other hand nearly three-fifths of the whole net revenue are derived from the *land*, about one-seventh from *opium*, and upward of one-ninth from *salt*. These resources together yield 85 per cent of the whole receipts.

As to minor items of expenditure and charges, it may suffice to state that the *Moturpha* revenue maintained in the Presidency of Madras, and levied on shops, looms, sheep, cattle, sundry professions, etc., yields somewhat about £50,000, while the yearly dinners of the East India House[44] cost about the same sum.

The great bulk of the revenue is derived from the land. As the various kinds of Indian land-tenure have recently been described in so many places, and in popular style, too,

I propose to limit my observations on the subject to a few general remarks on the zemindari and ryotwari systems.

The zemindari and the ryotwari were both of them agrarian revolutions, effected by British ukases, and opposed to each other; the one aristocratic, the other democratic; the one a caricature of English landlordism, the other of French peasant-proprietorship; but pernicious, both combining the most contradictory character—both made not for the people, who cultivate the soil, nor for the holder, who owns it, but for the Government that taxes it.

By the zemindari system, the people of the Presidency of Bengal were depossessed at once of their hereditary claims to the soil, in favour of the native tax-gatherers called *zemindars.* By the ryotwari system introduced into the Presidencies of Madras and Bombay, the native nobility, with their territorial claims, merassis, jagirs, etc., were reduced with the common people to the holding of minute fields, cultivated by themselves, in favour of the Collector of the East India Company.[45] But a curious sort of English landlord was the zemindar, receiving only one-tenth of the rent, while he had to make over nine-tenths of it to the Government. A curious sort of French peasant was the ryot, without any permanent title in the soil, and with the taxation changing every year in proportion to his harvest. The original class of zemindars, notwithstanding their unmitigated and uncontrolled rapacity against the depossessed mass of the exhereditary landholders, soon melted away under the pressure of the Company, in order to be replaced by mercantile speculators who now hold all the land of Bengal, with exception of the estates returned under the direct management of the Government. These speculators have introduced a variety of the zemindari tenure called *patni.* Not content to be placed with regard to the British Government in the situation of middlemen, they have created in their turn a class of "hereditary" middlemen called *patnidars*, who created again their subpatnidars, etc., so that a perfect scale of hierarchy of middlemen has sprung up, which presses with its entire weight on the unfortunate cultivator. As to the ryots in Madras and Bombay, the system soon degenerated into one of forced cultivation, and the land lost all its value.

"The land," says Mr. Campbell, "would be sold for balances by the collector, as in Bengal, but generally is not, for a very good reason, viz.: that nobody will buy it."

Thus, in Bengal, we have a combination of English landlordism, of the Irish middlemen system, of the Austrian system, transforming the landlord into the tax-gatherer, and of the Asiatic system making the State the real landlord. In Madras and Bombay we have a French peasant proprietor who is at the same time a serf, and a *métayer* of the State. The drawbacks of all these various systems accumulate upon him without his enjoying any of their redeeming features. The ryot is subject, like the French peasant, to the extortion of the private usurer; but he has no hereditary, no permanent title in his land, like the French peasant. Like the serf he is forced to cultivation, but he is not secured against want like the serf. Like the *métayer* he has to divide his produce with the State, but the State is not obliged, with regard to him, to advance the funds and the stock, as it is obliged to do with regard to the *métayer*. In Bengal, as in Madras and Bombay, under the *zemindari* as under the *ryotwari*, the ryots—and they form 11/12ths of the whole Indian population—have been wretchedly pauperized; and if they are, morally speaking, not sunk as low as the Irish cottiers, they owe it to their climate, the men of the South being possessed of less wants, and of more imagination than the men of the North.

Conjointly with the land-tax we have to consider the salt-tax. Notoriously the Company retain the monopoly of that article which they sell at three times its mercantile value—and this in a country where it is furnished by the sea, by the lakes, by the mountains and the earth itself. The practical working of this monopoly was described by the Earl of Albemarle in the following words:

"A great proportion of the salt for inland consumption throughout the country is purchased from the Company by large wholesale merchants at less than 4 rupees per *maund*;* these mix a fixed proportion of sand, chiefly got a few miles to the south-west of Dacca, and send the mixture to a second, or counting the Government as the first, to a

---

* An Indian dry measure varying locally. On the average it is 26.4 lbs.—*Ed.*

third monopolist at about 5 or 6 rupees. This dealer adds more earth or ashes, and thus passing through more hands, from the large towns to villages, the price is still raised from 8 to 10 rupees and the proportion of adulteration from 25 to 40 per cent. It appears then that the people pay from £21, 17s. 2d. to £27, 6s. 2d. for their salt, or in other words, from 30 to 36 times as much as the wealthy people of Great Britain."

As an instance of English bourgeois morals, I may allege, that Mr. Campbell defends the opium monopoly because it prevents the Chinese from consuming too much of the drug, and that he defends the brandy monopoly (licences for spirit-selling in India) because it has wonderfully increased the consumption of brandy in India.

The zemindar tenure, the ryotwar, and the salt-tax, combined with the Indian climate, were the hotbeds of the cholera—India's ravages upon the Western World—a striking and severe example of the solidarity of human woes and wrongs.

Written on July 19, 1853

Published in the *New-York Daily Tribune*, No. 3838, August 5, 1853

Printed according to the text of the newspaper

Karl Marx

THE FUTURE RESULTS OF THE BRITISH RULE IN INDIA

London, Friday, July 22, 1853

I propose in this letter to conclude my observations on India. How came it that English supremacy was established in India? The paramount power of the Great Mogul was broken by the Mogul Viceroys. The power of the Viceroys was broken by the Mahrattas.[46] The power of the Mahrattas was broken by the Afghans, and while all were struggling against all, the Briton rushed in and was enabled to subdue them all. A country not only divided between Mohammedan and Hindu, but between tribe and tribe, between caste and caste; a society whose framework was based on a sort of equilibrium, resulting from a general repulsion and constitutional exclusiveness between all its members. Such a country and such a society, were they not the predestined prey of conquest? If we knew nothing of the past history of Hindustan, would there not be the one great and incontestable fact, that even at this moment India is held in English thraldom by an Indian army maintained at the cost of India? India, then, could not escape the fate of being conquered, and the whole of her past history, if it be anything, is the history of the successive conquests she has undergone. Indian society has no history at all, at least no known history. What we call its history, is but the history of the successive intruders who founded their empires on the passive basis of that unresisting and unchanging society. The question, therefore, is not whether the English had a right to conquer India, but whether we are to prefer India conquered by the Turk, by the Persian, by the Russian, to India conquered by the Briton.

England has to fulfil a double mission in India: one destructive, the other regenerating—the annihilation of old Asiatic society, and the laying of the material foundations of Western society in Asia.

Arabs, Turks, Tartars, Moguls, who had successively overrun India, soon became *Hinduized*, the barbarian conquerors being, by an eternal law of history, conquered themselves by the superior civilization of their subjects. The British were the first conquerors superior, and, therefore, inaccessible to Hindu civilization. They destroyed it by breaking up the native communities, by uprooting the native industry, and by levelling all that was great and elevated in the native society. The historic pages of their rule in India report hardly anything beyond that destruction. The work of regeneration hardly transpires through a heap of ruins. Nevertheless it has begun.

The political unity of India, more consolidated, and extending farther than it ever did under the Great Moguls, was the first condition of its regeneration. That unity, imposed by the British sword, will now be strengthened and perpetuated by the electric telegraph. The native army, organized and trained by the British drill-sergeant, was the *sine qua non* of Indian self-emancipation, and of India ceasing to be the prey of the first foreign intruder. The free press, introduced for the first time into Asiatic society, and managed principally by the common offspring of Hindus and Europeans, is a new and powerful agent of reconstruction. The *zemindari* and *ryotwari* themselves, abominable as they are, involve two distinct forms of private property in land—the great desideratum of Asiatic society. From the Indian natives, reluctantly and sparingly educated at Calcutta, under English superintendence, a fresh class is springing up, endowed with the requirements for government and imbued with European science. Steam has brought India into regular and rapid communication with Europe, has connected its chief ports with those of the whole southeastern ocean, and has revindicated it from the isolated position which was the prime law of its stagnation. The day is not far distant when, by a combination of railways and steam vessels, the distance between England and India, measured by time, will be shortened to eight days, and when that once fabulous country will thus be actually annexed to the Western world.

The ruling classes of Great Britain have had, till now, but an accidental, transitory and exceptional interest in the progress of India. The aristocracy wanted to conquer it, the moneyocracy to plunder it, and the millocracy to undersell it. But now the tables are turned. The millocracy have discovered that the transformation of India into a reproductive country has become of vital importance to them, and that, to that end, it is necessary, above all, to gift her with means of irrigation and of internal communication. They intend now drawing a net of railways over India. And they will do it. The results must be inappreciable.

It is notorious that the productive powers of India are paralyzed by the utter want of means for conveying and exchanging its various produce. Nowhere, more than in India, do we meet with social destitution in the midst of natural plenty, for want of the means of exchange. It was proved before a Committee of the British House of Commons, which sat in 1848, that

> "when grain was selling from 6s. to 8s. a quarter at Khandesh, it was sold at 64s. to 70s. at Poona, where the people were dying in the streets of famine, without the possibility of gaining supplies from Khandesh, because the clay roads were impracticable."

The introduction of railways may be easily made to subserve agricultural purposes by the formation of tanks, where ground is required for embankment, and by the conveyance of water along the different lines. Thus irrigation, the *sine qua non* of farming in the East, might be greatly extended, and the frequently recurring local famines, arising from the want of water, would be averted. The general importance of railways, viewed under this head, must become evident, when we remember that irrigated lands, even in the districts near Ghauts, pay three times as much in taxes, afford ten or twelve times as much employment, and yield twelve or fifteen times as much profit, as the same area without irrigation.

Railways will afford the means of diminishing the amount and the cost of the military establishments. Col. Warren, Town Major of the Fort St. William, stated before a Select Committee of the House of Commons:

"The practicability of receiving intelligence from distant parts of the country in as many hours as at present it requires days and even weeks, and of sending instructions with troops and stores, in the more brief period, are considerations which cannot be too highly estimated. Troops could be kept at more distant and healthier stations than at present, and much loss of life from sickness would by this means be spared. Stores could not to the same extent be required at the various dépôts, and the loss by decay, and the destruction incidental to the climate, would also be avoided. The number of troops might be diminished in direct proportion to their effectiveness."

We know that the municipal organization and the economical basis of the village communities have been broken up, but their worst feature, the dissolution of society into stereotype and disconnected atoms, has survived their vitality. The village isolation produced the absence of roads in India, and the absence of roads perpetuated the village isolation. On this plan a community existed with a given scale of low conveniences, almost without intercourse with other villages, without the desires and efforts indispensable to social advance. The British having broken up this self-sufficient *inertia* of the villages, railways will provide the new want of communication and intercourse. Besides,

"one of the effects of the railway system will be to bring into every village affected by it such knowledge of the contrivances and appliances of other countries, and such means of obtaining them, as will first put the hereditary and stipendiary village artisanship of India to full proof of its capabilities, and then supply its defects." (Chapman, *The Cotton and Commerce of India.*)

I know that the English millocracy intend to endow India with railways with the exclusive view of extracting at diminished expenses the cotton and other raw materials for their manufactures. But when you have once introduced machinery into the locomotion of a country, which possesses iron and coals, you are unable to withhold it from its fabrication. You cannot maintain a net of railways over an immense country without introducing all those industrial processes necessary to meet the immediate and current wants of railway locomotion, and out of which there must grow the application of machinery to those branches of industry not immediately connected with railways. The railway system will therefore become, in India, truly the forerunner of modern industry. This is the more certain as the Hindus are allowed by British authorities themselves to possess particular aptitude for accommodating themselves to entirely new labour, and acquiring the requisite knowledge of machinery. Ample proof of this fact is afforded by the capacities and expertness of the native engineers in the Calcutta mint, where they have been for years employed in working the steam machinery, by the natives attached to the several steam-engines in the Hardwar coal districts, and by other instances. Mr. Campbell himself, greatly influenced as he is by the prejudices of the East India Company, is obliged to avow

> "that the great mass of the Indian people possesses a great *industrial* energy, is well fitted to accumulate capital, and remarkable for a mathematical clearness of head and talent for figures and exact sciences." "Their intellects," he says, "are excellent."

Modern industry, resulting from the railway system, will dissolve the hereditary divisions of labour, upon which rest the Indian castes, those decisive impediments to Indian progress and Indian power.

All the English bourgeoisie may be forced to do will neither emancipate nor materially mend the social condition of the mass of the people, depending not only on the development of the productive powers, but on their appropriation by the people. But what they will not fail to do is to lay down the material premises for both. Has the bourgeoisie ever done more? Has it ever effected a progress without dragging individuals and peoples through blood and dirt, through misery and degradation?

The Indians will not reap the fruits of the new elements of society scattered among them by the British bourgeoisie, till in Great Britain itself the now ruling classes shall have been supplanted by the industrial proletariat, or till the Hindus themselves shall have grown strong enough to throw off the English yoke altogether. At all events, we may safely expect to see, at a more or less remote period, the regeneration of that great and interesting country, whose gentle natives are, to use the expression of Prince Saltykov, even in the most inferior classes, "*plus fins et plus adroits que les italiens*,"* whose submission even is counterbalanced by

* "More subtle and adroit than the Italians." Marx quotes from A. D. Saltykov's book *Lettres sur l'Inde*. Paris, 1848, p. 61.—*Ed.*

a certain calm nobility, who, notwithstanding their natural languor, have astonished the British officers by their bravery, whose country has been the source of our languages, our religions, and who represent the type of the ancient German in the Jat[47] and the type of the ancient Greek in the Brahmin.

I cannot part with the subject of India without some concluding remarks.

The profound hypocrisy and inherent barbarism of bourgeois civilization lies unveiled before our eyes, turning from its home, where it assumes respectable forms, to the colonies, where it goes naked. They are the defenders of property, but did any revolutionary party ever originate agrarian revolutions like those in Bengal, in Madras, and in Bombay? Did they not, in India, to borrow an expression of that great robber, Lord Clive himself, resort to atrocious extortion, when simple corruption could not keep pace with their rapacity? While they prated in Europe about the inviolable sanctity of the national debt, did they not confiscate in India the dividends of the rajahs, who had invested their private savings in the Company's own funds? While they combated the French revolution under the pretext of defending "our holy religion," did they not forbid, at the same time, Christianity to be propagated in India, and did they not, in order to make money out of the pilgrims streaming to the temples of Orissa and Bengal, take up the trade in the murder and prostitution perpetrated in the temple of Juggernaut?[48] These are the men of "Property, Order, Family, and Religion."

The devastating effects of English industry, when contemplated with regard to India, a country as vast as Europe, and containing 150 millions of acres, are palpable and confounding. But we must not forget that they are only the organic results of the whole system of production as it is now constituted. That production rests on the supreme rule of capital. The centralization of capital is essential to the existence of capital as an independent power. The destructive influence of that centralization upon the markets of the world does but reveal, in the most gigantic dimensions, the inherent organic laws of political economy now at work in every civilized town. The bourgeois period of history has to create the material basis of the new world—on the one hand the universal intercourse founded upon the mutual dependency of mankind, and the means of that intercourse; on the other hand the development of the productive powers of man and the transformation of material production into a scientific domination of natural agencies. Bourgeois industry and commerce create these material conditions of a new world in the same way as geological revolutions have created the surface of the earth. When a great social revolution shall have mastered the results of the bourgeois epoch, the market of the world and the modern powers of production, and subjected them to the common control of the most advanced peoples, then only will human progress cease to resemble that hideous pagan idol, who would not drink the nectar but from the skulls of the slain.

Published in the
New-York Daily Tribune,
No. 3840, August 8, 1853

Printed according to the text
of the newspaper

Karl Marx

ANGLO-PERSIAN WAR

The declaration of war against Persia, by England or rather by the East India Company,[49] is the reproduction of one of those cunning and reckless tricks of Anglo-Asiatic diplomacy, by virtue of which England has extended her possessions on that continent. So soon as the Company casts a greedy look on any of the independent sovereigns, or on any region whose political and commercial resources or whose gold and jewels are valued, the victim is accused of having violated this or that ideal or actual convention, transgressed an imaginary promise or restriction, committed some nebulous outrage, and then war is declared, and the eternity of wrong, the perennial force of the fable of the wolf and the lamb, is again incarnadined in national history.

For many years England has coveted a position in the Persian Gulf, and above all the possession of the Island of Kareg, situated in the northern part of those waters. The celebrated Sir John Malcolm, several times Ambassador to Persia, expatiated on the value of that island to England, and affirmed that it could be made one of her most flourishing establishments in Asia, being in the neighbourhood of Bushire, Bandar Rig, Basra, Grien Barberia and Elkatif. Accordingly, the island and Bushire are already in the possession of England. Sir John considered it a central point for the commerce of Turkey, Arabia and Persia. The climate is excellent, and it contains all the facilities for becoming a flourishing spot. The Ambassador more than thirty-five years ago submitted his observations to Lord Minto, then Governor-General, and both sought to carry out the scheme. Sir John, in fact, received the command of an expedition to take the island, and had already set out, when he received orders to return to Calcutta, and Sir Harford Jones was sent on a diplomatic mission to Persia. During the first siege of Herat by Persia, in 1837-38, England, under the same ephemeral pretence as now—that is, to defend the Afghans, with whom she has constantly a deadly feud—seized upon Kareg, but was forced by circumstances, by the interference of Russia, to surrender her prey. The lately renewed and successful attempt of Persia against Herat has afforded England an occasion to accuse the Shah of violation of good faith toward her, and to take the island as a first step toward hostilities.

Thus, for half a century, England has striven continually, but rarely with success, to establish her preponderance in the Cabinet of the Persian Shahs. The latter, however, are a match for their wheedling foes, and squirm out of such treacherous embraces. Aside from having under their eyes English dealings in India, the Persians very likely keep in view this advice, given to Feth-ali Shah, in 1805: "Distrust the counsel of a nation of greedy merchants, which in India traffics with the lives and crowns of sovereigns." Set a thief to catch a thief. In Teheran, the capital of Persia, English influence is very low; for, not counting Russian intrigues there, France occupies a prominent standing, and of the three filibusters, Persia may most dread the British. At the present moment an embassy from Persia is on the way to or has already reached Paris, and there very likely the Persian complication will be the subject of diplomatic disputes. France, indeed, is not indifferent to the occupation of the island in the Persian Gulf. The question is rendered yet more knotty by the fact that France disentombs some buried parchment by which Kareg has already been twice ceded to her by the Persian Shahs—one so far back as in 1708, under Louis XIV, and then in 1808—on both occasions conditionally, it is true, but in terms sufficient to constitute some rights, or justify pretensions from the present imitator of those sovereigns, who were sufficiently anti-English.

In a recent answer to the *Journal des Débats, The London Times* gives up in the name of England to France every pretension to the leadership in European affairs, reserving for the English nation the undisputed direction of the affairs of Asia and America, where no other European power must interfere. It may, nevertheless, be doubted if Louis Bonaparte will accept this division of the world. At any rate, French diplomacy in Teheran during the late misunderstandings did not heartily support England; and the French press exhuming and ventilating Gallic pretensions to Kareg seems to foreshadow that England will not find it an easy game to attack and dismember Persia.

Written on October 30, 1856

Published in the *New-York Daily Tribune*, No. 4904, January 7, 1857

Printed according to the text of the newspaper

Karl Marx

THE BRITISH QUARREL WITH CHINA

The mails of the *America* which reached us yesterday morning bring a variety of documents concerning the British quarrel with the Chinese authorities at Canton, and the warlike operations of Admiral Seymour. The result which a careful study of the official correspondence between the British and Chinese authorities at Hongkong and Canton must, we think, produce upon every impartial mind, is that the British are in the wrong in the whole proceeding. The alleged cause of the quarrel, as stated by the latter, is that instead of appealing to the British Consul, certain Chinese officers had violently removed some Chinese criminals from a lorcha lying in Canton River, and hauled down the British flag which was flying from its mast. But, as says *The London Times*, "there are, indeed, matters in dispute such as whether the lorcha was carrying British colours, and whether the Consul was entirely justified in the steps that he took". The doubt thus admitted is confirmed when we remember that the provision of the treaty,[50] which the Consul insists should be applied to this lorcha, relates to British ships alone; while the lorcha, as it abundantly appears, was not in any just sense British. But in order that our readers may have the whole case before them, we proceed to give what is important in the official correspondence. First, we have a communication dated Oct. 21, from Mr. Parkes, the British Consul at Canton, to Governor-General Yeh, as follows:

"On the morning of the 8th inst. the British lorcha *Arrow*, when lying among the shipping anchored before the city, was boarded, without any previous reference being made to the British Consul, by a large force of Chinese officers and soldiers in uniform, who, in the face of the remonstrance of the master, an Englishman, seized, bound and carried away twelve Chinese out of her crew of fourteen and hauled down her colours. I reported all the particulars of this public insult to the British flag, and grave violation of the ninth article of the Supplementary Treaty, to your Excellency the same day, and appealed to you to afford satisfaction for the insult, and cause the provision of the treaty to be in this case faithfully observed. But your Excellency, with a strange disregard both to justice and treaty engagement, has offered no reparation or apology for the injury, and, by retaining the men you have seized in your custody, signify your approval of this violation of the treaty, and leave her Majesty's Government without assurance that a similar event shall not again occur."

It seems that the Chinese on board the lorcha were seized by the Chinese officers, because the latter had been informed that some of the crew had participated in a piracy committed against a Chinese merchantman. The British Consul accuses the Chinese Governor-General of seizing the crew, of hauling down the British flag, of declining to offer any apology, and of retaining the men seized in his custody. The Chinese Governor, in a letter addressed to Admiral Seymour, affirms that, having ascertained that nine of the captives were innocent, he directed, on Oct. 10, an officer to put them on board of their vessel again, but that Consul Parkes refused to receive them. As to the lorcha itself, he states that when the Chinese on board were seized, she was supposed to be a Chinese vessel, and rightly so, because she was built by a Chinese, and belonged to a Chinese, who had fraudulently obtained possession of a British ensign, by entering his vessel on the colonial British register—a method, it seems, habitual with Chinese smugglers. As to the question of the insult to the flag, the Governor remarks:

"It has been the invariable rule with lorchas of your Excellency's nation, to haul down the flag when they drop anchor, and to hoist it again when they get under way. When the lorcha was boarded, in order that the prisoners might be seized, it has been satisfactorily proved that no flag was flying. How then could a flag have been hauled down? Yet Consul Parkes, in one dispatch after another, pretends that satisfaction is required for the insult offered to the flag."

From these premises the Chinese Governor concludes that no breach of any treaty has been committed. On Oct. 12, nevertheless, the British Plenipotentiary[51] demanded not only the surrender of the whole of the arrested crew, but also an apology. The Governor thus replies:

"Early in the morning of Oct. 22, I wrote to Consul Parkes, and at the same time forwarded to him twelve men, namely, Li Ming-tai and Li Chi-fu, convicted on the inquiry I had instituted, and the witness, Wu Ai-ya, together with nine previously tendered. But Consul Parkes would neither receive the twelve prisoners nor my letter."

Parkes might, therefore, have now got back the whole of his twelve men, together with what was most probably an apology, contained in a letter which he did not open. In the evening of the same day, Governor Yeh again made inquiry why the prisoners tendered by him were not received, and why he received no answer to his letter. No notice was taken of this step, but on the 24th fire was opened on the forts, and several of them were taken; and it was not until Nov. 1 that Admiral Seymour explained the apparently incomprehensible conduct of Consul Parkes in a message to the Governor. The men, he says, had been restored to the Consul, but "not *publicly* restored to their vessel, nor had the required apology been made for the violation of the Consular jurisdiction". To this quibble, then, of not restoring in state a set of men numbering three convicted criminals, the whole case is reduced. To this the Governor of Canton answers, first, that the twelve men had been actually handed over to the Consul, and that there had not been "any refusal to return them to their vessel." What was still the matter with this British Consul, the Chinese Governor only learned after the city had been bombarded for six days. As to an apology, Governor Yeh insists that none could be given, as no fault had been committed. We quote his words:

"No foreign flag was seen by my executive at the time of the capture, and as, in addition to this, it was ascertained on examination of the prisoners by the officer deputed to conduct it, that the lorcha was in no respect a foreign vessel, I maintain that there was no mistake committed."

Indeed, the force of these Chinaman's dialectics disposes so effectually of the whole question—and there is no other apparent case—that Admiral Seymour at last has no resource left him but a declaration like the following:

"I must positively decline any further argument on the merits of the case of the lorcha *Arrow*. I am perfectly satisfied of the facts as represented to your Excellency by Mr. Consul Parkes."

But after having taken the forts, breached the walls of the city, and bombarded Canton for six days, the Admiral suddenly discovers quite a new object for his measures, as we find him writing to the Chinese Governor on Oct. 30:

"It is now for your Excellency, by immediate consultation with me, to terminate a condition of things of which the present evil is not slight, but which, if not amended, can scarcely fail to be productive of the most serious calamities."

The Chinese Governor answers, that according to the Convention of 1849,[52] he had no right to ask for such a consultation. He further says:

"In reference to the admission into the city, I must observe that, in April, 1849, his Excellency the Plenipotentiary Bonham issued a public notice at the factories here, to the effect that he thereby prohibited foreigners from entering the city. The notice was inserted in the newspapers of the time, and will, I presume, have been read by your Excellency. Add to this that the exclusion of foreigners from the city is by the unanimous vote of the whole population of Canton. It may be supposed how little to their liking has been this storming of the forts and this destruction of their dwellings; and, apprehensive as I am of the evil that may hence befall the officials and citizens of your Excellency's nation, I can suggest nothing better than a continued adherence to the policy of the Plenipotentiary Bonham, as to the correct course to be pursued. As to the consultation proposed by your Excellency, I have already, some days ago, deputed Tsang, Prefect of Liuchow."

Admiral Seymour now makes a clean breast of it, declaring that he does not care for the convention of Mr. Bonham:

"Your Excellency's reply refers me to the notification of the British Plenipotentiary of 1849, prohibiting foreigners from entering Canton. Now, I must remind you that, although we have indeed serious matter of complaint against the Chinese Government for breach of the promise given in 1847 to admit foreigners into Canton at the end of two years, my demand now made is in no way connected with former negotiations on the same subject, neither am I demanding admission of any but the foreign officials, and this only for the simple and sufficient reasons above assigned. On my proposal to treat personally with your Excellency, you do me the honour to remark that you sent a Prefect some days ago. I am compelled therefore to regard your Excellency's whole letter as unsatisfactory in the extreme, and have only to add that, unless I immediately receive an explicit assurance of your assent to what I have proposed, I shall at once resume offensive operations."

Governor Yeh retorts by again entering into the details of the Convention of 1849:

"In 1848 there was a long controversial correspondence on the subject between my predecessor Hsü and the British Plenipotentiary, Mr. Bonham, and Mr. Bonham being satisfied that an interview within the city was utterly out of the question, addressed a letter to Hsü in the April of 1849, in which he said, 'At the present time I can have no more discussion with your Excellency on this subject.' He further issued a notice from the factories to the effect that no foreigner was to enter the city, which was inserted in the papers, and he communicated this to the British Government. There was not a Chinese or foreigner of any nation who did not know that the question was never to be discussed again."

Impatient of argument, the British Admiral hereupon forces his way into the City of Canton to the residence of the Governor, at the same time destroying the Imperial fleet in the river. Thus there are two distinct acts in this diplomatic and military drama—the first introducing the bombardment of Canton on the pretext of a breach of the Treaty of 1842 committed by the Chinese Governor, and the second, continuing that bombardment on an enlarged scale, on the pretext that the Governor clung stubbornly to the Convention of 1849. First Canton is bombarded for breaking a treaty, and next it is bombarded for observing a treaty. Besides, it is not even pretended that redress was not given in the first instance, but only that redress was not given in the orthodox manner.

The view of the case put forth by *The London Times* would do no discredit even to General William Walker of Nicaragua.

"By this outbreak of hostilities," says that journal, "existing treaties are annulled, and we are left free to change our relations with the Chinese Empire as we please. The recent proceedings at Canton warn us that we ought to enforce that right of free entrance into the country and into the ports open to us, which was stipulated for in the Treaty of 1842. We must not again be told that our representatives must be excluded from the presence of the Chinese Governor-General, because *we have waived* the performance of the article which enabled foreigners to penetrate beyond the precincts of our factories."

In other words, "we" have commenced hostilities in order to break an existing treaty and to enforce a claim which "we" have waived by an express convention! We are happy to say, however, that another prominent organ of British opinion expresses itself in a more humane and becoming tone.

"It is," says *The Daily News*, "a monstrous fact, that in order to avenge the irritated pride of a British official, and punish the folly of an Asiatic governor, we prostitute our strength to the wicked work of carrying fire and sword, and desolation and death, into the peaceful homes of unoffending men, on whose shores we were originally intruders. Whatever may be the issue of this Canton bombardment, the deed itself is a bad and base one—a reckless and wanton waste of human life at the shrine of a false etiquette and a mistaken policy."

It is, perhaps, a question whether the civilized nations of the world will approve this mode of invading a peaceful country, without previous declaration of war, for an alleged infringement of the fanciful code of diplomatic etiquette. If the first Chinese war,[53] in spite of its infamous pretext, was patiently looked upon by other powers, because it held out the prospect of opening the trade with China, is not this second war likely to obstruct that trade for an indefinite period? Its first result must be the cutting off of Canton from the tea-growing districts, as yet, for the most part, in the hands of the imperialists—a circumstance which cannot profit anybody but the Russian overland tea traders.

Written on January 7, 1857

Published in the
New-York Daily Tribune,
No. 4918, January 23, 1857

Printed according to the text
of the newspaper

Karl Marx

THE WAR AGAINST PERSIA

To understand the policy and object of the war lately undertaken by the British against Persia, and which, according to the most recent accounts, has been so energetically pushed as to lead to submission on the part of the Shah, it is necessary to take a slight retrospect of Persian affairs. The Persian dynasty, founded in 1502 by Ismael, who claimed to be descended from the ancient Persian kings, after maintaining for more than two centuries the power and dignity of a great State, received, about 1720, a severe shock in the rebellion of the Afghans inhabiting its eastern provinces. Western Persia was invaded by them, and two Afghan princes succeeded in keeping themselves for a few years on the Persian throne. They were, however, speedily expelled by the famous Nadir, acting at first in the capacity of General to the Persian claimant. Afterward he assumed the crown himself, and not only reduced the rebellious Afghans, but by his famous invasion of India contributed much to that disorganization of the declining Mogul empire, which opened the way for the rise of the British power in India.

Amid the anarchy that ensued in Persia after the death of Nadir Shah in 1747, there sprang up, under the rule of Ahmed Duranee, an independent Afghan kingdom comprising the Principalities of Herat, Cabul, Candahar, Pechawur, and the whole of the territories afterward owned by the Sikhs. This kingdom, only superficially cemented, collapsed at the death of its founder, and was again broken up into its constituent parts, the independent Afghan tribes with separate chiefs, divided by interminable feuds and only exceptionally rallied under the common pressure of a collision with Persia. This political antagonism between the Afghans and Persians, founded on diversity of race, blended with historical reminiscences, kept alive by frontier quarrels and rival claims, is also, as it were, sanctioned by religious antagonism, the Afghans being Mohammedans of the Suni sect, that is to say, of the orthodox Mahometan faith, while Persia forms the stronghold of the heretical Shiites.[54]

In spite of this intense and universal antagonism, there existed one point of contact between the Persians and Afghans—their common hostility to Russia. Russia invaded Persia for the first time under Peter the Great, but without much advantage. Alexander I, more successful, deprived Persia, by the treaty of Ghulistan, of twelve provinces—the greater part of them south of the Caucasus. Nicholas, by the war of 1826-27, ending in the treaty of Turkmanchai, stripped Persia of several additional districts, and interdicted her from the navigation on her own shores along the Caspian Sea. The memory of past spoliations, the endurance of present restrictions, and the fear of future encroachments, alike concurred to spur Persia into deadly opposition to Russia. The Afghans, on their part, although never involved in actual quarrels with Russia, were used to consider her as the eternal foe of their religion, and a giant which was to swallow Asia. From considering Russia as their natural foe, both races—Persians and Afghans—were induced to consider England as their natural ally. Thus, to maintain her supremacy, England had but to play the benevolent mediator between Persia and Afghanistan, and to prove the decided adversary of Russian encroachment. A show of amity on the one hand, and an earnest of resistance on the other—nothing else was required.

It cannot be said, however, that the advantages of this position have been very successfully improved. In 1834, in the matter of the selection of an heir to the Shah of Persia, the English were induced to co-operate in favour of the prince proposed by Russia, and the next year to aid that prince with money and the active assistance of British military officers in maintaining his claim by arms against his rival.[55] The English Ambassadors dispatched to Persia were charged to warn the Persian Government against allowing itself to be pushed on to make war against the Afghans, which could only result in a waste of resources; but when these Ambassadors earnestly called for authority to prevent a threatened war of this sort, they were put in mind by the Ministry at home of an article in an old treaty of 1814, by which, in case of war between Persia and the Afghans, the English were not to interfere unless their mediation should be solicited. The idea of the British envoys and of the British Indian authorities was that this war was planned by Russia, which power desired to employ the extension of Persian authority eastward as the means of opening a road by which at some time or other a Russian army might enter India. These representations seem, however, to have made little or no impression on Lord Palmerston, then at the head of the Department of Foreign Affairs, and in September 1837, a Persian army invaded Afghanistan. Various small successes carried it to Herat, before which town it encamped and began siege operations under the personal direction of Count Simonich, the Russian Ambassador at the Persian Court. During the progress of these warlike acts, McNeill, the British Ambassador, found himself paralyzed by contradictory instructions. On the one hand, Lord Palmerston enjoined him "to refrain from making the relations of Persia" with Herat a "subject of discussion", as England had nothing to say between Persia and Herat. On the other hand, Lord Auckland, the Governor-General of India, wanted him to dissuade the Shah from pushing on his operations. At the very outset of the expedition Mr. Ellis had recalled the British officers serving in the Persian army, but Palmerston had them reinstated. So, again, the Indian Governor-General instructing McNeill to withdraw the British officers, Palmerston again reversed that decision. On March 8, 1838, McNeill proceeded to the Persian camp and offered his mediation, not in the name of England, but of India.

Toward the end of May 1838, the siege having now lasted about nine months, Palmerston sent a menacing dispatch to the Persian Court, for the first time making the affair of Herat a subject of remonstrance, and for the first time inveighing against "Persia's connection with Russia". Simultaneously, a hostile expedition was ordered by the Indian Government to sail to the Persian Gulf and seize upon the Island of Karak—the same lately occupied by the English. At a still later epoch the English Envoy withdrew from Teheran to Erzeroum, and the Persian Ambassador sent to England was refused admission. In the mean time, in spite of a very protracted blockade, Herat had held out, the Persian assaults were beaten back, and on Aug. 15, 1838, the Shah was forced to raise the siege and to retreat in hurried marches from Afghanistan. Here one would have supposed the operations of the English might have ended; but so far from that, matters took a most extraordinary turn. Not content with repelling the attempts of Persia, made, it was alleged, at the instigation and in the interest of Russia, to seize a part of Afghanistan, the English undertook to occupy the whole of it for themselves. Hence the famous Afghan war,[56] the ultimate result of which was so disastrous to the English, and the real responsibility for which still remains so much a mystery.

The present war against Persia has been undertaken on grounds very similar to that which preceded the Afghan war, namely, an attack upon Herat by the Persians, resulting, on the present occasion, in the capture of that city. A striking circumstance, however, is that the English have now been acting as the allies and defenders of the same Dost Mohamed, whom, in the Afghan struggle, they so unsuccesfully undertook to dethrone. It remains to be seen whether this war is to have sequences as extraordinary and unexpected as those which attended the former one.

Written about January 27, 1857

Published as an editorial in the *New-York Daily Tribune*, No. 4937, February 14, 1857

Printed according to the text of the newspaper

Karl Marx

PARLIAMENTARY DEBATES ON THE CHINESE HOSTILITIES

London, February 27, 1857

The Earl of Derby's resolution, and that of Mr. Cobden, both of them passing condemnation upon the Chinese hostilities, were moved according to notices given, the one on the 24th of February, in the House of Lords, the other on the 27th of February, in the House of Commons. The debates in the Lords ended on the same day when the debates in the Commons began. The former gave the Palmerston Cabinet a shock by leaving it in the comparatively weak majority of 36 votes. The latter may result in its defeat. But whatever interest may attach to the discussion in the Commons, the debates in the House of Lords have exhausted the argumentative part of the controversy—the mastery speeches of Lords Derby and Lyndhurst forestalling the eloquence of Mr. Cobden, Sir E. Bulwer, Lord John Russell, and *tutti quanti*.

The only law authority on the part of the Government, the Lord Chancellor*, remarked that "unless England had a good case with regard to the *Arrow*, all proceedings from the last to first were wrong." Derby and Lyndhurst proved beyond doubt that England had no case at all with regard to that lorcha. The line of argument followed by them coincides so much with that taken up in the columns of *The Tribune*** on the first publication of the English dispatches that I am able to condense it here into a very small compass.

---

* Robert Cranworth.—*Ed.*

** See this collection, pp. 91-96.—*Ed.*

What is the charge against the Chinese Government upon which the Canton massacres are pretended to rest? The infringement of Art. 9 of the supplemental treaty of 1843. That article prescribes that any Chinese offenders, being in the Colony of Hongkong, or on board a British man-of-war, or on board a British merchant ship, are not to be seized by the Chinese authorities themselves, but should be demanded from the British Consul, and by him be handed over to the native authorities. Chinese pirates were seized in the River of Canton on board the lorcha *Arrow*, by Chinese officers, without the intervention of the British Consul. The question arises, therefore, was the *Arrow* a British vessel? It was, as Lord Derby shows,

> "a vessel Chinese built, Chinese captured, Chinese sold, Chinese bought and manned, and Chinese owned."

By what means, then, was this Chinese vessel converted into a British merchantman? By purchasing at Hongkong a British register or sailing licence. The legality of this register relies upon an ordinance of the local legislation of Hongkong, passed in March, 1855. That ordinance not only infringed the treaty existing between England and China, but annulled the law of England herself. It was, therefore, void and null. Some semblance of English legality it could but receive from the Merchant Shipping Act, which, however, was passed only two months after the issue of the ordinance. And even with the legal provisions of that act it had never been brought into consonance. The ordinance, therefore, under which the lorcha *Arrow* received its register, was so much waste paper. But even according to this worthless paper the *Arrow* had forfeited its protection by the infringement of the provisions prescribed, and the expiration of its licence. This point is conceded by Sir J. Bowring himself. But then, it is said, whether or not the *Arrow* was an English vessel, it had, at all events, hoisted the English flag, and that flag was insulted. Firstly, if the flag was flying, it was not legally flying. But was it flying at all? On this point there exists discrepancy between the English and Chinese declarations. The latter have, however, been corroborated by depositions, forwarded by the Consuls, of the master and crew of the Portuguese lorcha

No. 83. With reference to these depositions, *The Friend of China*[57] of Nov. 13 states that "it is now notorious at Canton that the British flag had not been flying on board the lorcha for six days previous to its seizure." Thus falls to the ground the punctilio of honour, together with the legal case.*

Lord Derby had in this speech the good taste altogether to forbear from his habitual waggishness, and thus to give his argument a strictly judicial character. No efforts, however, on his part were wanted to impregnate his speech with a deep current of irony. The Earl of Derby, the chief of the hereditary aristocracy of England, pleading against the late Doctor, now Sir John Bowring, the pet disciple of Bentham; pleading for humanity against the professional humanitarian; defending the real interest of nations against the systematic utilitarian insisting upon a punctilio of diplomatic etiquette; appealing to the "*vox populi—vox dei*" against the greatest-benefit-of-the-greatest-number[58] man; the descendant of the conquerors preaching peace where a member of the Peace Society[59] preached red-hot shell; a Derby branding the acts of the British navy as "miserable proceedings" and "inglorious operations," where a Bowring congratulates it upon cowardly outrages which met with no resistance, upon "its brilliant achievements, unparalleled bravery, and splendid union of military skill and valour"—such contrasts were the more keenly satirical the less the Earl of Derby seemed to be aware of them. He had the advantage of that great historical irony which does not flow from the wit of individuals, but from the humour of situations. The whole parliamentary history of England has, perhaps, never exhibited such an intellectual victory of the aristocrat over the parvenu.

Lord Derby declared at the outset that he "should have to rely upon statements and documents exclusively furnished by the very parties whose conduct he was about to impugn," and that he was content "to rest his case upon these documents." Now it has been justly remarked that those documents, as laid before the public by the Government, would have allowed the latter to shift the whole

* The manuscript ends here.—*Ed.*

responsibility upon its subordinates. So much is this the case that the attacks made by the parliamentary adversaries of the Government were exclusively directed to Bowring and Co., and could have been endorsed by the home Government itself, without at all impairing its own position. I quote from his Lordship:

"I do not wish to say anything disrespectful of Dr. Bowring. He may be a man of great attainments; but it appears to me that on the subject of his admission into Canton he is possessed with a perfect monomania [*Hear, hear, and laughter*]. I believe he dreams of his entrance into Canton. I believe he thinks of it the first thing in the morning, the last thing at night, and in the middle of the night, if he happens to be awake [*Laughter*]. I do not believe that he would consider any sacrifice too great, any interruption of commerce to be deplored, any bloodshed to be regretted, when put in the scale with the immense advantage to be derived from the fact that Sir J. Bowring had obtained an official reception in the Yamen* of Canton [*Laughter*]."

Next came Lord Lyndhurst:

"Sir J. Bowring, who is a distinguished humanitarian as well as plenipotentiary [*Laughter*], himself admits the register is void, and that the lorcha was not entitled to hoist the English flag. Now, mark what he says: 'The vessel had no protection, but the Chinese do not know this. For God's sake do not whisper it to them.' He persevered, too, for he said in effect: We know the Chinese have not been guilty of any violation of treaty, but we will not tell them so; we will insist upon reparation and a return of the men they have seized in a particular form. If the men were not returned in the form, what was to be the remedy? Why, to seize a junk—a war junk. If that was not sufficient, seize more, until we compelled them to submit, although we knew they had the right on their side and we had no justice on ours [*Hear*]. Was there ever conduct more abominable, more flagrant, in which—I will not say more fraudulent, but what is equal to fraud in our country—more false pretence has been put forward by a public man in the service of the British Government [*Hear*]? It is extraordinary that Sir J. Bowring should think he had the right of declaring war. I can understand a man in such a position having necessarily a power of carrying on defensive operations, but to carry on offensive operations upon such a ground—upon such a pretence—is one of the most extraordinary proceedings to be found in the history of the world. It is quite clear from the papers laid on the table, that from the first moment at which Sir J. Bowring was appointed to the station he now fills, his ambition was to procure what his predecessors had completely failed to effect—namely, the entry within the walls of Canton. Bent only upon carrying this object of gaining admission within the walls

* Chinese mandarin's official residence.—*Ed.*

of Canton into execution, he has, for no necessary purpose whatever, plunged the country into a war; and what is the result? Property, to the large amount of $1,500,000, belonging to British subjects, is now impounded in the City of Canton, and in addition to that our factories are burned to the ground, and all this is only owing to the mischievous policy of one of the most mischievous of men.

> "—But man, proud man,
> Dressed in a little brief authority,
> Most ignorant of what he's most assured,
> This glassy essence,—like an angry ape,
> Plays such fantastic tricks before high heaven
> As make the angels weep."*

And, lastly, Lord Grey:

"If your Lordships will refer to the papers you will find that when Sir J. Bowring applied for an interview with Commissioner Yeh, the Commissioner was ready to meet him, but he appointed for that purpose the house of the merchant Wu Hao-kuan, without the city. Sir J. Bowring's dignity would not allow him to go anywhere but to the official residence of the Commissioner. I expect, if no other result, at least the good result from the adoption of the resolution—the instant recall of Sir J. Bowring."

Sir J. Bowring met with similar treatment at the hands of the Commons, and Mr. Cobden even opened his speech with a solemn repudiation of his "friend of twenty years' standing."

The literal quotations from the speeches of Lords Derby, Lyndhurst and Grey prove that, to parry the attack, Lord Palmerston's Administration had only to drop Sir J. Bowring instead of identifying itself with that "distinguished humanitarian." That it owed this facility of escape neither to the indulgence nor the tactics of his adversaries, but exclusively to the papers laid before Parliament, will become evident from the slightest glance at the papers themselves as well as the debates founded upon them.

Can there remain any doubt as to Sir J. Bowring's "monomania" with respect to his entrance into Canton? Is it not proved that that individual, as *The London Times* says, "has taken a course entirely out of his own head, without either advice from his superiors at home or any reference to their politics"? Why, then, should Lord Palmerston, at a moment when his Government is tottering, when his way

* Shakespeare, *Measure for Measure,* Act II, Scene II.—*Ed.*

is beset with difficulties of all sorts—financial difficulties, Persian war difficulties, secret-treaty difficulties, electoral reform difficulties, coalition difficulties—when he is conscious that the eyes of the House are "upon him more earnestly but less admiringly than ever before," why should he single out just that moment to exhibit, for the first time in his political life, an unflinching fidelity to another man and to a subaltern too—at the hazard of not only impairing still more his own position, but of completely breaking it up? Why should he push his new-fangled enthusiasm to such a point as to offer himself as the expiatory sacrifice for the sins of a Dr. Bowring? Of course no man in his senses thinks the noble Viscount capable of any such romantic aberrations. The line of policy he has followed up in this Chinese difficulty affords conclusive evidence of the defective character of the papers he has laid before Parliament. Apart from published papers there must exist secret papers and secret instructions which would go far to show that if Dr. Bowring was possessed of the "monomania" of entering into Canton, there stood behind him the cool-headed chief of Whitehall[60] working upon his monomania and driving it, for purposes of his own, from the state of latent warmth into that of consuming fire.

Published in the *New-York Daily Tribune*, No. 4962, March 16, 1857

Printed according to the text of the newspaper

Karl Marx

THE COMING ELECTION IN ENGLAND

London, March 13, 1857

"And stand between two churchmen, good my Lord;
For on that ground I'll build a holy descant."*

Palmerston does not exactly comply with the advice tendered by Buckingham to Richard III. He stands between the churchman on the one side, and the opium-smuggler on the other. While the Low Church bishops, whom the veteran impostor allowed the Earl of Shaftesbury, his kinsman, to nominate, vouch his "righteousness," the opium-smugglers, the dealers in "sweet poison for the age's tooth,"** vouch his faithful service to "commodity, the bias of the world."*** Burke, the Scotchman, was proud of the London "Resurrectionists."[61] So is Palmerston of the Liverpool "poisoners." These smooth-faced gentlemen are the worthy representatives of a town, the pedigree of whose greatness may be directly traced back to the slave-trade. Liverpool, otherwise not famous for poetical production, may at least claim the original merit of having enriched poetry with odes on the slave-trade. While Pindar commenced his hymn on the Olympian victors with the celebrated "water is the best thing" (*Ariston men hudor*),**** a modern Liverpool Pindar might, therefore, be fairly expected to open his hymn on the Downing Street prize-fighters with the more ingenious exordium, "Opium is the best thing."

---

* Shakespeare, *The Tragedy of King Richard III*, Act III, Scene VII.—*Ed.*

** Shakespeare, *The Life and Death of King John*, Act I, Scene I.—*Ed.*

*** Ibid., Act II, Scene I.—*Ed.*

**** From Pindar's *First Olympian Ode*.—*Ed.*

Along with the holy bishops and the unholy opium-smugglers, there go the large tea-dealers, for the greater part directly or indirectly engaged in the opium traffic, and, therefore, interested in oversetting the present treaties with China. They are, besides, actuated by motives of their own. Having in the past year ventured upon enormous speculations in tea, the prolongation of hostilities will at once enhance the huge stocks they hold, and enable them to postpone the large payments to their creditors at Canton. Thus, war will allow them to cheat at once their British buyers and their Chinese sellers, and consequently realize their notions of "national glory" and "commercial interests." Generally the British manufacturers disagree from the tenets of this Liverpool catechism, upon the same lofty principle which puts in opposition the Manchester man, wanting low cotton prices, to the Liverpool gentleman, wanting high ones. During the first Anglo-Chinese war, extending from 1839 to 1842, the British manufacturers had flattered themselves with false hopes of marvellously extended exports. Yard by yard they had measured the cotton stuffs the Celestials were to be clothed in. Experience broke the padlock Palmerstonian politicians had put upon their mind. From 1854 to 1857 the British manufactured exports to China did not average more than £1,250,000 sterling, an amount frequently reached in years preceding the first war with China.

"In fact," as Mr. Cobden, the spokesman of the British manufacturers, stated in the House of Commons, "since 1842 we" (the United Kingdom) "have not added to our exports to China at all, at least as far as our manufactures are concerned. We have increased our consumption of tea; that is all."

Hence the broader views which British manufacturers, in contradistinction to British bishops, opium-smugglers, and tea-dealers, are able to take of Chinese politics. If we pass over the tax-eaters and place-hunters who hang on the skirts of every administration, and the silly coffee-house patriots who believe "the nation to pluck up a heart" under Pam's* auspices, we have in fact enumerated all the

* Palmerston's.—*Ed.*

bona fide partisans of Palmerston. Still we must not forget *The London Times* and *Punch*, the Grand Cophta and the Clown of the British press,[62] both of whom are riveted to the present administration by golden and official links, and, consequently, write up a factitious enthusiasm for the hero of the Canton massacres. But then, it ought to be considered that the vote of the House of Commons betokened a rebellion against Palmerston as much as against *The Times.* The imminent elections have, therefore, to decide not only whether Palmerston shall engross all the power of the State, but also whether *The Times* shall monopolize the whole manufacture of public opinion.

Upon which principle, then, is Palmerston likely to appeal to the general election? Extension of trade with China? But he has destroyed the very port upon which that commerce depended. For a more or less protracted period he has transferred it from the sea to the land, from the five ports to Siberia, from England to Russia. In the United Kingdom he has raised the duty upon tea—the greatest bar against the extension of the Chinese trade. The safety of the British merchant-adventurers? But the Blue Book, entitled "Correspondence Respecting Insults in China," laid upon the table of the Commons by the Ministry itself, proves that, since the last seven years, there occurred but six cases of insult, in two of which the English were the aggressors, while in the four others the Chinese authorities exerted themselves to the full satisfaction of the British authorities in order to punish the offenders. If, then, the fortunes and the lives of the British merchants in Hongkong, Singapore, etc., are at present endangered, their perils are conjured up by Palmerston himself. But the honour of the British flag! Palmerston has sold it for £50 a piece to the smugglers of Hongkong, and stained it by the "wholesale massacre of helpless British customers." Yet, these pleas of extension of trade, safety of British merchant-adventurers, and honour of the British flag, are the only ones put up by the Government oracles which till now have addressed their constituents. They wisely refrain from touching any point of internal policy, as the cry of "no reform," and "more taxes," would not do. One member of the Palmerstonian Cabinet, Lord Mulgrave, the Household Treasurer, tells his constituents that he has "no political theories to propound." Another one, Bob Lowe, in his Kidderminster address, girds at the ballot, the extension of suffrage, and similar "humbug." A third one, Mr. Labouchere, the same clever fellow who defended the Canton bombardment on the plea that, should the Commons brand it as unjust, the English people must prepare to pay a bill of about £5,000,000 to the foreign merchants whose Canton property had been destroyed—this same Labouchere, in his appeal to his Taunton constituents, ignores politics altogether, simply resting his claims upon the high deeds of Bowring, Parkes and Seymour.

The remark, then, of a British provincial paper, that Palmerston has got, not only no "good cry for the hustings, but no cry at all," is perfectly true. Yet his case is by no means desperate. Circumstances are altogether altered since the vote of the Commons. The local outrage on Canton has led to a general war with China. There remains the question only, who is to carry on the war? The man who asserts that war to be just, is he not better enabled to push it on with vigour than his adversaries, getting in by passing sentence upon it?

During his interregnum will Palmerston not embroil matters to such a degree as to remain the indispensable man?

Then the mere fact of there taking place an electoral battle, will it not decide the question in his favour? For the greater part of the British electoral bodies, as at present constituted, an electoral battle means a battle between Whigs and Tories. Now, as he is the actual head of the Whigs, as his overthrow must bring the Tories in, will not the greater part of the so-called Liberals vote for Palmerston in order to oust Derby? Such are the true considerations upon which the Ministerialists rely. If their calculations prove correct, Palmerston's dictatorship, till now silently suffered, would be openly proclaimed. The new Parliamentary majority would owe their existence to the explicit profession of passive obedience to the Minister. A *coup d'état* might then, in due course of time, follow Palmerston's appeal from the Parliament to the people, as it followed Bonaparte's appeal from the *Assemblée Nationale* to the nation. That same people might then learn to their damage that Palmerston is the old colleague of the Castlereagh-Sidmouth Cabinet, who gagged the press, suppressed public meetings, suspended the Habeas Corpus Act, made it legal for the Cabinet to imprison and expulse at pleasure, and lastly butchered the people at Manchester for protesting against the Corn Laws.[63]

Published in the
New-York Daily Tribune,
No. 4975, March 31, 1857

Printed according to the text
of the newspaper

Karl Marx

ENGLISH FEROCITY IN CHINA

A few years since, when the frightful system of torture in India was exposed in Parliament, Sir James Hogg, one of the Directors of the Most Honourable East India Company, boldly asserted that the statements made were unfounded. Subsequent investigation, however, proved them to be based upon facts which should have been well known to the Directors, and Sir James had left him to admit either "wilful ignorance" or "criminal knowledge" of the horrible charge laid at the Company's doors. Lord Palmerston, the present Premier of England, and the Earl of Clarendon, the Minister of Foreign Affairs, seem just now to be placed in a similar unenviable position. At the late Lord Mayor's banquet, the Premier said, in his speech, while attempting to justify the atrocities committed upon the Chinese:

"If the Government had, in this case, approved of unjustifiable proceedings, they had undoubtedly followed a course which deserved to incur the censure of Parliament and of the country. We were persuaded, however, on the contrary, that these proceedings were necessary and vital. We felt that a great wrong had been inflicted on our country. We felt that our fellow-countrymen in a distant part of the globe had been exposed to a series of insults, outrages and atrocities which could not be passed over in silence [*Cheers*]. We felt that the treaty rights of this country had been broken, and that those locally charged with the defence of our interests in that quarter of the world were not only justified, but obliged to resent those outrages, so far as the power in their hands would enable them to do so. We felt that we should be betraying the trust which the citizens of the country had reposed in us if we had not approved of the proceedings which we thought to be right, and which we, if placed in the same circumstances, should have deemed it our duty to have pursued [*Cheers*]."

Now, however much the people of England and the world at large may be deceived by such plausible statements, his Lordship himself certainly does not believe them to be true, or if he does, he has betrayed a wilful ignorance almost as unjustifiable as "criminal knowledge." Ever since the first report reached us of English hostilities in China, the Government journals of England and a portion of the American press have been heaping wholesale denunciations upon the Chinese—sweeping charges of violation of treaty obligations—insults to the English flag—degradation of foreigners residing on their soil, and the like; yet not one single distinct charge has been made or a single fact instanced in support of these denunciations, save the case of the lorcha *Arrow*, and, with respect to this case, the circumstances have been so misrepresented and glossed over by Parliamentary rhetoric as utterly to mislead those who really desire to understand the merits of the question.

The lorcha *Arrow* was a small Chinese vessel, manned by Chinese, but employed by some Englishmen. A licence to carry the English flag had been temporarily granted to her, which licence had expired prior to the alleged "insult." She is said to have been used to smuggle salt, and had on board of her some very bad characters—Chinese pirates and smugglers—whom, being old offenders against the laws, the authorities had long been trying to arrest. While lying at anchor in front of Canton—with sails furled, and no flag whatever displayed—the police became aware of the presence on board of these offenders, and arrested them—precisely such an act as would have taken place here, had the police along our wharves known that river-thieves and smugglers were secreted in a native or foreign vessel near by. But, as this arrest interfered with the business of the owners, the captain went to the English Consul and complained. The Consul, a young man recently appointed, and, as we are informed, a person of a quick and irritable disposition, rushes on board *in propria persona*, gets into an excited parley with the police who have only discharged their simple duty, and consequently fails in obtaining satisfaction. Thence he rushes back to the Consulate, writes an imperative demand for restitution and apology to the Governor-General of the Kwangtung Province, and a note to Sir John Bowring and Admiral Seymour at Hongkong, representing that he and his country's flag have been insulted beyond endurance, and intimating in pretty broad terms that now is the time for a demonstration against Canton, such as had long been waited for.

Gov. Yeh politely and calmly responds to the arrogant demands of the excited young British Consul. He states the reason of the arrest, and regrets that there should have been any misunderstanding in the matter; at the same time he unqualifiedly denies the slightest intention of insulting the English flag, and sends back the men, whom, although lawfully arrested, he desired not to detain at the expense of so serious a misunderstanding. But this is not satisfactory to Mr. Consul Parkers—he must have an official apology, and a more formal restitution, or Gov. Yeh must abide the consequences. Next arrives Admiral Seymour with the British fleet, and then commences another correspondence, dogmatic and threatening on the side of the Admiral; cool, unimpassioned, polite, on the side of the Chinese official. Admiral Seymour demands a personal interview within the walls of Canton. Gov. Yeh says this is contrary to all precedent, and that Sir George Bonham had agreed that it should not be required.[64] He would readily consent to an interview, as usual, outside the walled town if necessary, or meet the Admiral's wishes in any other way not contrary to Chinese usage and hereditary etiquette. But this did not suit the bellicose representative of British power in the East.

Upon the grounds thus briefly stated—and the official accounts now before the people of England fully bear out this statement—this most unrighteous war has been waged. The unoffending citizens and peaceful tradesmen of Canton have been slaughtered, their habitations battered to the ground, and the claims of humanity violated, on the flimsy pretence that "English life and property are endangered by the aggressive acts of the Chinese!" The British Government and the British people—at least those who have chosen to examine the question—know how false and hollow are such charges. An attempt has been made to divert investigation from the main issue, and to impress the public mind with the idea that a long series of injuries, preceding the case of the lorcha *Arrow*, form of themselves a sufficient *casus belli*. But these sweeping assertions are baseless. The Chinese have at least ninety-nine injuries to complain of to one on the part of the English.

How silent is the press of England upon the outrageous violations of the treaty daily practised by foreigners living in China under British protection! We hear nothing of the illicit opium trade, which yearly feeds the British treasury at the expense of human life and morality. We hear nothing of the constant bribery of sub-officials, by means of which the Chinese Government is defrauded of its rightful revenue on incoming and outgoing merchandise. We hear nothing of the wrongs inflicted "even unto death" upon misguided and bonded emigrants sold to worse than slavery on the coast of Peru and into Cuban bondage. We hear nothing of the bullying spirit often exercised against the timid nature of the Chinese, or of the vice introduced by foreigners at the ports open to their trade. We hear nothing of all this and of much more, first, because the majority of people out of China care little about the social and moral condition of that country; and secondly, because it is the part of policy and prudence not to agitate topics where no pecuniary advantage would result. Thus, the English people at home, who look no farther than the grocer's where they buy their tea, are prepared to swallow all the misrepresentations which the Ministry and the Press choose to thrust down the public throat.

Meanwhile, in China, the smothered fires of hatred kindled against the English during their opium war have burst into a flame of animosity, which no tenders of peace and friendship will be very likely to quench.

Written about March 22, 1857

Published in the
New-York Daily Tribune,
No. 4984, April 10, 1857

Printed according to the text of the newspaper

Frederick Engels

THE NEW ENGLISH EXPEDITION IN CHINA

Should the quarrel which the English have picked with the Chinese be pushed to extremity, it may be expected to end in a new military and naval expedition similar to that undertaken in 1841-42, on the basis of the opium quarrel. The easy success of the English on that occasion, in extorting an immense sum of silver from the Chinese, will be apt to recommend a new experiment of the same sort to a people who, with all their horror of *our* filibustering propensities, still retain, not less than ourselves, not a little of the old plundering buccaneering spirit which distinguished our common ancestors of the 16th and 17th centuries. Yet remarkable changes in the position of things in China, which have occurred since that former successful plundering inroad on behalf of the opium trade, make it very doubtful whether a similar expedition at the present day would be attended by anything like a similar result. The new expedition would doubtless set out, like that of 1841-42, from the Island of Hongkong. That expedition consisted of a fleet of two seventy-fours, eight frigates, a great number of sloops and brigs-of-war, twelve steamers, and forty transports, having on board a military force, marines included, amounting to fifteen thousand men. The new expedition would hardly be attempted with any smaller force; indeed, some of the considerations we are about to state would indicate the policy of making it much larger.

The expedition of 1841-42, sailing from Hongkong on the 21st of August, 1841, took possession first of Amoy, and then, on the 1st of October, of the Island of Chusan, which they made the base of their future operations. The object of these operations was to penetrate into and ascend the great central river Yangtze Kiang as far as the City of Nanking, about two hundred miles from its mouth. The river Yangtze Kiang divides China into two quite distinct portions—the North and the South. About forty miles below Nanking the Imperial Canal enters and crosses the great river, affording the means of commercial intercourse between the northern and southern provinces. The theory of the campaign was that the possession of this important communication would be a fatal thing for Peking, and would force the Emperor to make peace forthwith. On the 13th of June, 1842, the English forces, under Sir Henry Pottinger, appeared off Wusung, at the entrance of the small river of that name. This river flows from the south, entering the estuary of the Yangtze Kiang very near its debouch into the Yellow Sea. The mouth of the Wusung River forms the harbour of Shanghai, situated a short distance up. The banks of the Wusung were covered with batteries, all of which were stormed and carried without difficulty. A column of the invading force then marched on Shanghai, which surrendered without any attempt at resistance. But, though little resistance was as yet experienced from the peaceful and timid inhabitants on the banks of the Yangtze Kiang, who, after a prolonged peace of nearly two hundred years, had now their first experience of war, the estuary itself, and the approach to it from the sea, were found to present great impediments. The broad estuary of the Yangtze Kiang enters the sea from between shores half covered with mud, and hardly discernible, as the sea for many leagues off is a muddy yellow, whence comes its name. Ships intending to enter the Yangtze Kiang are obliged to move cautiously along the southern shore, keeping the lead constantly going, in order to avoid the bars of movable sand with which the approach is impeded. These banks extend up the estuary as high as the upper end of the great Island of Chungming, which lies midway in it and divides it into two channels. Above this island, which is some thirty miles long, the shores begin to show themselves above the water, but the course of the channel becomes very serpentine. The tide flows up as far as Chingkiangfu, about half way to Nanking, and where, in fact, what has hitherto been an estuary or arm of the sea, first takes on, for ascending vessels, the character of a river. Before making this point, the English fleet met with some serious difficulties. It took them fifteen days to make the distance of eighty miles from their anchorage at Chusan. Near the Island of Chungming several of the larger ships ran aground, but succeeded in getting off by the help of the rising tide. Having conquered these difficulties and approached the City of Chingkiang, the English found abundant proof that, however deficient the Tartar-Chinese soldiers might be in military skill, they were not lacking in courage and spirit. These Tartar soldiers, who were only fifteen hundred in number, fought with the utmost desperation, and were killed to a man. Before they marched to the battle, as if anticipating the result, they strangled or drowned all their women and children, great numbers of whose dead bodies were afterward drawn from the wells into which they had been thrown. The Commander-in-Chief, seeing that the day was lost, set fire to his house and perished in the flames. The English lost a hundred and eighty-five men in the attack—a loss which they revenged by the most horrible excesses in sacking the town—the war having been conducted by the English throughout in a spirit of brutal ferocity, which was a fitting counterpart to the spirit of smuggling cupidity in which it had originated. Had the invaders met with a similar resistance everywhere they never would have reached Nanking. But such was not the case. The City of Kuachou, on the opposite side of the river, submitted and paid a ransom of three millions of dollars, which the English freebooters of course pocketed with immense satisfaction.

Above this point, the channel of the river had a depth of thirty fathoms, and, so far as the bottom was concerned, the navigation became easy, but at some points the current ran with great swiftness, not less than six and seven miles an hour. There was nothing, however, to prevent ships-of-the-line from ascending to Nanking, under the walls of which the English at length cast anchor on the 9th of August. The effect thus produced was exactly what had been anticipated. The Emperor* was frightened into signing the treaty of the 29th of August, the pretended violation of which is now

* Tao Kuang.—*Ed.*

made the occasion of new demands which threaten a new war.

That new war, should it occur, will probably be conducted on the model of the former one. But there are several reasons why the English could not anticipate a similar easy success. The experience of that war has not been lost on the Chinese. In the recent military operations in Canton River they have exhibited such improved skill in gunnery and the art of defence as to lead to the suspicion of their having Europeans among them. In everything practical, and war is eminently practical, the Chinese far surpass all the Orientals, and there is no doubt that in military matters the English will find them apt scholars. Again, it is likely that the English may encounter artificial obstacles to the ascent of the Yangtze Kiang, should they again attempt it, such as do not appear to have been met with on the former occasion. But,—what is the most serious consideration of all—the reoccupation of Nanking cannot be supposed to be attended with anything like the same terror and alarm to the Imperial Court at Peking which it caused on the former occasion. Nanking, for a considerable period past, as well as large portions of the surrounding districts, has been in possession of the rebels, one or more of whose chiefs make that city their head-quarters. In this state of the case its occupation by the English might be rather agreeable to the Emperor than otherwise. They might do him good service in driving the rebels from a city which, when they had got it, might prove a possession rather difficult, troublesome and dangerous to keep, and which, as recent experience has shown, may be held by a hostile power without any immediately fatal results to Peking or the Imperial rule.

Written at the beginning of April, 1857

Published in the *New-York Daily Tribune*, No. 4990, April 17, 1857

Printed according to the text of the newspaper

Frederick Engels

PERSIA AND CHINA

London, May 22, 1857

The English have just concluded an Asiatic war, and are entering upon another.[65] The resistance offered by the Persians, and that which the Chinese have so far opposed to British invasion, form a contrast worth our attention. In Persia, the European system of military organization has been engrafted upon Asiatic barbarity; in China, the rotting semi-civilization of the oldest State in the world meets the Europeans with its own resources. Persia has been signally defeated, while distracted, half-dissolved China has hit upon a system of resistance which, if followed up, will render impossible repetition of the triumphal marches of the first Anglo-Chinese war.

Persia was in a state similar to that of Turkey during the war of 1828-29 against Russia. English, French, Russian officers had in turns tried their hands at the organization of the Persian army. One system had succeeded another, and each in its turn had been thwarted by the jealousy, the intrigues, the ignorance, the cupidity and corruption of the Orientals whom it was to form into European officers and soldiers. The new regular army had never had an opportunity of trying its organization and strength in the field. Its only exploits had been confined to a few campaigns against Kurds, Turcomans and Afghans, where it served as a sort of nucleus or reserve to the numerous irregular cavalry of Persia. The latter did most of the actual fighting; the regulars had generally but to impose upon the enemy by the demonstrative effect of their seemingly formidable arrays. At last, the war with England broke out.

The English attacked Bushire, and met with a gallant

though ineffective resistance. But the men who fought at Bushire were not regulars; they were composed of the irregular levies of the Persian and Arab inhabitants of the coast. The regulars were only concentrating, some sixty miles off, in the hills. At last they advanced. The Anglo-Indian army met them half way; and, though the Persians used their artillery with credit to themselves, and formed their squares on the most approved principles, a single charge of one single Indian cavalry regiment swept the whole Persian army, guards and line, from the field. And to know what these Indian regular cavalry are considered to be worth in their own service, we have only to refer to Capt. Nolan's book on the subject. They are, among Anglo-Indian officers, considered worse than useless, and far inferior to the irregular Anglo-Indian cavalry. Not a single action can Capt. Nolan find where they were creditably engaged. And yet, these were the men, six hundred of whom drove ten thousand Persians before them! Such was the terror spread among the Persian regulars that never since have they made a stand anywhere—the artillery alone excepted. At Mohammerah, they kept out of harm's way, leaving the artillery to defend the batteries, and retired as soon as these were silenced; and when, on a reconnaissance, the British landed three hundred riflemen and fifty irregular horse, the whole of the Persian host marched off, leaving baggage, stores and guns in the possession of the—victors you cannot call them—the invaders.

All this, however, neither brands the Persians as a nation of cowards, nor condemns the introduction of European tactics among Orientals. The Russo-Turkish wars of 1806-12 and 1828-29 offer plenty of such examples. The principal resistance offered to the Russians was made by the irregular levies both from the fortified towns and from the mountain provinces. The regulars, wherever they showed themselves in the open field, were at once upset by the Russians, and very often ran away at the first shot; while a single company of Arnaut* irregulars, in a ravine at Varna, successfully opposed the Russian siege operations for weeks together. Yet, during the late war, the Turkish regular army have

* Turkish name of the Albanians.—*Ed.*

defeated the Russians in every single engagement from Oltenitza and Cetata to Kars and to Ingur.

The fact is that the introduction of European military organization with barbaric nations is far from being completed when the new army has been subdivided, equipped and drilled after the European fashion. That is merely the first step toward it. Nor will the enactment of some European military code suffice; it will no more ensure European discipline than a European set of drill-regulations will produce, by itself, European tactics and strategy. The main point, and at the same time the main difficulty, is the creation of a body of officers and sergeants, educated on the modern European system, totally freed from the old national prejudices and reminiscences in military matters, and fit to inspire life into the new formation. This requires a long time, and is sure to meet with the most obstinate opposition from Oriental ignorance, impatience, prejudice, and the vicissitudes of fortune and favour inherent to Eastern courts. A Sultan or Shah is but too apt to consider his army equal to anything as soon as the men can defile in parade, wheel, deploy and form column without getting into hopeless disorder. And as to military schools, their fruits are so slow in ripening that under the instabilities of Eastern governments they can scarcely ever be expected to show any. Even in Turkey, the supply of educated officers is but scanty, and the Turkish army could not have done at all, during the late war, without the great number of renegades and the European officers in its ranks.

The only arm which everywhere forms an exception is the artillery. Here the Orientals are so much at fault and so helpless that they have to leave the whole management to their European instructors. The consequence is that as in Turkey, so in Persia, the artillery was far ahead of the infantry and cavalry.

That under these circumstances the Anglo-Indian army, the oldest of all Eastern armies organized on the European system, the only one that is subject not to an Eastern, but an exclusively European government, and officered almost entirely by Europeans—that this army, supported by a strong reserve of British troops and a powerful navy, should easily disperse the Persian regulars, is but a matter of course. The reverse will do the Persians the more good the more signal it was. They will now see, as the Turks have seen before, that European dress and parade-drill is no talisman in itself, and maybe, twenty years hence, the Persians will turn out as respectable as the Turks did in their late victories.

The troops which conquered Bushire and Mohammerah will, it is understood, be at once sent to China. There they will find a different enemy. No attempts at European evolutions, but the irregular array of Asiatic masses, will oppose them there. Of these they no doubt will easily dispose; but what if the Chinese wage against them a national war, and if barbarism be unscrupulous enough to use the only weapons which it knows how to wield?

There is evidently a different spirit among the Chinese now to what they showed in the war of 1840 to 1842. Then, the people were quiet; they left the Emperor's soldiers to fight the invaders, and submitted after a defeat with Eastern fatalism to the power of the enemy. But now, at least in the southern provinces, to which the contest has so far been confined, the mass of the people take an active, nay, a fanatical part in the struggle against the foreigners. They poison the bread of the European community at Hongkong by wholesale, and with the coolest premeditation. (A few loaves have been sent to Liebig for examination. He found large quantities of arsenic pervading all parts of them, showing that it had already been worked into the dough. The dose, however, was so strong that it must have acted as an emetic, and thereby counteracted the effects of the poison.) They go with hidden arms on board trading steamers, and, when on the journey, massacre the crew and European passengers and seize the boat. They kidnap and kill every foreigner within their reach. The very coolies emigrating to foreign countries rise in mutiny, and as if by concert, on board every emigrant ship, and fight for its possession, and, rather than surrender, go down to the bottom with it, or perish in its flames. Even out of China, the Chinese colonists, the most submissive and meek of subjects hitherto, conspire and suddenly rise in nightly insurrection, as at Sarawak; or, as at Singapore, are held down by main force and vigilance only. The piratical policy of the British Government has caused this universal outbreak of all Chinese against all foreigners, and marked it as a war of extermination.

What is an army to do against a people resorting to such means of warfare? Where, how far, is it to penetrate into the enemy's country, how to maintain itself there? Civilization-mongers who throw hot shell on a defenceless city and add rape to murder, may call the system cowardly, barbarous, atrocious; but what matters it to the Chinese if it be only successful? Since the British treat them as barbarians, they cannot deny to them the full benefit of their barbarism. If their kidnappings, surprises, midnight massacres are what we call cowardly, the civilization-mongers should not forget that according to their own showing they could not stand against European means of destruction with their ordinary means of warfare.

In short, instead of moralizing on the horrible atrocities of the Chinese, as the chivalrous English press does, we had better recognize that this is a war *pro aris et focis*, a popular war for the maintenance of Chinese nationality, with all its overbearing prejudice, stupidity, learned ignorance and pedantic barbarism if you like, but yet a popular war. And in a popular war the means used by the insurgent nation cannot be measured by the commonly recognized rules of regular warfare, nor by any other abstract standard, but by the degree of civilization only attained by that insurgent nation.

The English are this time placed in a difficult position. Thus far, the national Chinese fanaticism seems to extend no further than over those southern provinces which have not adhered to the great rebellion. Is the war to be confined to these? Then it would certainly lead to no result, no vital point of the Empire being menaced. At the same time, it would be a very dangerous war for the English if the fanaticism extends to the people of the interior. Canton may be totally destroyed and the coasts nibbled at in all possible points, but all the forces the British could bring together would not suffice to conquer and hold the two provinces of Kwangtung and Kwangsi. What, then, can they do further? The country north of Canton, as far as Shanghai and Nanking, is in the hands of the Chinese insurgents, whom it would be bad policy to offend; and north of

Nanking the only point an attack on which might lead to a decisive result is Peking. But where is the army to form a fortified and garrisoned base of operations on the shore, to overcome every obstacle on the road, to leave detachments to secure the communications with the shore, and to appear in anything like formidable strength before the walls of a town, the size of London, a hundred miles from its landing place? On the other side, a successful demonstration against the capital would shake to its groundworks the very existence of the Chinese Empire—accelerate the upsetting of the Ching dynasty and pave the way, not for British, but for Russian progress.

The new Anglo-Chinese war presents so many complications that it is utterly impossible to guess the turn it may take. For some months the want of troops, and for a still longer time the want of decision, will keep the British pretty inactive except, perhaps, on some unimportant point, to which under actual circumstances Canton too may be said to belong.

One thing is certain, that the death-hour of old China is rapidly drawing nigh. Civil war has already divided the South from the North of the Empire, and the Rebel King seems to be as secure from the Imperialists (if not from the intrigues of his own followers) at Nanking, as the Heavenly Emperor from the rebels at Peking. Canton carries on, so far, a sort of independent war with the English, and all foreigners in general; and while British and French fleets and troops flock to Hongkong, slowly but steadily the Siberian-line Cossacks advance their stanitzas from the Daurian mountains to the banks of the Amur, and the Russian marines close in by fortifications the splendid harbours of Manchuria. The very fanaticism of the southern Chinese in their struggle against foreigners seems to mark a consciousness of the supreme danger in which old China is placed; and before many years pass away, we shall have to witness the death-struggle of the oldest empire in the world, and the opening day of a new era for all Asia.

Published in the
New-York Daily Tribune,
No. 5032, June 5, 1857

Printed according to the text
of the newspaper

Karl Marx

THE PERSIAN TREATY

London, June 12, 1857

Some time ago a question respecting the Persian war was addressed to Lord Palmerston in his own House of Commons, he tauntingly replied: "As soon as the *peace* is ratified the House may express its opinions on the war." The treaty of peace signed at Paris, March 4, 1857, and ratified at Bagdad, May 2, 1857, has now been laid before the House. It consists of fourteen Articles, eight of them being freighted with the usual treaty-of-peace ballast. Article V stipulates that the Persian troops are to withdraw, from the territory and city of Herat, and from every part of Afghanistan, within three months from the date of the exchange of the ratifications of the treaty. By Art. XIV the British Government on its part, engages, so soon as the above stipulation be carried into effect, "to withdraw without delay the British troops from all ports, places and islands belonging to Persia". Now it should be recollected that the evacuation of Herat by the Persian troops was spontaneously offered by Feroukh Khan, the Persian Ambassador, during his protracted conferences at Constantinople with Lord Stratford de Redcliffe, and before the capture of Bushire had yet occurred. The only new profit accruing to England from this stipulation is, therefore, limited to the privilege of enchaining, during the most unhealthy season, her troops to the most pestilential spot of the Persian Empire. The terrible ravages the sun and the swamps and the sea inflict during the summer months, even on the native population of Bushire and Mohammerah, are chronicled by old and modern writers, but why refer to them since a few weeks ago, Sir Henry Rowlinson, a very competent judge, and Palmerstonian too, publicly declared that the Anglo-Indian troops were sure to sink under the horrors of the climate? *The London Times*, on receiving the news of the Mohammerah victory, proclaimed at once the necessity of advancing despite the treaty of peace to Shiraz, in order to save the troops. The suicides, too, of the British Admiral and General, placed at the head of the expedition, were due to their profound anxiety as to the probable fate of the troops, whom, by Governmental instruction, they were not to push beyond Mohammerah. A Crimean catastrophe on a smaller scale may thus be safely expected; this time proceeding neither from the necessities of war, nor from the blunders of the Administration, but from a treaty written with the sword of the victor. There occurs one phrase in the articles quoted which, *if it suits* Palmerston, may be worked into "a small bone of contention."

Art. XIV stipulates the "withdrawal of the British troops from all ports, places and islands *belonging to Persia*". Now it is a controvertible matter whether or not the town of Mohammerah *does* belong to Persia. The Turks have never renounced their claims to that place, which, situated on the Delta of the Euphrates, was their only seaport on that river always accessible, the port of Bassora being at certain seasons too shallow for ships of large burden. Thus, if Palmerston pleases, he may hold Mohammerah on the pretext of its not "belonging" to Persia, and of waiting for the final settlement of the boundary question between Turkey and Persia.

Art. VI stipulates that Persia agrees to

> "relinquish all claims to sovereignty over the territory and city of Herat and the counties of Afghanistan"; to "abstain from all interference with the internal affairs of Afghanistan"; to "recognize the independence of Herat and the whole of Afghanistan, and never to attempt to interfere with the independence of those States; to refer, in case of differences with Herat and Afghanistan, for adjustment to the friendly offices of the British Government, and not to take up arms unless those friendly offices fail of effect."

The British Government, on their part, engage

> "at all times to exert their influence with the States of Afghanistan to prevent any causes of umbrage being given by them," and "to use their best endeavours to compose differences in a manner just and honourable to Persia."

Now, if this article is stripped of its red tape, it means nothing beyond the acknowledgment by Persia of the independence of Herat, a concession to make which Feroukh Khan had declared himself ready at the Constantinople conferences. It is true that, by virtue of this article the British Government is appointed the official intermeddler between Persia and Afghanistan, but that part it was, since the commencement of this century, always acting. Whether it be able or not to continue it, is a question, not of right but of might. Besides, if the Shah harbours at the Court of Teheran any Hugo Grotius, the latter will point out that any stipulation by which an independent State gives a foreign Government the right of interfering with its international relations is null and void according to the *jus gentium*, and that the stipulation with England is the more so, since it converts Afghanistan, a merely poetical term for various tribes and States, into a real country. The country of Afghanistan exists, in a diplomatic sense, no more than the country of Panslavia.

Art. VII which stipulates that, in case of any violation of the Persian frontier by the Afghan States, "the Persian Government shall have the right to undertake military operations for the repression and punishment of the aggressors," but "must retire within its own territory so soon as its object is accomplished," is but a literal repetition of just that clause of the treaty of 1852 which gave the immediate occasion for the Bushire expedition.

By Art. IX Persia admits the establishment and recognition of British Consuls-General, Consuls, Vice-Consuls, and Consular Agents to be placed on the footing of the most favourite nation; but by Art. XII the British Government renounces

> "the right of protecting here after any Persian subject not actually in the employment of the British mission or of British Consuls-General, Consuls, Vice-Consuls and Consular Agents."

The establishment of British Consulates in Persia being agreed to by Feroukh Khan before the commencement of the war, the present treaty adds only the renunciation, on the part of England, of her right of protectorate over Persian subjects, which right formed one of the ostensible causes of the war. Austria, France and other States have obtained the establishment of Consulates in Persia without recurring to any piratical expeditions.

Lastly, the treaty forces Mr. Murray back on the Court of Teheran, and prescribes the apology to be made to that gentleman, for being characterized in a letter addressed to Sadir Azim by the Shah, as a "stupid, ignorant and insane man"; as a "simpleton", and as the author of a "rude, unmeaning and disgusting document". The apology to be made to Mr. Murray was likewise offered by Feroukh Khan, but then declined by the British Government, who insisted upon the dismissal of Sadir Azim, and Mr. Murray's solemn entry into Teheran "to the sound of cornet, flute, harp, sackbut, psaltery, diclimer, and all manner of music". By accepting, as Consul-General in Egypt, personal favours from Mons. Barrot; by sending, on his first landing at Bushire, the tobacco then presented to him in the Shah's name to the bazaars, there to be publicly sold; by acting the knight-errant of a Persian lady of dubious virtue, Mr. Murray has failed to impress on the Oriental mind very high notions of British integrity or dignity. His forced readmission at the Persian Court must, therefore, be considered a rather questionable success. On the whole, the treaty contains, beyond the offers Feroukh Khan made before the outbreak of the war, no stipulations worth the paper they are written upon, and still less the treasure spent and the blood shed. The clear profits of the Persian expedition may be summed up in the odium incurred by Great Britain throughout Central Asia; the disaffection of India, increased by the withdrawal of Indian troops, and the new burdens thrown on the Indian Exchequer; the almost inevitable recurrence of another Crimean catastrophe ; the acknowledgment of Bonaparte's official mediation between England and Asiatic States; lastly, the acquisition by Russia of two strips of land of great importance—the one on the Caspian, the other on the north-coast frontier of Persia.

Published in the
New-York Daily Tribune,
No. 5048, June 24, 1857

Printed according to the text
of the newspaper

Karl Marx

THE REVOLT IN THE INDIAN ARMY[66]

The Roman *divide et impera* was the great rule by which Great Britain, for about one hundred and fifty years, contrived to retain the tenure of her Indian Empire. The antagonism of the various races, tribes, castes, creeds and sovereignties, the aggregate of which forms the geographical unity of what is called Indian, continued to be the vital principle of British supremacy. In later times, however, the conditions of that supremacy have undergone a change. With the conquest of Scinde and the Punjab,[67] the Anglo-Indian Empire had not only reached its natural limits, but it had trampled out the last vestiges of independent Indian States. All warlike native tribes were subdued, all serious internal conflicts were at an end, and the late incorporation of Oudh[68] proved satisfactorily that the remnants of the so-called independent Indian principalities exist on sufferance only. Hence a great change in the position of the East India Company. It no longer attacked one part of India by the help of another part, but found itself placed at the head, and the whole of India at its feet. No longer conquering, it had become *the* conqueror. The armies at its disposition no longer had to extend its dominion, but only to maintain it. From soldiers they were converted into policemen; 200,000,000 natives being curbed by a native army of 200,000 men, officered by Englishmen, and that native army, in its turn, being kept in check by an English army numbering 40,000 only. On first view, it is evident that the allegiance of the Indian people rests on the fidelity of the native army, in creating which the British rule simultaneously organized the first general centre of resistance which the Indian people was ever possessed of. How far that native army may be relied upon is clearly shown by its recent mutinies, breaking out as soon as the war with Persia had almost denuded the Presidency of Bengal of its European soldiers. Before this there had been mutinies in the Indian army, but the present revolt is distinguished by characteristic and fatal features. It is the first time that sepoy regiments have murdered their European officers; that Mussulmans and Hindus, renouncing their mutual antipathies, have combined against their common masters; that "disturbances beginning with the Hindus, have actually ended in placing on the throne of Delhi a Mohammedan emperor;" that the mutiny has not been confined to a few localities; and lastly, that the revolt in the Anglo-Indian army has coincided with a general disaffection exhibited against English supremacy on the part of the great Asiatic nations, the revolt of the Bengal army being, beyond doubt, intimately connected with the Persian and Chinese wars.

The alleged cause of the dissatisfaction which began to spread four months ago in the Bengal army was the apprehension on the part of the natives lest the Government should interfere with their religion. The serving out of cartridges, the paper of which was said to have been greased with the fat of bullocks and pigs, and the compulsory biting of which was, therefore, considered by the natives as an infringement of their religious prescriptions, gave the signal for local disturbances. On the 22d of January an incendiary fire broke out in cantonments a short distance from Calcutta. On the 25th of February the 19th Native Regiment mutinied at Berhampore, the men objecting to the cartridges served out to them. On the 31st of March that regiment was disbanded; at the end of March the 34th Sepoy Regiment, stationed at Barrackpore, allowed one of its men to advance with a loaded musket upon the parade-ground in front of the line, and, after having called his comrades to mutiny, he was permitted to attack and wound the Adjutant and Sergeant-Major of his regiment. During the hand-to-hand conflict that ensued, hundreds of sepoys looked passively on, while others participated in the struggle, and attacked the officers with the butt ends of their muskets. Subsequently that regiment was also disbanded. The month of April was signalized by incendiary fires in several cantonments of the Bengal army at Allahabad, Agra, Ambala, by a mutiny of the 3d Regiment of Light Cavalry at Meerut, and by similar appearances of disaffection in the Madras and Bombay armies. At the beginning of May an *émeute* was preparing at Lucknow, the capital of Oudh, which was, however, prevented by the promptitude of Sir H. Lawrence. On the 9th of May the mutineers of the 3d Light Cavalry of Meerut were marched off to jail, to undergo the various terms of imprisonment to which they were sentenced. On the evening of the following day the troopers of the 3d Cavalry, together with the two native regiments, the 11th and 20th, assembled upon the parade-ground, killed the officers endeavouring to pacify them, set fire to the cantonments, and slew all the Englishmen they were able to lay hands on. Although the British part of the brigade mustered a regiment of infantry, another of cavalry, and an overwhelming force of horse and foot artillery, they were not able to move until nightfall. Having inflicted but little harm on the mutineers, they allowed them to betake themselves to the open field and to throw themselves into Delhi, some forty miles distant from Meerut. There they were joined by the native garrison, consisting of the 38th, 54th and 74th regiments of infantry, and a company of native artillery. The British officers were attacked, all Englishmen within reach of the rebels were murdered, and the heir* of the late Mogul** of Delhi proclaimed King of India. Of the troops sent to the rescue of Meerut, where order had been re-established, six companies of native sappers and miners, who arrived on the 15th of May, murdered their commanding officer, Major Frazer, and made at once for the open country, pursued by troops of horse artillery and several of the 6th Dragoon Guards. Fifty or sixty of the mutineers were shot, but the rest contrived to escape to Delhi. At Ferozeppore, in the Punjab, the 57th and 45th native infantry regiments mutinied, but were put down by

* Bahadur Shah II.—*Ed.*
** Akbar II.—*Ed.*

force. Private letters from Lahore state the whole of the native troops to be in an undisguised state of mutiny. On the 19th of May, unsuccessful efforts were made by the sepoys stationed at Calcutta to get possession of Fort St. William. Three regiments arrived from Bushire at Bombay were at once dispatched to Calcutta.

In reviewing these events, one is startled by the conduct of the British commander at Meerut—his late appearance on the field of battle being still less incomprehensible than the weak manner in which he pursued the mutineers. As Delhi is situated on the right and Meerut on the left bank of the Jumna—the two banks being joined at Delhi by one bridge only—nothing could have been easier than to cut off the retreat of the fugitives.

Meanwhile, martial law has been proclaimed in all the disaffected districts; forces, consisting of natives mainly, are concentrating against Delhi from the north, the east and the south; the neighbouring princes are said to have pronounced for the English; letters have been sent to Ceylon to stop Lord Elgin and Gen. Ashburnham's forces, on their way to China; and finally, 14,000 British troops were to be dispatched from England to India in about a fortnight. Whatever obstacles the climate of India at the present season, and the total want of means of transportation, may oppose to the movements of the British forces, the rebels at Delhi are very likely to succumb without any prolonged resistance. Yet, even then, it is only the prologue of a most terrible tragedy that will have to be enacted.

Written on June 30, 1857

Published in the
New-York Daily Tribune,
No. 5065, July 15, 1857

Printed according to the text
of the newspaper

Karl Marx

THE REVOLT IN INDIA

London, July 17, 1857

On the 8th of June, just a month had passed since Delhi fell into the hands of the revolted sepoys and the proclamation by them of a Mogul Emperor.* Any notion, however, of the mutineers being able to keep the ancient capital of India against the British forces would be preposterous. Delhi is fortified only by a wall and a simple ditch, while the heights surrounding and commanding it are already in the possession of the English, who, even without battering the walls, might enforce its surrender in a very short period by the easy process of cutting off its supply of water. Moreover, a motley crew of mutineering soldiers who have murdered their own officers, torn asunder the ties of discipline, and not succeeded in discovering a man upon whom to bestow the supreme command, are certainly the body least likely to organize a serious and protracted resistance. To make confusion more confused, the checkered Delhi ranks are daily swelling from the fresh arrivals of new contingents of mutineers from all parts of the Bengal Presidency, who, as if on a preconcerted plan, are throwing themselves into the doomed city. The two sallies which, on the 30th and 31st of May, the mutineers risked without the walls, and in both of which they were repulsed with heavy losses, seem to have proceeded from despair rather than from any feeling of self-reliance or strength. The only thing to be wondered at is the slowness of the British operations, which, to some degree, however, may be accounted for by the horrors of the season

* Bahadur Shah II.—*Ed.*

and the want of means of transport. Apart from Gen. Anson, the commander-in-chief, French letters state that about 4,000 European troops have already fallen victims of the deathly heat, and even the English papers confess that in the engagements before Delhi the men suffered more from the sun than from the shot of the enemy. In consequence of its scanty means of conveyance, the main British force stationed at Ambala consumed about twenty-seven days in its march upon Delhi, so that it moved at the rate of about one and a half hours per day. A further delay was caused by the absence of heavy artillery at Ambala, and the consequent necessity of bringing over a siege-train from the nearest arsenal, which was as far off as Phillaur, on the further side of the Sutlej.

With all that, the news of the fall of Delhi may be daily expected; but what next? If the uncontested possession by the rebels during a month of the traditionary centre of the Indian Empire acted perhaps as the most powerful ferment in completely breaking up the Bengal army, in spreading mutiny and desertion from Calcutta to the Punjab in the north, and to Rajputana in the west, and in shaking the British authority from one end of India to the other, no greater mistake could be committed than to suppose that the fall of Delhi, though it may throw consternation among the ranks of the sepoys, should suffice either to quench the rebellion, to stop its progress, or to restore the British rule. Of the whole native Bengal army, mustering about 80,000 men—composed of about 28,000 Rajputs, 23,000 Brahmins,[69] 13,000 Mohammedans, 5,000 Hindus of inferior castes, and the rest Europeans—30,000 have disappeared in consequence of mutiny, desertion, or dismission from the ranks. As to the rest of that army, several of the regiments have openly declared that they will remain faithful and support the British authority, excepting in the matter in which the native troops are now engaged: They will not aid the authorities against the mutineers of the native regiments, and will, on the contrary, assist their "bhaies" (brothers). The truth of this has been exemplified in almost every station from Calcutta. The native regiments remained passive for a time; but, as soon as they fancied themselves strong enough, they mutinied. An Indian correspondent of

The London Times leaves no doubt as to the "loyalty" of the regiments which have not yet pronounced, and the native inhabitants who have not yet made common cause with the rebels.

> "If you read," he says, "that *all is quiet,* understand it to mean that the native troops have not yet risen in open mutiny; that the discontented part of the inhabitants are not yet in open rebellion; that they are either too weak, or fancy themselves to be so, or that they are waiting for a more fitting time. Where you read of the 'manifestation of loyalty' in any of the Bengal native regiments, cavalry or infantry, understand it to mean that one half of the regiments thus favourably mentioned only are really faithful; the other half are but acting a part, the better to find the Europeans off their guard, when the proper time arrives, or, by warding off suspicion, have it the more in their power to aid their mutinous companions."

In the Punjab, open rebellion has only been prevented by disbanding the native troops. In Oudh, the English can only be said to keep Lucknow, the residency, while everywhere else the native regiments have revolted, escaped with their ammunition, burned all the bungalows to the ground, and joined with the inhabitants who have taken up arms. Now, the real position of the English army is best demonstrated by the fact that it was thought necessary, in the Punjab as well as the Rajputana, to establish flying corps. This means that the English cannot depend either on their sepoy troops or on the natives to keep the communication open between their scattered forces. Like the French during the Peninsular war, they command only the spot of ground held by their own troops, and the next neighbourhood domineered by that spot; while for communication between the disjoined members of their army they depend on flying corps, the action of which, most precarious in itself, loses naturally in intensity in the same measure that it spreads over a greater extent of space. The actual insufficiency of the British forces is further proved by the fact that, for removing treasures from disaffected stations, they were constrained to have them conveyed by sepoys themselves, who, without any exception, broke out in rebellion on the march, and absconded with the treasures confided to them. As the troops sent from England will, in the best case, not arrive before November, and as it would be still more dangerous to draw off European troops from the presidencies of Madras and Bombay—the 10th Regiment of Madras sepoys, having already shown symptoms of disaffection—any idea of collecting the regular taxes throughout the Bengal Presidency must be abandoned, and the process of decomposition be allowed to go on. Even if we suppose that the Burmese will not improve the occasion, that the Maharajah of Gwalior* will continue supporting the English, and the Ruler of Nepal,** commanding the finest Indian army, remain quiet; that disaffected Peshawar will not combine with the restless hill tribes, and that the Shah of Persia*** will not be silly enough to evacuate Herat—still, the whole Bengal Presidency must be reconquered, and the whole Anglo-Indian army remade. The cost of this enormous enterprise will altogether fall upon the British people. As to the notion put forward by Lord Granville in the House of Lords, of the East India Company being able to raise, by Indian loans, the necessary means, its soundness may be judged from the effects produced by the disturbed state of the north-western provinces on the Bombay money market. An immediate panic seized the native capitalists, very large sums were withdrawn from the banks, government securities proved almost unsaleable, and hoarding to a great extent commenced not only in Bombay but in its environs also.

Published in the
New-York Daily Tribune,
No. 5082, August 4, 1857

Printed according to the text
of the newspaper

* Sindhia.—*Ed.*
** Jang Bahadur.—*Ed.*
*** Nasr-ed-Din.—*Ed.*

Karl Marx

THE INDIAN QUESTION

London, July 28, 1857

The three hours' speech delivered last night in "The Dead House," by Mr. Disraeli, will gain rather than lose by being read instead of being listened to. For some time, Mr. Disraeli affects an awful solemnity of speech, an elaborate slowness of utterance and a passionless method of formality, which, however consistent they may be with his peculiar notions of the dignity becoming a Minister in expectance, are really distressing to his tortured audience. Once he succeeded in giving even commonplaces the pointed appearance of epigrams. Now he contrives to bury even epigrams in the conventional dullness of respectability. An orator who, like Mr. Disraeli, excels in handling the dagger rather than in wielding the sword, should have been the last to forget Voltaire's warning, that "*Tous les genres sont bons excepté le genre ennuyeux.*"*

Beside these technical peculiarities which characterize Mr. Disraeli's present manner of eloquence, he, since Palmerston's accession to power, has taken good care to deprive his Parliamentary exhibitions of every possible interest of actuality. His speeches are not intended to carry his motions, but his motions are intended to prepare for his speeches. They might be called self-denying motions, since they are so constructed as neither to harm the adversary, if carried, nor to damage the proposer, if lost. They mean, in fact, to be neither carried nor lost, but simply to be dropped. They

* "All genres are good except the dull ones." Voltaire. Introduction to the comedy *The Prodigal Son.—Ed.*

belong neither to the acids nor to the alkalis, but are born neutrals. The speech is not the vehicle of action, but the hypocrisy of action affords the opportunity for a speech. Such, indeed, may be the classical and final form of parliamentary eloquence; but then, at all events, the final form of parliamentary eloquence must not demur to sharing the fate of all final forms of parliamentarism—that of being ranged under the category of nuisances. Action, as Aristotle said, is the ruling law of the drama.* So it is of political oratory. Mr. Disraeli's speech on the Indian revolt might be published in the tracts of the Society for the Propagation of Useful Knowledge, or it might be delivered to a mechanics' institution, or tendered as a prize essay to the Academy of Berlin. This curious impartiality of his speech as to the place where, and the time when, and the occasion on which it was delivered, goes far to prove that it fitted neither place, time, nor occasion. A chapter on the decline of the Roman Empire which might read exceedingly well in Montesquieu or Gibbon would prove an enormous blunder if put in the mouth of a Roman Senator, whose peculiar business it was to stop that very decline. It is true that in our modern parliaments, a part lacking neither dignity nor interest might be imagined of an independent orator who, while despairing of influencing the actual course of events, should content himself to assume a position of ironical neutrality. Such a part was more or less successfully played by the late M. Garnier-Pagès—not the Garnier-Pagès of Provisional Government but the well-known member of Louis Philippe's Chamber of Deputies; but Mr. Disraeli, the avowed leader of an obsolete faction, would consider even success in this line as a supreme failure. The revolt of the Indian army afforded certainly a magnificent opportunity for oratorical display. But, apart from his dreary manner of treating the subject, what was the gist of the motion which he made the pretext for his speech? It was no motion at all. He feigned to be anxious for becoming acquainted with two official papers, the one of which he was not quite sure to exist, and the other of which he was sure not immediately to bear on the subject in question. Consequently his speech and his motion lacked any

* Aristotle, *Poetics*, Chapter VI.—*Ed.*

point of contact save this, that the motion heralded a speech without an object, and that the object confessed itself not worth a speech. Still, as the highly elaborated opinion of the most distinguished out-of-office statesman of England, Mr. Disraeli's speech ought to attract the attention of foreign countries. I shall content myself with giving in his *ipsissima verba* a short analysis of his "considerations on the decline of the Anglo-Indian Empire."

"Does the disturbance in India indicate a military mutiny, or is it a national revolt? Is the conduct of the troops the consequence of a sudden impulse, or is it the result of an organised conspiracy?"

Upon these points Mr. Disraeli asserts the whole question to hinge. Until the last ten years, he affirmed, the British Empire in India was founded on the old principle of *divide et impera*—but that principle was put into action by respecting the different nationalities of which India consisted, by avoiding to tamper with their religion, and by protecting their landed property. The sepoy army served as a safety-valve to absorb the turbulent spirits of the country. But of late years a new principle has been adopted in the government of India—the principle of destroying nationality. The principle has been realized by the forcible destruction of native princes, the disturbance of the settlement of property, and the tampering with the religion of the people. In 1848 the financial difficulties of the East India Company had reached that point that it became necessary to augment its revenues one way or the other. Then a minute in Council was published, in which was laid down the principle, almost without disguise, that the only mode by which an increased revenue could be obtained was by enlarging the British territories at the expense of the native princes. Accordingly, on the death of the Rajah of Satara,* his adoptive heir was not acknowledged by the East India Company, but the Raj absorbed in its own dominions. From that moment the system of annexation was acted upon whenever a native prince died without natural heirs. The principle of adoption—the very corner-stone of Indian society—was systematically set aside

* Appa Sahib.—*Ed.*

by the Government. Thus were forcibly annexed to the British Empire the Rajs of more than a dozen independent princes from 1848 to 1854. In 1854 the Raj of Berar, which comprised 80,000 square miles of land, a population from 4,000,000 to 5,000,000, and enormous treasures, was forcibly seized. Mr. Disraeli ends the list of forcible annexations with Oudh, which brought the East Indian Government in collision not only with the Hindus, but also with the Mohammedans. Mr. Disraeli then goes on showing how the settlement of property in India was disturbed by the new system of government during the last ten years.

"The principle of the law of adoption," he says, "is not the prerogative of princes and principalities in India, it applies to every man in Hindustan who has landed property, and who professes the Hindu religion."

I quote a passage:

"The great feudatory, or jagirdar, who holds his lands by public service to his lord; and the enamdar, who holds his land free of all land-tax, who corresponds, if not precisely, in a popular sense, at least, with our freeholder[70]—both of these classes—classes most numerous in India—always, on the failure of their natural heirs, find in this principle the means of obtaining successors to their estates. Those classes were all touched by the annexation of Satara, they were touched by the annexation of the territories of the ten inferior but independent princes to whom I have already alluded, and they were more than touched, they were terrified to the last degree, when the annexation of the Raj of Berar took place. What man was safe? What feudatory, what freeholder who had not a child of his own loins was safe throughout India? [*Hear, hear*]. These were not idle fears; they were extensively acted upon and reduced to practice. The resumption of jagirs and of enams commenced for the first time in India. There have been, no doubt, impolitic moments when attempts have been made to inquire into titles, but no one had ever dreamt of abolishing the law of adoption; therefore, no authority, no government had ever been in a position to resume jagirs and enams the holders of which had left no natural heirs. Here was a new source of revenue; but while all these things were acting upon the minds of these classes of Hindus, the Government took another step to disturb the settlement of property, to which I must now call the attention of the House. The House is aware, no doubt, from reading the evidence taken before the Committee of 1853, that there are great portions of the land of India which are exempt from the land-tax. Being free from land-tax in India is far more than equivalent to freedom from the land-tax, in this country, for, speaking generally and popularly, the land-tax in India is the whole taxation of the State.

"The origin of these grants is difficult to penetrate, but they are undoubtedly of great antiquity. They are of different kinds. Beside the private freeholds, which are very extensive, there are large grants of land free from the land-tax with which mosques and temples have been endowed."

On the pretext of fraudulent claims of exemption, the British Governor-General* took upon himself to examine the titles of the Indian landed estates. Under the new system, established in 1848,

"that plan of investigating titles was at once embraced, as a proof of a powerful Government, a vigorous Executive, and most fruitful source of public revenue. Therefore commissions were issued to inquire into titles to landed estates in the Presidency of Bengal and adjoining country. They were also issued in the Presidency of Bombay, and surveys were ordered to be made in the newly-settled provinces, in order that these commissions might be conducted, when the surveys were completed, with due efficiency. Now there is no doubt that, during the last nine years, the action of these commissions of inquiry into the freehold property of landed estates in India has been going on at an enormous rate, and immense results have been obtained."

Mr. Disraeli computes that the resumption of estates from their proprietors is not less than £500,000 a year in the Presidency of Bengal; £370,000 in the Presidency of Bombay; £200,000 in the Punjab, etc. Not content with this one method of seizing upon the property of the natives, the British Government discontinued the pensions to the native grandees, to pay which it was bound by treaty.

"This," says Mr. Disraeli, "is confiscation by a new means, but upon a most extensive, startling and shocking scale."

Mr. Disraeli then treats the tampering with the religion of the natives, a point upon which we need not dwell. From all his premises he arrives at the conclusion that the present Indian disturbance, is not a military mutiny, but a national revolt, of which the sepoys are the acting instruments only. He ends his harangue by advising the Government to turn their attention to the internal improvement of India, instead of pursuing its present course of aggression.

Published in the *New-York Daily Tribune*, No. 5091, August 14, 1857

Printed according to the text of the newspaper

---

* Dalhousie.—*Ed.*

Frederick Engels

AFGHANISTAN

(Excerpt)

AFGHANISTAN, an extensive country of Asia, north-west of India. It lies between Persia and the Indies, and in the other direction between the Hindoo-koosh and the Indian Ocean. It formerly included the Persian provinces of Khorassan and Kohistan, together with Herat, Beloochistan, Cashmere, and Scinde, and a considerable part of the Punjab. In its present limits there are probably not more than 4,000,000 inhabitants. . . .

The geographical position of Afghanistan, and the peculiar character of the people, invest the country with a political importance that can scarcely be over-estimated in the affairs of Central Asia. The government is a monarchy, but the king's authority over his high-spirited and turbulent subjects, is personal and very uncertain. The kingdom is divided into provinces, each superintended by a representative of the sovereign, who collects the revenue and remits it to the capital. The Afghans are a brave, hardy, and independent race; they follow pastoral or agricultural occupations only, eschewing trade and commerce, which they contemptuously resign to Hindoos, and to other inhabitants of towns. With them, war is an excitement and relief from the monotonous occupation of industrial pursuits. The Afghans are divided into clans, over which the various chiefs exercise a sort of feudal supremacy. Their indomitable hatred of rule, and their love of individual independence, alone prevents their becoming a powerful nation; but this very irregularity and uncertainty of action makes them dangerous neighbours, liable to be blown about by the wind of caprice, or to be stirred up by political intriguers, who artfully excite their passions. The two principal tribes are the Dooranees and Ghiljies, who are always at feud with each other. The Dooranee is the more powerful; and in virtue of their supremacy their ameer or khan made himself king of Afghanistan. He has a revenue of about $10,000,000. His authority is supreme only in his tribe. The military contingents are chiefly furnished by the Dooranees; the rest of the army is supplied either by the other clans, or by military adventurers who enlist into the service in hopes of pay or plunder. Justice in the towns is administered by cadis, but the Afghans rarely resort to law. Their khans have the right of punishment even to the extent of life or death. Avenging of blood is a family duty; nevertheless, they are said to be a liberal and generous people when unprovoked, and the rights of hospitality are so sacred that a deadly enemy who eats bread and salt, obtained even by stratagem, is sacred from revenge, and may even claim the protection of his host against all other danger. In religion they are Mohammedans, and of the Soonee sect; but they are not bigoted, and alliances between Sheeahs and Soonees are by no means uncommon. Afghanistan has been subjected alternately to Mogul and Persian dominion. Previous to the advent of the British on the shores of India the foreign invasions which swept the plains of Hindostan always proceeded from Afghanistan. Sultan Mahmoud the Great, Genghis Khan, Tamerlane, and Nadir Shah, all took this road. In 1747 after the death of Nadir, Shah Ahmed, who had learned the art of war under that military adventurer, determined to shake off the Persian yoke. Under him Afghanistan reached its highest point of greatness and prosperity in modern times. He belonged to the family of the Suddosis, and his first act was to seize upon the booty which his late chief had gathered in India. In 1748 he succeeded in expelling the Mogul governor from Cabool and Peshawar, and crossing the Indus he rapidly overran the Punjab. His kindgom extended from Khorassan to Delhi, and he even measured swords with the Mahratta powers. These great enterprises did not, however, prevent him from cultivating some of the arts of peace, and he was favourably known as a poet and historian. He died in 1773, and left his crown to his son Timour, who, however, was unequal to the weighty charge. He abandoned the city of Candahar, which had been founded by his father, and had, in a few years, become a wealthy and populous town, and removed the seat of government back to Cabool. During his reign the internal dissensions of the tribes, which had been repressed by the firm hand of Shah Ahmed, were revived. In 1793 Timour died, and Siman succeeded him. This prince conceived the idea of consolidating the Mohammedan power of India, and this plan, which might have seriously endangered the British possessions, was thought so important that Sir John Malcolm was sent to the frontier to keep the Afghans in check, in case of their making any movement, and at the same time negotiations were opened with Persia, by whose assistance the Afghans might be placed between two fires. These precautions were, however, unnecessary; Siman Shah was more than sufficiently occupied by conspiracies, and disturbances at home, and his great plans were nipped in the bud. The king's brother, Mahmud, threw himself into Herat with the design of erecting an independent principality, but failing in his attempt he fled into Persia. Siman Shah had been assisted in attaining the throne by the Bairukshee family, at the head of which was Sheir Afras Khan. Siman's appointment of an unpopular vizier excited the hatred of his old supporters, who organized a conspiracy which was discovered, and Sheir Afras was put to death. Mahmud was now recalled by the conspirators, Siman was taken prisoner and his eyes put out. In opposition to Mahmud, who was supported by the Dooranees, Shah Soojah was put forward by the Ghiljies, and held the throne for some time; but he was at last defeated, chiefly through the treachery of his own supporters, and was forced to take refuge amongst the Sikhs. In 1809 Napoleon had sent Gen. Gardane to Persia in the hope of inducing the shah to invade India, and the Indian government sent a representative to the court of Shah Soojah to create an opposition to Persia. At this epoch, Runjeet Singh rose into power and fame. He was a Sikh chieftain, and by his genius made his country independent of the Afghans, and erected a kingdom in the Punjab, earning for himself the title of Maharajah (chief rajah), and the respect of the Anglo-Indian government. The usurper Mahmud was, however, not destined to enjoy his triumph long. Futteh Khan, his vizier, who had alternately fluctuated between Mahmud and Shah Soojah, as ambition or temporary interest prompted, was seized by the king's son Kamran, his eyes put out, and afterward cruelly put to death. The powerful family of the murdered vizier swore to avenge his death. The puppet Shah Soojah was again brought forward and Mahmud expelled. Shah Soojah having given offence, however, was presently deposed, and another brother crowned in his stead. Mahmud fled to Herat, of which he continued in possession, and in 1829 on his death his son Kamran succeeded him in the government of that district. The Bairukshee family, having now attained chief power, divided the territory among themselves, but following the national usage quarrelled, and were only united in presence of a common enemy. One of the brothers, Mohammed Khan, held the city of Peshawar, for which he paid tribute to Runjeet Singh; another held Ghuznee; a third Candahar; while in Cabool, Dost Mohammed, the most powerful of the family, held sway. To this prince, Capt. Alexander Burnes was sent as ambassador in 1835, when Russia and England were intriguing against each other in Persia and Central Asia. He offered an alliance which the Dost was but too eager to accept; but the Anglo-Indian government demanded everything from him, while it offered absolutely nothing in return. In the mean time, in 1838, the Persians, with Russian aid and advice, laid siege to Herat, the key of Afghanistan and India; a Persian and a Russian agent arrived at Cabool, and the Dost, by the constant refusal of any positive engagement on the part of the British, was, at last, actually compelled to receive overtures from the other parties. Burnes left, and Lord Auckland, then governor-general of India, influenced by his secretary W. McNaghten, determined to punish Dost Mohammed, for what he himself had compelled him to do. He resolved to dethrone him, and to set up Shah Soojah, now a pensioner of the Indian government. A treaty was concluded with Shah Soojah, and with the Sikhs; the shah began collecting an army, paid and officered by the British, and an Anglo-Indian force was concentrated on the Sutlej. McNaghten, seconded by Burnes, was to accompany the expedition in the quality of envoy in Afghanistan. In the mean time the Persians had raised the siege of Herat, and thus the only valid reason for interference in Afghanistan was removed, but, nevertheless, in December 1838, the army marched toward Scinde, which country was coerced into submission, and the payment of a contribution for the benefit of the Sikhs and Shah Soojah. Feb. 20, 1839, the British army passed the Indus. It consisted of about 12,000 men, with above 40,000 camp-followers, beside the new levies of the shah. The Bolan pass was traversed in March; want of provisions and forage began to be felt; the camels dropped by hundreds, and a great part of the baggage was lost. April 7, the army entered the Kojuk pass, traversed it without resistance, and on April 25 entered Candahar, which the Afghan princes, brothers of Dost Mohammed, had abandoned. After a rest of two months, Sir John Keane, the commander, advanced with the main body of the army toward the north, leaving a brigade under Nott, in Candahar. Ghuznee, the impregnable stronghold of Afghanistan, was taken. July 22, a deserter having brought information that the Cabool gate was the only one which had not been walled up; it was accordingly blown down, and the place was then stormed. After this disaster, the army which Dost Mohammed had collected, at once disbanded, and Cabool too opened its gates, August 6. Shah Soojah was installed in due form but the real direction of government remained in the hands of McNaghten, who also paid all Shah Soojah's expenses out of the Indian treasury. The conquest of Afghanistan seemed accomplished, and a considerable portion of the troops was sent back. But the Afghans were noways content to be ruled by the *Feringhee Kafirs* (European infidels), and during the whole of 1840 and '41, insurrection followed on insurrection in every part of the country. The Anglo-Indian troops had to be constantly on the move. Yet, McNaghten declared this to be the normal state of Afghan society, and wrote home that everything went on well, and Shah Soojah's power was taking root. In vain were the warnings of the military officers and the other political agents. Dost Mohammed had surrendered to the British in October, 1840, and was sent to India; every insurrection during the summer of '41 was successfully repressed, and toward October, McNaghten, nominated governor of Bombay, intended leaving with another body of troops for India. But then the storm broke out. The occupation of Afghanistan cost the Indian treasury £1,250,000 per annum: 16,000 troops, Anglo-Indian, and Shah Soojah's, had to be paid in Afghanistan; 3,000 more lay in Scinde, and the Bolan pass; Shah Soojah's regal splendors, the salaries of his functionaries, and all expenses of his court and government, were paid by the Indian treasury, and finally, the Afghan chiefs were subsidized, or rather bribed, from the same source, in order to keep them out of mischief. McNaghten was informed of the impossibility of going on at this rate of spending money. He attempted retrenchment, but the only possible way to enforce it was to cut down the allowances of the chiefs. The very day he attempted this, the chiefs formed a conspiracy for the extermination of the British, and thus McNaghten himself was the means of bringing about the concentration of those insurrectionary forces, which hitherto had struggled against the invaders singly, and without unity or concert; though it is certain, too, that by this time the hatred of British dominion among the Afghans had reached the highest point. The English in Cabool were commanded by Gen. Elphinstone, a gouty, irresolute, completely helpless old man, whose orders constantly contradicted each other. The troops occupied a sort of fortified camp, which was so extensive that the garrison was scarcely sufficient to man the ramparts, much less to detach bodies to act in the field. The works were so imperfect that ditch and parapet could be ridden over on horseback. As if this was not enough, the camp was commanded almost within musket range by the neighbouring heights, and to crown the absurdity of the arrangements, all provisions, and medical stores, were in two detached forts at some distance from camp, separated from it, moreover, by walled gardens and another small fort not occupied by the English. The citadel or Bala Hissar of Cabool would have offered strong and splendid winter quarters for the whole army, but to please Shah Soojah, it was not occupied. Nov. 2, 1841, the insurrection broke out. The house of Alexander Burnes, in the city, was attacked and he himself murdered. The British general did nothing, and the insurrection grew strong by impunity. Elphinstone, utterly helpless, at the mercy of all sorts of contradictory advice, very soon got everything into that confusion which Napoleon described by the three words, *ordre, contreordre, désordre*. The Bala Hissar was, even now, not occupied. A few companies were sent against the thousands of insurgents, and of course were beaten. This still more emboldened the Afghans. Nov. 3, the forts close to the camp were occupied. On the 9th, the commissariat fort (garrisoned by only 80 men) was taken by the Afghans, and the British were thus reduced to starvation. On the 5th, Elphinstone already talked of buying a free passage out of the country. In fact, by the middle of November, his irresolution and incapacity had so demoralized the troops that neither Europeans nor Sepoys were any longer fit to meet the Afghans in the open field. Then the negotiations began. During these, McNaghten was murdered in a conference with Afghan chiefs. Snow began to cover the ground, provisions were scarce. At last, Jan. 1, a capitulation was concluded. All the money, £190,000, was to be handed over to the Afghans, and bills signed for £140,000 more. All the artillery and ammunition, except 6 six-pounders and 3 mountain guns, were to remain. All Afghanistan was to be evacuated. The chiefs, on the other hand, promised a safe conduct, provisions, and baggage cattle. Jan. 5, the British marched out, 4,500 combatants and 12,000 camp-followers. One march sufficed to dissolve the last remnant of order, and to mix up soldiers and camp-followers in one hopeless confusion, rendering all resistance impossible. The cold and snow and the want of provisions acted as in Napoleon's retreat from Moscow. But instead of Cossacks keeping a respectful distance, the British were harassed by infuriated Afghan marksmen, armed with long-range matchlocks, occupying every height. The chiefs who signed the capitulation neither could nor would restrain the mountain tribes. The Koord-Cabool pass became the grave of nearly all the army, and the small remnant, less than 200 Europeans, fell at the entrance of the Jugduluk pass. Only one man, Dr. Brydon, reached Jelalabad to tell the tale. Many officers, however, had been seized by the Afghans, and kept in captivity. Jelalabad was held by Sale's brigade. Capitulation was demanded of him, but he refused to evacuate the town, so did Nott at Candahar. Ghuznee had fallen; there was not a single man in the place that understood any thing about artillery, and the Sepoys of the garrison had succumbed to the climate. In the mean time, the British authorities on the frontier, at the first news of the disaster of Cabool, had concentrated at Peshawar the troops destined for the relief of the regiments in Afghanistan. But transportation was wanting and the Sepoys fell sick in great numbers. Gen. Pollock, in February, took the command, and by the end of March, 1842, received further reinforcements. He then forced the Khyber pass, and advanced to the relief of Sale at Jelalabad; here Sale had a few days before completely defeated the investing Afghan army. Lord Ellenborough, now governor-general of India, ordered the troops to fall back; but both Nott and Pollock found a welcome excuse in the want of transportation. At last, by the beginning of July, public opinion in India forced Lord Ellenborough to do something for the recovery of the national honour and the prestige of the British army; accordingly, he authorized an advance on Cabool, both from Candahar and Jelalabad. By the middle of August, Pollock and Nott had come to an understanding respecting their movements, and Aug. 20, Pollock moved towards Cabool, reached Gundamuck, and beat a body of Afghans on the 23d, carried the Jugduluk pass Sept. 8, defeated the assembled strength of the enemy on the 13th at Tezeen, and encamped on the 15th under the walls of Cabool. Nott, in the mean time, had, Aug. 7, evacuated Candahar, and marched with all his forces toward Ghuznee. After some minor engagements, he defeated a large body of Afghans, Aug. 30, took possession of Ghuznee, which had been abandoned by the enemy, Sept. 6, destroyed the works and town, again defeated the Afghans in the strong position of Alydan, and, Sept. 17, arrived near Cabool, where Pollock at once established his communication with him. Shah Soojah had, long before, been murdered by some of the chiefs, and since then no regular government had existed in Afghnistan; nominally, Futteh Jung, his son, was king. Pollock despatched a body of cavalry after the Cabool prisoners, but these had succeeded in bribing their guard, and met him on the road. As a mark of vengeance, the bazaar of Cabool was destroyed, on which occasion the soldiers plundered part of the town and massacred many inhabitants. Oct. 12, the British left Cabool and marched by Jelalabad and Peshawar to India. Futteh Jung, despairing of his position, followed them. Dost Mohammed was now dismissed from captivity, and returned to his kingdom. Thus ended the attempt of the British to set up a prince of their own making in Afghanistan.

Written about August 10, 1857

Published in the *New American Cyclopaedia*, Vol. I, 1858

Printed according to the text in the *New American Cyclopaedia*

Karl Marx

THE INDIAN REVOLT

London, September 4, 1857

The outrages committed by the revolted sepoys in India are indeed appalling, hideous, ineffable—such as one is prepared to meet only in wars of insurrection, of nationalities, of races, and above all of religion; in one word, such as respectable England used to applaud when perpetrated by the Vendeans on the "Blues," by the Spanish guerrillas on the infidel Frenchmen, by Serbians on their German and Hungarian neighbours, by Croats on Viennese rebels, by Cavaignac's Garde Mobile or Bonaparte's Decembrists on the sons and daughters of proletarian France.[71] However infamous the conduct of the sepoys, it is only the reflex, in a concentrated form, of England's own conduct in India, not only during the epoch of the foundation of her Eastern Empire, but even during the last ten years of a long-settled rule. To characterize that rule, it suffices to say that torture formed an organic institution of its financial policy.* There is something in human history like retribution; and it is a rule of historical retribution that its instrument be forged not by the offended, but by the offender himself.

The first blow dealt to the French monarchy proceeded from the nobility, not from the peasants. The Indian revolt does not commence with the ryots, tortured, dishonoured and stripped naked by the British, but with the sepoys, clad, fed, petted, fatted and pampered by them. To find parallels to the sepoy atrocities, we need not, as some London papers pretend, fall back on the Middle Ages, nor

---

* See this collection, pp. 162-67.—*Ed.*

even wander beyond the history of contemporary England. All we want is to study the first Chinese war, an event, so to say, of yesterday. The English soldiery then committed abominations for the mere fun of it; their passions being neither sanctified by religious fanaticism nor exacerbated by hatred against an overbearing and conquering race, nor provoked by the stern resistance of a heroic enemy. The violations of women, the spittings of children, the roastings of whole villages, were then mere wanton sports, not recorded by mandarins, but by British officers themselves.

Even at the present catastrophe it would be an unmitigated mistake to suppose that all the cruelty is on the side of the sepoys, and all the milk of human kindness flows on the side of the English. The letters of the British officers are redolent of malignity. An officer writing from Peshawar gives a description of the disarming of the 10th Irregular Cavalry for not charging the 55th Native Infantry when ordered to do so. He exults in the fact that they were not only disarmed, but stripped of their coats and boots, and after having received 12d. per man, were marched down to the river side, and there embarked in boats and sent down the Indus, where the writer is delighted to expect every mother's son will have a chance of being drowned in the rapids. Another writer informs us that, some inhabitants of Peshawar having caused a night alarm by exploding little mines of gunpowder in honour of a wedding (a national custom), the persons concerned were tied up next morning, and "received such a flogging as they will not easily forget." News arrived from Pindee that three native chiefs were plotting. Sir John Lawrence replied by a message ordering a spy to attend to the meeting. On the spy's report, Sir John sent a second message, "Hang them." The chiefs were hanged. An officer in the civil service, from Allahabad, writes: "We have power of life and death in our hands, and we assure you we spare not." Another, from the same place: "Not a day passes but we string up from ten to fifteen of them (non-combatants)." One exulting officer writes: "Holmes is hanging them by the score, like a 'brick.'" Another, in allusion to the summary hanging of a large body of the natives: "Then our fun commenced." A third: "We hold court-martials on horseback, and every nigger we meet with we either string up or shoot." From Benares we are informed that thirty zemindars were hanged on the mere suspicion of sympathizing with their own countrymen, and whole villages were burned down on the same plea. An officer from Benares, whose letter is printed in *The London Times*, says: "The European troops have become fiends when opposed to natives."

And then it should not be forgotten that, while the cruelties of the English are related as acts of martial vigour, told simply, rapidly, without dwelling on disgusting details, the outrages of the natives, shocking as they are, are still deliberately exaggerated. For instance, the circumstantial account first appearing in *The Times*, and then going the round of the London press, of the atrocities perpetrated at Delhi and Meerut, from whom did it proceed? From a cowardly parson residing at Bangalore, Mysore, more than a thousand miles, as the bird flies, distant from the scene of action. Actual accounts of Delhi evince the imagination of an English parson to be capable of breeding greater horrors than even the wild fancy of a Hindu mutineer. The cutting of noses, breasts, etc., in one word, the horrid mutilations committed by the sepoys, are of course more revolting to European feeling than the throwing of red-hot shell on Canton dwellings by a Secretary of the Manchester Peace Society, or the roasting of Arabs pent up in a cave by a French Marshal,[72] or the flaying alive of British soldiers by the cat-o'-nine-tails under drum-head court-martial, or any other of the philanthropical appliances used in British penitentiary colonies. Cruelty, like every other thing, has its fashion, changing according to time and place. Caesar, the accomplished scholar, candidly narrates how he ordered many thousand Gallic warriors to have their right hands cut off. Napoleon would have been ashamed to do this. He preferred dispatching his own French regiments, suspected of republicanism, to Santo Domingo, there to die of the blacks and the plague.

The infamous mutilations committed by the sepoys remind one of the practices of the Christian Byzantine Empire, or the prescriptions of Emperor Charles V's criminal law, or the English punishments for high treason, as still recorded by Judge Blackstone. With Hindus, whom their religion has made virtuosi in the art of self-torturing, these tortures inflicted on the enemies of their race and creed appear quite natural, and must appear still more so to the English, who, only some years since, still used to draw revenues from the Juggernaut festivals, protecting and assisting the bloody rites of a religion of cruelty.

The frantic roars of the "bloody old *Times*," as Cobbett used to call it—its playing the part of a furious character in one of Mozart's operas, who indulges in most melodious strains in the idea of first hanging his enemy, then roasting him, then quartering him, then spitting him, and then flaying him alive—its tearing the passion of revenge to tatters and to rags—all this would appear but silly if under the pathos of tragedy there were not distinctly perceptible the tricks of comedy. *The London Times* overdoes its part, not only from panic. It supplies comedy with a subject even missed by Molière, the Tartuffe of Revenge. What it simply wants is to write up the funds and to screen the Government. As Delhi has not, like the walls of Jericho, fallen before mere puffs of wind, John Bull is to be steeped in cries for revenge up to his very ears, to make him forget that his Government is responsible for the mischief hatched and the colossal dimensions it has been allowed to assume.

Published in the *New-York Daily Tribune*, No. 5119, September 16, 1857

Printed according to the text of the newspaper

Frederick Engels

ALGERIA
(Excerpt)

ALGERIA, a division of northern Africa, formerly the Turkish pashalic of Algiers, but since 1830 included in the foreign dominions of France. It is bounded N. by the Mediterranean, E. by Tunis, W. by Morocco, S. by the Great Sahara. . . .

The Berbers, Kabyles, or Mazidh, for they are known by the three names, are believed to have been the aboriginal inhabitants. Of their history as a race little is known, further than that they once occupied the whole of north-western Africa, and are to be found also on the eastern coast. The Kabyles live in the mountain district. The other inhabitants are Arabs. The descendants of the Mussulman invaders, Moors, Turks, Kouloughs,[73] Jews, and Negroes, and lastly the French, are found in the country. The population in 1852 was 2,078,035, of which 134,115 were Europeans of all nations, beside a military force of 100,000 men. The Kabyles are an industrious race, living in regular villages, excellent cultivators, and working in mines, in metals, and in coarse woollen and cotton factories. They make gunpowder and soap, gather honey and wax, and supply the towns with poultry, fruit, and other provisions. The Arabs follow the habits of their ancestors, leading a nomadic life, and shifting their camps from place to place according as the necessities of pasturage or other circumstances compel them. The Moors are probably the least respectable of the inhabitants. Living in the towns, and more luxurious than either the Arabs or Kabyles, they are, from the constant oppression of their Turkish rulers, a timid race, reserving nevertheless their cruelty and vindictiveness, while in moral character they stand very low. The chief towns of Algeria are Algiers, the capital, Constantine, population about 20,000, and Bona; a fortified town on the sea-coast, population about 10,000 in 1847. Near this are the coral fisheries, frequented by the fishers from France and Italy. Bougiah is on the gulf of the same name. The capture of this place was hastened by the outrages of the Kabyles in the neighbourhood, who wrecked a French brig by cutting her cable and then plundered her and massacred the crew. There are some remains of antiquity in the interior, especially in the province of Constantine, among others those of the ancient city of Lambessa; with remains of the city gates, parts of an amphitheatre, and a mausoleum supported by Corinthian pillars. On the coast is Coleah Cherchell, the ancient Julia Caesarea, a place of some importance to the French. It was the residence of Juba, and in its neighbourhood are ancient remains. Oran is a fortified town. It remained in possession of the Spaniards until 1792. Tlemcen, once the residence of Abd el-Kader, is situated in a fertile country; the ancient city was destroyed by fire in 1670, and the modern town was almost destroyed by the French. It has manufactures of carpets and blankets. South of the Atlas is the Zaab, the ancient Gaetulia. The chief place is Biscara; the Biscareens are a peaceful race, much liked in the northern parts as servants and porters. Algeria has been successively conquered by the Roman, the Vandal, and the Arab. When the Moors were driven from Spain in 1492, Ferdinand sent an expedition against Algiers; seizing on Oxean, Bougjah, and Algiers he threatened the subjugation of the country. Unable to cope with the powerful invader, Selim Cutemi, the emir of the Metidjah, a fertile plain in the neighbourhood of Algiers, asked assistance from the Turks, and the celebrated corsair, Barbarossa Horush, was sent to his assistance. Horush appeared in 1516, and having first made himself master of the country and slain Selim Cutemi with his own hand, he attacked the Spaniards, and after a war of varying fortunes, was obliged to throw himself into Tlemcen, where a Spanish army besieged him, and having succeeded in capturing him, put him to death in 1518. His brother Khair-ed-Deen succeeded him, sought assistance from the sultan, Selim I, and acknowledged that prince as his sovereign. Selim accordingly appointed him pasha of Algiers, and sent him a body of troops with which he was able to repulse the Spaniards, and eventually to make himself master of the country. His exploits against the Christians in the Mediterranean gained him the dignity of capudan pasha from Solyman I. Charles V made an attempt to reinstate the Spanish authority, and a powerful expedition of 370 vessels and 30,000 men crossed the Mediterranean in 1541. But a terrible storm and earthquake dispersed the fleet, and cut off all communication between it and the army. Without shelter, and exposed to the harassing attacks of a daring enemy, the troops were compelled to re-embark, and make their escape with a loss of 8,000 men, 15 vessels of war, and 140 transports. From this time forward there were unceasing hostilities between the Barbary powers, and the knights of Malta; thence sprang that system of piracy which made the Algerine corsairs so terrible in the Mediterranean, and which was so long submitted to by the Christian powers. The English under Blake, the French under Duquesne, the Dutch, and other powers, at various times attacked Algiers; and Duquesne having twice bombarded it, the dey sent for the French consul of Louis XIV, and having learned from him the cost of the bombardment, jeeringly told him that he would himself have burnt down the city for half the money.... From the first occupation of Algeria by the French[74] to the present time, the unhappy country has been the arena of unceasing bloodshed, rapine, and violence. Each town, large and small, has been conquered in detail at an immense sacrifice of life. The Arab and Kabyle tribes, to whom independence is precious, and hatred of foreign domination a principle dearer than life itself, have been crushed and broken by the terrible razzias in which dwellings and property are burnt and destroyed, standing crops cut down, and the miserable wretches who remain massacred, or subjected to all the horrors of lust and brutality. This barbarous system of warfare has been persisted in by the French against all the dictates of humanity, civilization, and Christianity. It is alleged in extenuation, that the Kabyles are ferocious, addicted to murder, torturing their prisoners, and that with savages lenity is a mistake.

The policy of a civilized government resorting to the *lex talionis* may well be doubted. And judging of the tree by its fruits, after an expenditure of probably $100,000,000, and a sacrifice of hundreds of thousands of lives, all that can be said of Algeria is that it is a school of war for French generals and soldiers, in which all the French officers who won laurels in the Crimean war received their military training and education. As an attempt at colonization, the numbers of Europeans compared with the natives show its present almost total failure; and this in one of the most fertile countries of the world, the ancient granary of Italy, within 20 hours of France, where security of life and property alike from military friends and savage enemies alone are wanted. Whether the failure is attributable to an inherent defect in the French character, which unfits them for emigration, or to injudicious local administration, it is not within our province to discuss. Every important town, Constantine, Bona, Bougiah, Arzew, Mostaganem, Tlemcen, was carried by storm with all the accompanying horrors. The natives submitted with an ill grace to their Turkish rulers, who had at least the merit of being co-religionists; but they found no advantage in the so-called civilization of the new government, against which, beside, they had all the repugnance of religious fanaticism. Each governor came but to renew the severities of his predecessors; proclamations announced the most gracious intentions, but the army of occupation, the military movements, the terrible cruelties practised on both sides, all refuted the professions of peace and good-will. In 1831, Baron Pichon had been appointed civil intendant, and he endeavoured to organize a system of civil administration which should move with the military government, but the check which his measures would have placed on the governor-in-chief offended Savary, duc de Rovigo, Napoleon's ancient minister of police, and on his representation Pichon was recalled. Under Savary, Algeria was made the exile of all those whose political or social misconduct had brought them under the lash of the law; and a foreign legion, the soldiers of which were forbidden to enter the cities, was introduced into Algeria. In 1833, a petition was presented to the chamber of deputies, stating, "'for 3 years we have suffered every possible act of injustice. Whenever complaints are preferred to the authorities, they are only answered by new atrocities, particularly directed against those by whom the complaints were brought forward. On that account no one dares to move, for which reason there are no signatures to this petition. O my lords, we beseech you in the name of humanity, to relieve us from this crushing tyranny: to ransom us from the bonds of slavery. If the land is to be under martial law, if there is to be no civil power, we are undone; there will never be peace for us."

This petition led to a commission of inquiry, the consequence of which was the establishment of a civil administration. After the death of Savary, under the *ad interim* rule of Gen. Voirol, some measures had been commenced calculated to allay the irritation; the draining of swamps, the improvement of the roads, the organization of a native militia. This, however, was abandoned on the return of Marshal Clausel, under whom a first and most unfortunate expedition against Constantine was undertaken. His government was so unsatisfactory, that a petition praying inquiry into its abuses signed by 54 leading persons connected with the province, was forwarded to Paris in 1836. This led eventually to Clausel's resignation. The whole of Louis Philippe's reign was occupied in attempts at colonization which only resulted in land-jobbing operations; in military colonization, which was useless, as the cultivators were not safe away from the guns of their own block-houses; in attempts to settle the eastern part of Algeria, and to drive out Abd el-Kader from Oran and the west.[75] The fall of that restless and intrepid chieftain so far pacified the country, that the great tribe of the Hamianes Garabas sent in their submission at once. On the revolution of 1848, Gen. Cavaignac was appointed to supersede the Duke Aumale in the governorship of the province, and he and the Prince de Joinville, who was also in Algeria, then retired. But the republic did not seem more fortunate than the monarchy in the administration of this province. Several governors succeeded each other during its brief existence. Colonists were sent out to till the lands, but they died off, or quitted in disgust. In 1849, Gen. Pelissier marched against several tribes, and the villages of the Beni Sillem; their crops and all accessible property were burnt and destroyed as usual, because they refused tribute. In Zaab, a fertile district on the edge of the desert, great excitement having arisen in consequence of the preaching of a marabout,[76] an expedition was despatched against them 1,200 strong, which they succeeded in defeating; and it was found that the revolt was widespread, and fomented by secret associations called the Sidi Abderrahman, whose principal object was the extirpation of the French. The rebels were not put down until an expedition under Generals Canrobert and Herbillon had been sent against them; and the siege of Zoatchs, an Arab town, proved that the natives had neither lost courage nor contracted affection for their invaders. The town resisted the efforts of the besiegers for 51 days, and was taken by storm at last. Little Kabylia did not give in its surrender till 1851, when Gen. St. Arnaud subdued it, and thereby established a line of communication between Philippeville and Constantine. The French bulletins and French papers abound in statements of the peace and prosperity of Algeria. These are, however, a tribute to national vanity. The country is even now as unsettled in the interior as ever. The French supremacy is perfectly illusory, except on the coast and near the towns. The tribes still assert their independence and detestation of the French regime, and the atrocious system of razzias has not been abandoned; for in the year 1857 a successful razzia was made by Marshal Randon on the villages and dwelling-places of the hitherto unsubdued Kabyles, in order to add their territory to the French dominions. The natives are still ruled with a rod of iron, and continual outbreaks show the uncertain tenure of the French occupation, and hollowness of peace maintained by such means. Indeed, a trial which took place at Oran in August, 1857, in which Captain Doineau, the head of the Bureau Arabe,[77] was proved guilty of murdering a prominent and wealthy native, revealed a habitual exercise of the most cruel and despotic power on the part of the French officials, even of subordinate rank, which justly attracted the attention of the world.

Written about September 17, 1857

Published in the *New American Cyclopaedia*, Vol. I, 1858

Printed according to the text in the *New American Cyclopaedia*

Karl Marx

INVESTIGATION OF TORTURES IN INDIA

Our London correspondent, whose letter with regard to the Indian revolt we published yesterday,* very properly referred to some of the antecedents which prepared the way for this violent outbreak. We propose today to devote a moment to continuing that line of reflections, and to showing that the British rulers of India are by no means such mild and spotless benefactors of the Indian people as they would have the world believe. For this purpose, we shall resort to the official Blue Books on the subject of East India torture, which were laid before the House of Commons during the sessions of 1856 and 1857. The evidence, it will be seen, is of a sort which cannot be gainsaid.

We have first the report of the Torture Commission at Madras, which states its "belief in the general existence of torture for revenue purposes." It doubts whether

> "anything like an equal number of persons is annually subjected to violence on criminal charges, as for the fault of non-payment of revenue."

It declares that there was

> "one thing which had impressed the Commission even more painfully than the conviction that torture exists; it is the difficulty of obtaining redress which confronts the injured parties."

The reasons for this difficulty given by the Commissioners are: 1. The distances which those who wish to make complaints personally to the collector have to travel, involving

* See this collection, pp. 152-55.—*Ed.*

expense and loss of time in attending upon his office; 2. The fear that applications by letter "will be returned with the ordinary endorsement of a reference to the tahsildar," the district police and revenue officer—that is, to the very man who, either in his person or through his petty police subordinates, has wronged him; 3. The inefficient means of procedure and punishment provided by law for officers of Government, even when formally accused or convicted of these practices. It seems that if a charge of this nature were proved before a magistrate, he could only punish by a fine of fifty rupees, or a month's imprisonment. The alternative consisted of handing over the accused "to the criminal judge to be punished by him, or committed for trial before the Court of the Circuit."

The report adds that

"these seem to be tedious proceedings, applicable only to one class of offences, abuse of authority—namely, in police charges, and totally inadequate to the necessities of the case."

A police or revenue officer, who is the same person, as the revenue is collected by the police, when charged with extorting money, is first tried by the assistant collector; he then can appeal to the collector; then to the Revenue Board. This Board may refer him to the Government or to the civil courts.

"In such a state of the law, no poverty-stricken ryot could contend against any wealthy revenue officer; and we are not aware of any complaints having been brought forward under these two regulations (of 1822 and 1828) by the people".

Further, this extorting of money applies only to taking the public money, or forcing a further contribution from the ryot for the officer to put into his own pocket. There is, therefore, no legal means of punishment whatever for the employment of force in collecting the public revenue.

The report from which these quotations are made applies only to the Presidency of Madras; but Lord Dalhousie himself, writing, in September, 1855, to the Directors,* says that

"he has long ceased to doubt that torture in one shape or other is practised by the lower subordinates in every British province."

* Court of directors of the East India Company.—*Ed.*

The universal existence of torture as a financial institution of British India is thus officially admitted, but the admission is made in such a manner as to shield the British Government itself. In fact, the conclusion arrived at by the Madras Commission is that the practice of torture is entirely the fault of the lower Hindu officials, while the European servants of the Government had always, however unsuccessfully, done their best to prevent it. In answer to this assertion the Madras Native Association presented, in January, 1856, a petition to Parliament, complaining of the torture investigation on the following grounds: 1. That there was scarcely any investigation at all, the Commission sitting only in the city of Madras, and for but three months, while it was impossible, except in very few cases, for the natives who had complains to make to leave their homes; 2. That the Commissioners did not endeavour to trace the evil to its source; had they done so, it would have been discovered to be in the very system of collecting the revenue; 3. That no inquiry was made of the accused native officials as to what extent their superiors were acquainted with the practice.

"The origin of this coercion," say the petitioners, "is not with the physical perpetrators of it, but descends to them from the officials immediately their superiors, which latter again are answerable for the estimated amount of the collection to their European superiors, these also being responsible on the same head to the highest authority of the Government."

Indeed, a few extracts from the evidence on which the Madras Report professes to be founded, will suffice to refute its assertion that "no blame is due to Englishmen." Thus, Mr. W. D. Kohlhoff, a merchant, says:

"The modes of torture practised are various, and suitable to the fancy of the tahsildar or his subordinates, but whether any redress is received from higher authorities, it is difficult for me to tell, *as all complaints are generally referred to the tahsildars* for investigation and information."

Among the cases of complaint from natives, we find the following:

"Last year, as our peasanum (principal paddy or rice crops) failed for want of rain, we were unable to pay as usual. When the jamabandi was made we claimed a remission on account of the losses, according to the terms of the agreement entered into in 1837, by us, when Mr. Eden was our collector. As this remission was not allowed, we refused to take our puttahs. The tahsildar then commenced to compel us to pay with great severity, from the month of June to August. I and others were placed in charge of persons who used to take us in the sun. There we were made to stoop and stones were put on our backs, and we were kept in the burning sand. After 8 o'clock, we were let to go to our rice. Such like ill treatment was continued during three months, during which we sometimes went to give our petitions to the collector, who refused to take them. We took these petitions and appealed to the Sessions Court, who transmitted them to the collector. Still we got no justice. In the month of September, a notice was served upon us, and twenty-five days after, our property was distrained, and afterward sold. Besides what I have mentioned, our women were also ill treated; the kittee was put upon their breasts."

A native Christian states in reply to questions put by the Commissioners:

"When a European or native regiment passes through, all the ryots are pressed to bring in provisions, etc., *for nothing*, and should any of them ask for the price of the articles, they are severely tortured."

There follows the case of a Brahmin, in which he, with others of his own village and of the neighbouring villages, was called on by the tahsildar to furnish planks, charcoal, firewood, etc., gratis, that he might carry on the Coleroon bridge-work; on refusing, he is seized by twelve men and maltreated in various ways. He adds:

"I presented a complaint to the sub-collector, Mr. W. Cadell, but he made no inquiry and tore my complaint. As he is desirous of completing cheaply the Coleroon bridge-work at the expense of the poor and of acquiring a good name from the Government, whatever may be the nature of the murder committed by the tahsildar, he takes no cognizance of it."

The light in which illegal practices, carried to the last degree of extortion and violence, were looked upon by the highest authority, is best shown by the case of Mr. Brereton, the Commissioner in charge of the Ludhiana District in the Punjab in 1855. According to the Report of the Chief Commissioner for the Punjab*, it was proved that

"in matters under the immediate cognizance or direction of the Deputy Commissioner, Mr. Brereton himself, the houses of wealthy citizens had been causelessly searched; that property seized on such

* John Lawrence.—*Ed.*

occasions was detained for lengthened periods; that many parties were thrown into prison, and lay there for weeks, without charges being exhibited against them; and that the laws relating to security for bad character had been applied with sweeping and indiscriminating severity. That the Deputy Commissioner had been followed about from district to district by certain police officers and informers, whom he employed wherever he went, and that these men had been the main authors of mischief."

In his minute on the case, Lord Dalhousie says:

"We have irrefragable proof—proof, indeed, undisputed by Mr. Brereton himself—that that officer has been guilty of each item in the heavy catalogue of irregularities and illegalities with which the Chief Commissioner has charged him, and which have brought disgrace on one portion of the British administration, and have subjected a large number of British subjects to gross injustice, to arbitrary imprisonment and cruel torture."

Lord Dalhousie proposes "to make a great public example," and, consequently, is of opinion that

"Mr. Brereton cannot, *for the present*, be fitly entrusted with the authority of a Deputy Commissioner, but ought to be removed from that grade to the grade of a first class Assistant."

These extracts from the Blue Books may be concluded with the petition from the inhabitants of Taluk in Canara, on the Malabar coast, who, after stating that they had presented several petitions to the Government to no purpose, thus contrast their former and present condition:

"While we were cultivating wet and dry lands, hill tracts, low tracts and forests, paying the light assessment fixed upon us, and thereby enjoying tranquillity and happiness under the administration of 'Ranee', Bahadur and Tippoo, the then Circar* servants, levied an additional assessment, but we never paid it. We were not subjected to privations, oppressions or ill-usages in collecting the revenue. On the surrender of this country to the Honourable Company,** they devised all sorts of plans to squeeze out money from us. With this pernicious object in view, they invented rules and framed regulations, and directed their collectors and civil judges to put them in execution. But the then collectors and their subordinate native officials paid for some time due attention to our grievances, and acted in consonance with our wishes. On the contrary, the present collectors and their subordinate officials, *desirous of obtaining promotion on any account whatever,* neglect the welfare and interests of the people in general, turn a deaf ear to our grievances, and subject us to all sorts of oppression."

* Government.—*Ed.*

** East India Company.—*Ed.*

We have here given but a brief and mildly-coloured chapter from the real history of British rule in India. In view of such facts, dispassionate and thoughtful men may perhaps be led to ask whether a people are not justified in attempting to expel the foreign conquerors who have so abused their subjects. And if the English could do these things in cold blood, is it surprising that the insurgent Hindus should be guilty, in the fury of revolt and conflict, of the crimes and cruelties alleged against them?

Written on August 28, 1857

Published in the
New-York Daily Tribune,
No. 5120, September 17, 1857

Printed according to the text of the newspaper

Karl Marx

BRITISH INCOMES IN INDIA

The present state of affairs in Asia suggests the inquiry, What is the real value of their Indian dominion to the British nation and people? Directly, that is in the shape of tribute, of surplus of Indian receipts over Indian expenditures, nothing whatever reaches the British Treasury. On the contrary, the annual outgo is very large. From the moment that the East India Company entered extensively on the career of conquest—now just about a century ago—their finances fell into an embarrassed condition, and they were repeatedly compelled to apply to Parliament, not only for military aid to assist them in holding the conquered territories, but for financial aid to save them from bankruptcy. And so things have continued down to the present moment, at which so large a call is made for troops on the British nation, to be followed, no doubt, by corresponding calls for money. In prosecuting its conquests hitherto, and building up its establishments, the East India Company has contracted a debt of upward of £50,000,000 sterling, while the British Government has been at the expense, for years past, of transporting to and from and keeping up in India, in addition to the forces, native and European, of the East India Company, a standing army of thirty thousand men. Such being the case, it is evident that the advantage to Great Britain from her Indian Empire must be limited to the profits and benefits which accrue to individual British subjects. These profits and benefits, it must be confessed, are very considerable.

First, we have the stockholders in the East India Company, to the number of about 3,000 persons, to whom under the recent Charter[78] there is guaranteed, upon a paid-up capital of six millions of pounds sterling, an annual dividend of ten and a half per cent, amounting to £630,000 annually. As the East India stock is held in transferable shares, anybody may become a stockholder who has money enough to buy the stock, which, under the existing Charter, commands a premium of from 125 to 150 per cent. Stock to the amount of £500, costing say $6,000, entitles the holder to speak at the proprietors' meetings, but to vote he must have £1,000 of stock. Holders of £3,000 have two votes, of £6,000 three votes, and of £10,000 or upward four votes. The proprietors, however, have but little voice, except in the election of the Board of Directors, of whom they choose twelve, while the Crown appoints six; but these appointees of the Crown must be qualified by having resided for ten years or more in India. One-third of the Directors go out of office each year, but may be re-elected or re-appointed. To be a Director, one must be a proprietor of £2,000 of stock. The Directors have a salary of £500 each, and their Chairman and Deputy Chairman twice as much; but the chief inducement to accept the office is the great patronage attached to it in the appointment of all Indian officers, civil, and military—a patronage, however, largely shared, and, as to the most important offices, engrossed substantially, by the Board of Control. This Board consists of six members, all Privy Councillors, and in general two or three of them Cabinet Ministers, the President of the Board being always so, in fact a Secretary of State for India.

Next come the recipients of this patronage, divided into five classes—civil, clerical, medical, military and naval. For service in India, at least in the civil line, some knowledge of the languages spoken there is necessary, and to prepare young men to enter their civil service, the East India Company has a college at Haileybury. A corresponding college for the military service, in which, however, the rudiments of military science are the principal branches taught, has been established at Addiscombe, near London. Admission to these colleges was formerly a matter of favour on the part of the Directors of the Company, but under the latest modifications of the Charter it has been opened to competition in the way of a public examination of candidates. On first reaching India, a civilian is allowed about $150 a month, till having passed a necessary examination in one or more of the native languages (which must be within twelve months after his arrival), he is attached to the service with emoluments which vary from $2,500 to near $50,000 per annum. The latter is the pay of the members of the Bengal Council; the members of the Bombay and Madras Councils* receive about $30,000 per annum. No person not a member of Council can receive more than about $25,000 per annum, and, to obtain an appointment worth $20,000 or over, he must have been a resident in India for twelve years. Nine years' residence qualifies for salaries of from $15,000 to $20,000, and three years' residence for salaries of from $7,000 to $15,000. Appointments in the civil service go nominally by seniority and merit, but really to a great extent by favour. As they are the best paid, there is great competition to get them, the military officers leaving their regiments for this purpose whenever they can get a chance. The average of all the salaries in the civil service is stated at about $8,000, but this does not include perquisites and extra allowances, which are often very considerable. These civil servants are employed as Governors, Councillors, Judges, Ambassadors, Secretaries, Collectors of the Revenue, etc.—the number in the whole being generally about 800. The salary of the Governor-General of India is $125,000, but the extra allowances often amount to a still larger sum. The Church service includes three bishops and about one hundred and sixty chaplains. The Bishop of Calcutta has $25,000 a year; those of Madras and Bombay half as much; the chaplains from $2,500 to 7,000, besides fees. The medical service includes some 800 physicians and surgeons, with salaries of from $1,500 to $10,000.

The European military officers employed in India, including those of the contingents which the dependent princes are obliged to furnish, number about 8,000. The fixed pay in the infantry is, for ensigns, $1,080; lieutenants, $1,344; captains, $2,226; majors, $3,810; lieutenant-colonels, $5,520;

* Councils under the British Governor-Generals.—*Ed.*

colonels, $7,680. This is the pay in cantonment. In active service, it is more. The pay in the cavalry, artillery and engineers, is somewhat higher. By obtaining staff situations or employments in the civil service, many officers double their pay.

Here are about ten thousand British subjects holding lucrative situations in India, and drawing their pay from the Indian service. To these must be added a considerable number living in England, whither they have retired upon pensions, which in all the services are payable after serving a certain number of years. These pensions, with the dividends and interest on debts due in England, consume some fifteen to twenty millions of dollars drawn annually from India, and which may in fact be regarded as so much tribute paid to the English Government indirectly through its subjects. Those who annually retire from the several services carry with them very considerable amounts of savings from their salaries, which is so much more added to the annual drain on India.

Besides those Europeans actually employed in the service of the Government, there are other European residents in India to the number of 6,000 or more, employed in trade or private speculation. Except a few indigo, sugar and coffee planters in the rural districts, they are principally merchants, agents and manufacturers, who reside in the cities of Calcutta, Bombay and Madras, or their immediate vicinity. The foreign trade of India, including imports and exports to the amount of about fifty millions of dollars of each, is almost entirely in their hands, and their profits are no doubt very considerable.

It is thus evident that individuals gain largely by the English connection with India, and of course their gain goes to increase the sum of the national wealth. But against all this a very large offset is to be made. The military and naval expenses paid out of the pockets of the people of England on Indian account have been constantly increasing with the extent of the Indian dominion. To this must be added the expense of Burmese, Afghan, Chinese and Persian wars. In fact, the whole cost of the late Russian war may fairly be charged to the Indian account, since the fear and dread of Russia, which led to that war, grew entirely out of jealousy as to her designs on India. Add to this the career of endless conquest and perpetual aggression in which the English are involved by the possession of India, and it may well be doubted whether, on the whole, this dominion does not threaten to cost quite as much as it can ever be expected to come to.

Written at the beginning
of September 1857

Published in the
New-York Daily Tribune,
No. 5123, September 21, 1857

Printed according to the text
of the newspaper

Karl Marx

THE APPROACHING INDIAN LOAN

London, January 22, 1858

The buoyancy in the London money market, resulting from the withdrawal of an enormous mass of capital from the ordinary productive investments, and its consequent transfer to the security markets, has, in the last fortnight, been somewhat lessened by the prospects of an impending *Indian loan* to the amount of eight or ten million pounds sterling. This loan, to be raised in England, and to be authorized by Parliament immediately on its assembling in February, is required to meet the claims upon the East India Company by its home creditors, as well as the extra expenditure for war materials, stores, transport of troops, etc., necessitated by the Indian revolt. In August, 1857, the British Government had, before the prorogation of Parliament, solemnly declared in the House of Commons that no such loan was intended, the financial resources of the Company being more than sufficient to meet the crisis. The agreeable delusion thus palmed on John Bull was, however, soon dispelled when it oozed out that by a proceeding of a very questionable character, the East India Company had laid hold on a sum of about £3,500,000 sterling, entrusted to them by different companies, for the construction of Indian railways; and had, moreover, secretly borrowed £1,000,000 sterling from the Bank of England, and another million from the London Joint Stock banks. The public being thus prepared for the worst, the Government did no longer hesitate to drop the mask, and by semi-official articles in *The Times, Globe* and other government organs, avow the necessity of the loan.

It may be asked why a special act on the part of the legislative power is required for launching such a loan, and then, why such an event does create the least apprehension, since, on the contrary, every vent for British capital, seeking now in vain for profitable investment, should, under present circumstances, be considered a windfall, and a most salutary check upon the rapid depreciation of capital.

It is generally known that the commercial existence of the East India Company was terminated in 1834, when its principal remaining source of commercial profits, the monopoly of the China trade, was cut off. Consequently, the holders of East India stock having derived their dividends, nominally, at least, from the trade profits of the Company, a new financial arrangement with regard to them had become necessary. The payment of the dividends, till then chargeable upon the commercial revenue of the Company, was transferred to its political revenue. The proprietors of East India stocks were to be paid out of the revenues enjoyed by the East India Company in its governmental capacity, and, by act of Parliament, the Indian stock, amounting to £6,000,000 sterling, bearing ten per cent interest, was converted into a capital not to be liquidated except at the rate of £200 for every £100 of stock. In other words, the original East India stock of £6,000,000 sterling was converted into a capital of £12,000,000 sterling, bearing five per cent interest, and chargeable upon the revenue derived from the taxes of the Indian people. The debt of the East India Company was thus, by a Parliamentary sleight of hand, changed into a debt of the Indian people. There exists, besides, a debt exceeding £50,000,000 sterling, contracted by the East India Company in India, and exclusively chargeable upon the state revenues of that country; such loans contracted by the Company in India itself having always been considered to lie beyond the district of Parliamentary legislation, and regarded no more than the debts contracted by the colonial governments in Canada or Australia for instance.

On the other hand, the East India Company was prohibited from contracting interest-bearing debts in Great Britain herself, without the especial sanction of Parliament. Some years ago, when the Company set about establishing railways and electric telegraphs in India, it applied for the authorization of Indian bonds in the London market, a request which was granted to the amount of £7,000,000 sterling, to be issued in bonds bearing 4 per cent interest, and secured only on the Indian state revenues. At the commencement of the outbreak in India, this bond-debt stood at £3,894,400 sterling, and the very necessity of again applying to Parliament shows the East India Company to have, during the course of the Indian insurrection, exhausted its legal powers of borrowing at home.

Now it is no secret that before recurring to this step, the East India Company had opened a loan at Calcutta, which, however, turned out a complete failure. This proves, on the one hand, that Indian capitalists are far from considering the prospects of British supremacy in India in the same sanguine spirit which distinguishes the London press; and, on the other hand, exacerbates the feelings of John Bull to an uncommon pitch, since he is aware of the immense hoardings of capital having gone on for the last seven years in India, whither, according to a statement recently published by Messrs. Haggard & Pixley, there has been shipped in 1856 and 1857, from the port of London alone, bullion to the amount of £21,000,000. *The London Times*, in a most persuasive strain, has taught its readers that

> "of all the incentives to the loyalty of the natives, that of making them our creditors was the least doubtful; while, on the other hand, among an impulsive, secretive and avaricious people no temptation to discontent or treachery could be stronger than that created by the idea that they were annually taxed to send dividends to wealthy claimants in other countries."

The Indians, however, appear not to understand the beauty of a plan which would not only restore English supremacy at the expense of Indian capital, but at the same time, in a circuitous way, open the native hoards to British commerce. If, indeed, the Indian capitalists were as fond of British rule as every true Englishman thinks it an article of faith to assert, no better opportunity could have been afforded them of exhibiting their loyalty and getting rid of their silver. The Indian capitalists shutting up their hoards, John Bull must open his mind to the dire necessity of defraying himself in the first instance, at least, the expenses of the Indian insurrection, without any support on the part of the natives. The impending loan constitutes, moreover, a precedent only, and looks like the first leaf in a book, bearing the title, *Anglo-Indian Home Debt.* It is no secret that what the East India Company wants are not eight millions, or ten millions, but twenty-five to thirty million pounds, and even these as a first instalment only, not for expenses to be incurred, but for debts already due. The deficient revenue for the last three years amounted to £5,000,000; the treasure plundered by the insurgents up to the 15th October last, to £10,000,000, according to the statement of the *Phoenix*, an Indian governmental paper; the loss of revenue in the north-eastern provinces, consequent upon the rebellion, to £5,000,000, and the war expenses to at least £10,000,000.

It is true that successive loans by the Indian Company, in the London money market, would raise the value of money and prevent the increasing depreciation of capital; that is to say, the further fall in the rate of interest; but such a fall is exactly required for the revival of British industry and commerce. Any artificial check put upon the downward movement of the rate of discount is equivalent to an enhancement in the cost of production and the terms of credit, which, in its present weak state, English trade feels itself unable to bear. Hence the general cry of distress at the announcement of the Indian loan. Though the Parliamentary sanction adds no imperial guarantee to the loan of the Company, that guarantee, too, must be conceded, if money is not to be obtained on other terms; and despite all fine distinctions, as soon as the East India Company is supplanted by the British Government, its debt will be merged into the British debt. A further increase of the large national debt seems, therefore, one of the first financial consequences of the Indian revolt.

Published in the *New-York Daily Tribune*, No. 5243, February 9, 1858

Printed according to the text of the newspaper

Frederick Engels

DETAILS OF THE ATTACK ON LUCKNOW

At last we are in possession of detailed accounts of the attack and fall of Lucknow. The principal sources of information, in a military point of view, the dispatches of Sir Colin Campbell, have not yet, indeed, been published; but the correspondence of the British press, and especially the letters of Mr. Russel in *The London Times*, the chief portions of which have been laid before our readers, are quite sufficient to give a general insight into the proceedings of the attacking party.

The conclusions we drew from the telegraphic news, as to the ignorance and cowardice displayed in the defence, are more than confirmed by the detailed accounts. The works erected by the Hindus, formidable in appearance, were in reality of no greater consequence than the fiery dragons and grimacing faces painted by Chinese "braves" on their shields or on the walls of their cities. Every single work exhibited an apparently impregnable front, nothing but loopholed and embrasured walls and parapets, difficulties of access of every possible description, cannon and small arms bristling everywhere. But the flanks and rear of every position were completely neglected, a mutual support of the various works was never thought of, and even the ground between the works, as well as in front of them, had never been cleared, so that both front and flank attacks could be prepared without the knowledge of the defence, and could approach under perfect shelter to within a few yards from the parapet. It was just such a conglomerate of intrenchments as might be expected from a body of private sappers deprived of their officers, and serving in an army where ignorance and indiscipline reigned supreme. The intrenchments of Lucknow are but a translation of the whole method of sepoy warfare into baked clay walls and earthen parapets. The mechanical portion of European tactics had been partially impressed upon their minds; they knew the manual and platoon drill well enough; they could also build a battery and loophole a wall; but how to combine the movements of companies and battalions in the defence of a position, or how to combine batteries and loopholed houses and walls, so as to form an intrenched camp capable of resistance—of this they were utterly ignorant. Thus, they weakened the solid masonry walls of their palaces by over-loopholing them, heaped tier upon tier of loopholes and embrasures, placed parapeted batteries on their roofs, and all this to no purpose whatever, because it could all be turned in the easiest possible manner. In the same way, knowing their tactical inferiority, they tried to make up for it by cramming every post as full of men as possible, to no other purpose than to give terrible effect to the British artillery and to render impossible all orderly and systematic defence as soon as the attacking columns fell upon this motley host from an unexpected direction. And when the British, by some accidental circumstance, were compelled to attack even the formidable front of the works, their construction was so faulty that they could be approached, breached and stormed almost without any risk. At the Imambarah this was the case. Within a few yards from the building stood a pucka (sun-baked clay) wall. Up to this the British made a short sap (proof enough that the embrasures and loopholes on the higher part of the building had no plunging fire upon the ground immediately in front), and used this very wall as a breaching battery, prepared for them by the Hindus themselves! They brought up two 68-pounders (naval guns) behind this wall. The lightest 68-pounder in the British service weighs 87 cwt., without the carriage; but supposing even that an 8-inch gun for hollow shot only is alluded to, the lightest gun of that class weighs 50 cwt., and with the carriage at least three tons. That such guns could be brought up at all in such proximity to a palace several storeys high, with a battery on the roof, shows a contempt of commanding positions and an ignorance of military engineering which no private sapper in any civilized army could be capable of.

Thus much for the science against which the British had to contend. As to courage and obstinacy, they were equally absent from the defence. From the Martinière to the Musabagh, on the part of the natives, there was but one grand and unanimous act of bolting, as soon as a column advanced to the attack. There is nothing in the whole series of engagements that can compare even with the massacre (for fight it can scarcely be called) in the Secundarbagh during Campbell's relief of the Residency. No sooner do the attacking parties advance, than there is a general helter-skelter to the rear, and where there are but a few narrow exits so as to bring the crowded rabble to a stop, they fall pell-mell, and without any resistance, under the volleys and bayonets of the advancing British. The "British bayonet" has done more execution in any one of these onslaughts on panic-stricken natives than in all the wars of the English in Europe and America put together. In the East, such bayonet-battles, where one party only is active and the other abjectly passive, are a regular occurrence in warfare; the Burmese stockades in every case furnished an example. According to Mr. Russell's account, the chief loss suffered by the British was caused by Hindus cut off from retreat, and barricaded in the rooms of the palaces, whence they fired from the windows upon the officers in the courtyards and gardens.

In storming the Imambarah and the Kaisarbagh, the bolting of the Hindus was so rapid, that the place was not taken, but simply marched into. The interesting scene, however, was now only commencing; for, as Mr. Russell blandly observes, the conquest of the Kaisarbagh on that day was so unexpected that there was no time to guard against indiscriminate plunder. A merry scene it must have been for a true, liberty-loving John Bull to see his British grenadiers helping themselves freely to the jewels, costly arms, clothes, and all the toggery of his Majesty of Oudh. The Sikhs, Gurkhas and camp followers were quite ready to imitate the example, and a scene of plunder and destruction followed which evidently surpassed even the descriptive talent of Mr. Russell. Every fresh step in advance was accompanied with plunder and devastation. The Kaisarbagh had fallen on the 14th; and half an hour after, discipline was at an end, and the officers had lost all command over their men. On the 17th, Gen. Campbell was obliged to establish patrols to check plundering, and to remain in inactivity "until the present licence ceases." The troops were evidently completely out of hand. On the 18th, we hear that there is a cessation of the *grosser* sort of plunder, but devastation is still going on freely. In the city, however, while the vanguard were fighting against the natives' fire from the houses, the rear-guard plundered and destroyed to their hearts' content. In the evening, there is another proclamation against plundering; strong parties of every regiment to go out and fetch in their own men, and to keep their camp followers at home; nobody to leave the camp except on duty. On the 20th, a recapitulation of the same orders. On the same day, two British "officers and gentlemen," Lieuts. Cape and Thackwell, "went into the city *looting*, and were murdered in a house"; and on the 26th, matters were still so bad that the most stringent orders were issued for the suppression of plunder and outrage; hourly roll-calls were instituted; all soldiers strictly forbidden to enter the city; camp followers, if found armed in the city, to be hanged; soldiers not to wear arms except on duty, and all non-combatants to be disarmed. To give due weight to these orders, a number of triangles for flogging were erected "at proper places."

This is indeed a pretty state of things in a civilized army in the 19th century; and if any other troops in the world had committed one-tenth of these excesses, how would the indignant British press brand them with infamy! But these are the deeds of the British army, and therefore we are told that such things are but the normal consequences of war. British officers and gentlemen are perfectly welcome to appropriate to themselves any silver spoons, jewelled bracelets, and other little memorials they may find about the scene of their glory; and if Campbell is compelled to disarm his own army in the midst of war, in order to stop wholesale robbery and violence, there may have been military reasons for the step; but surely nobody will begrudge these poor fellows a week's holiday and a little frolic after so many fatigues and privations.

The fact is, there is no army in Europe or America with so much brutality as the British. Plündering, violence, massacre—things that everywhere else are strictly and completely banished—are a time-honoured privilege, a vested right of the British soldier. The infamies committed for days together, after the storming of Badajoz and San Sebastian, in the Peninsular war, are without a parallel in the annals of any other nation since the beginning of the Erench Revolution, and the mediaeval usage, proscribed everywhere else, of giving up to plunder a town taken by assault, is still the rule with the British. At Delhi imperious military considerations enforced an exception; but the army, though bought off by extra pay, grumbled, and now at Lucknow they have made up for what they missed at Delhi. For twelve days and nights there was no British army at Lucknow—nothing but a lawless, drunken, brutal rabble, dissolved into bands of robbers, far more lawless, violent and greedy than the sepoys who had just been driven out of the place. The sack of Lucknow in 1858 will remain an everlasting disgrace to the British military service.

If the reckless soldiery, in their civilizing and humanizing progress through India, could rob the natives of their personal property only, the British Government steps in immediately afterwards and strips them of their real estate as well. Talk of the first French Revolution confiscating the lands of the nobles and the church! Talk of Louis Napoleon confiscating the property of the Orleans family! Here comes Lord Canning, a British nobleman, mild in language, manners and feelings, and confiscates, by order of his superior, Viscount Palmerston, the lands of a whole people, every rood, perch and acre, over an extent of ten thousand square miles. A very nice bit of *loot* indeed for John Bull! And no sooner has Lord Ellenborough, in the name of the new Government, disapproved of this hitherto unexampled measure, than up rise *The Times* and a host of minor British papers to defend this wholesale robbery, and break a lance for the right of John Bull to confiscate everything he likes. But then, John is an exceptional being, and what is virtue in him, according to *The Times*, would be infamy in others.

Meanwhile—thanks to the complete dissolution of the British army for the purpose of plunder—the insurgents escaped, unpursued, into the open country. They concentrate in Rohilkhand, while a portion carry on petty warfare in Oudh, and other fugitives have taken the direction of Bundelkhand. At the same time, the hot weather and the rains are fast approaching; and it is not to be expected that the season will be so uncommonly favourable to European constitutions as last year. Then, the mass of the European troops were more or less acclimated; this year, most of them are newly arrived. There is no doubt that a campaign in June, July and August will cost the British an immense number of lives, and what with the garrisons that have to be left in every conquered city the active army will melt down very rapidly. Already are we informed that reinforcements of 1,000 men per month will scarcely keep up the army at its effective strength; and as to garrisons, Lucknow alone requires at least 8,000 men, over one-third of Campbell's army. The force organizing for the campaign of Rohilkhand will scarcely be stronger than this garrison of Lucknow. We are also informed that among the British officers the opinion is gaining ground that the guerrilla warfare which is sure to succeed the dispersion of the larger bodies of insurgents, will be far more harassing and destructive of life to the British than the present war with its battles and sieges. And, lastly, the Sikhs are beginning to talk in a way which bodes no good to the English. They feel that without their assistance the British would scarcely have been able to hold India, and that, had they joined the insurrection, Hindustan would certainly have been lost to England, at least, for a time. They say this soundly, and exaggerate it in their Eastern way. To them the English no longer appear as that superior race which beat them at Mudki, Ferozeshah and Aliwal. From such a conviction to open hostility there is but a step with Eastern nations; a spark may kindle the blaze.

Altogether, the taking of Lucknow has no more put down the Indian insurrection than the taking of Delhi. This summer's campaign may produce such events that the British will have, next winter, to go substantially over the same ground again, and perhaps even to reconquer the Punjab. But in the best of cases, a long and harassing guerrilla warfare is before them—not an enviable thing for Europeans under an Indian sun.

Written on May 8, 1858

Published in the *New-York Daily Tribune*, No. 5333, May 25, 1858

Printed according to the text of the newspaper

Karl Marx

THE ANNEXATION OF OUDH

About eighteen months ago, at Canton, the British Government propounded the novel doctrine in the law of nations that a state may commit hostilities on a large scale against a province of another state, without either declaring war or establishing a state of war against that other state. Now the same British Government, in the person of the Governor-General of India, Lord Canning, has made another forward move in its task of upsetting the existing law of nations. It has proclaimed that

> "the proprietary right in the soil of the Province of Oudh is confiscated to the British Government, which will dispose of that right in such manner as it may see fitting."

When, after the fall of Warsaw in 1831, the Russian Emperor confiscated "the proprietary right in the soil" hitherto held by numerous Polish nobles, there was one unanimous outburst of indignation in the British press and Parliament. When, after the battle of Novara, the Austrian Government did not confiscate, but merely sequestered, the estates of such Lombard noblemen as had taken an active part in the war of independence, that unanimous outburst of British indignation was repeated. And when, after the 2nd December, 1851, Louis Napoleon confiscated the estates of the Orleans family, which, by the common law of France, ought to have been united to the public domain on the accession of Louis Philippe, but which had escaped that fate by a legal quibble, then British indignation knew no bounds, and *The London Times* declared that by this act the very foundations of social order were upset, and that civil society could no longer exist. All this honest indignation has now been practically illustrated. England, by one stroke of the pen, has confiscated not only the estates of a few noblemen, or of a royal family, but the whole length and breadth of a kingdom nearly as large as Ireland, "the inheritance of a whole people," as Lord Ellenborough himself terms it.

But let us hear what pretexts—grounds we cannot call them—Lord Canning, in the name of the British Government, sets forth for this unheard-of proceeding: First, "The army is in possession of Lucknow." Second, "The resistance, begun by a mutinous soldiery, has found support from the inhabitants of the city and of the province at large." Third, "They have been guilty of a great crime, and have subjected themselves to a just retribution." In plain English: Because the British army have got hold of Lucknow, the Government has the right to confiscate all the land in Oudh which they have not yet got hold of. Because the native soldiers in British pay have mutinied, the natives of Oudh, who were subjected to British rule by force, have not the right to rise for their national independence. In short, the people of Oudh have rebelled against the legitimate authority of the British Government, and the British Government now distinctly declares that rebellion is a sufficient ground for confiscation. Leaving, therefore, out of the question all the circumlocution of Lord Canning, the whole question turns upon the point that he assumes the British rule in Oudh to have been legitimately established.

Now, British rule in Oudh was established in the following manner: When, in 1856, Lord Dalhousie thought the moment for action had arrived, he concentrated an army at Cawnpore which, the King of Oudh* was told, was to serve as a corps of observation against Nepal. This army suddenly invaded the country, took possession of Lucknow, and took the King prisoner. He was urged to cede the country to the British, but in vain. He was then carried off to Calcutta, and the country was annexed to the territories

* Wajid Ali Shah.—*Ed.*

of the East India Company. This treacherous invasion was based upon article 6 of the treaty of 1801, concluded by Lord Wellesley. This treaty was the natural consequence of that concluded in 1798 by Sir John Shore. According to the usual policy followed by the Anglo-Indian Government in their intercourse with native princes, this first treaty of 1798 was a treaty of offensive and defensive alliance on both sides. It secured to the East India Company a yearly subsidy of 76 lacs of rupees ($3,800,000); but by articles 12 and 13 the King was obliged to reduce the taxation of the country. As a matter of course, these two conditions, in open contradiction to each other, could not be fulfilled by the King at the same time. This result, looked for by the East India Company, gave rise to fresh complications, resulting in the treaty of 1801, by which a cession of territory had to make up for the alleged infractions of the former treaty; a cession of territory which, by the way, was at the time denounced in Parliament as a downright robbery, and would have brought Lord Wellesley before a Committee of Inquiry, but for the political influence then held by his family.

In consideration of this cession of territory, the East India Company, by article 3, undertook to defend the King's remaining territories against all foreign and domestic enemies; and by article 6 guaranteed the possession of these territories to him and his heirs and successors forever. But this same article 6 contained also a pit-fall for the King, viz.: The King engaged that he would establish such a system of administration, to be carried into effect by his own officers, as should be conducive to the prosperity of his subjects, and be calculated to secure the lives and property of the inhabitants. Now, supposing the King of Oudh had broken this treaty; had not, by his government, secured the lives and property of the inhabitants (say by blowing them from the cannon's mouth, and confiscating the whole of their lands), what remedy remained to the East India Company? The King was, by the treaty, acknowledged as an independent sovereign, a free agent, one of the contracting parties. The East India Company, on declaring the treaty broken and thereby annulled, could have but two modes of action: either by negotiation, backed by pressure, they might have come to a new arrangement, or else they might have declared war against the King. But to invade his territory without declaration of war, to take him prisoner unawares, dethrone him and annex his territory, was an infraction not only of the treaty, but of every principle of the law of nations.

That the annexation of Oudh was not a sudden resolution of the British Government is proved by a curious fact. No sooner was Lord Palmerston, in 1830, Foreign Secretary, than he sent an order to the then Governor-General* to annex Oudh. The subordinate at that time declined to carry out the suggestion. The affair, however, came to the knowledge of the King of Oudh,** who availed himself of some pretext to send an embassy to London. In spite of all obstacles, the embassy succeeded in acquainting William IV, who was ignorant of the whole proceeding, with the danger which had menaced their country. The result was a violent scene between William IV and Palmerston, ending in a strict injunction to the latter never to repeat such *coups d'état* on pain of instant dismissal. It is important to recollect that the actual annexation of Oudh and the confiscation of all the landed property of the country took place when Palmerston was again in power. The papers relating to this first attempt at annexing Oudh, in 1831, were moved for, a few weeks ago, in the House of Commons, when Mr. Baillie, Secretary of the Board of Control, declared that these papers had disappeared.

Again, in 1837, when Palmerston, for the second time, was Foreign Secretary, and Lord Auckland Governor-General of India, the King of Oudh*** was compelled to make a fresh treaty with the East India Company. This treaty takes up article 6 of the one of 1801, because "it provides no remedy for the obligation contained in it" (to govern the country well); and it expressly provides, therefore, by article 7,

> "that the King of Oudh shall immediately take into consideration, in concert with the British Resident, the best means of remedying the

* William Bentinck.—*Ed.*
** Nazr-ed-Din.—*Ed.*
*** Mohammed Ali Shah.—*Ed.*

defects in the police, and in the judicial and revenue administrations of his dominions; and that if his Majesty should neglect to attend to the advice and counsel of the British Government, and if gross and systematic oppression, anarchy and misrule should prevail within the Oudh dominions, such as seriously to endanger the public tranquillity, the British Government reserves to itself the right of appointing its own officers to the management of whatsoever portions of the Oudh territory, either to a small or great extent, in which such misrule shall have occurred, for so long a period as it may deem necessary; the surplus receipts in such case, after defraying all charges, to be paid into the King's Treasury, and a true and faithful account rendered to his Majesty of the receipts and expenditure."

By article 8, the treaty further provides:

"That in case the Governor-General of India in Council should be compelled to resort to the exercise of the authority vested in him by article 7, he will endeavour so far as possible to maintain, with such improvements as they may admit of, the native institutions and forms of administration within the assumed territories, so as to facilitate the restoration of these territories to the Sovereign of Oudh, when the proper period for such restoration shall arrive."

This treaty professes to be concluded between the Governor-General of British India in Council, on one hand, and the King of Oudh on the other. It was, as such, duly ratified, by both parties, and the ratifications were duly exchanged. But when it was submitted to the Board of Directors of the East India Company, it was annulled (April 10, 1838) as an infraction of the friendly relations between the Company and the King of Oudh, and an encroachment, on the part of the Governor-General, on the rights of that potentate. Palmerston had not asked the Company's leave to conclude the treaty, and he took no notice of their annulling resolution. Nor was the King of Oudh informed that the treaty had ever been cancelled. This is proved by Lord Dalhousie himself (minute Jan. 5, 1856):

"It is very probable that the King, in the course of the discussions which will take place with the Resident,* may refer to the treaty negotiated with his predecessor in 1837; the Resident is aware that the treaty was not continued in force, having been annulled by the Court of Directors as soon as it was received in England. The Resident is further aware that, although the King of Oudh was informed at the time that certain aggravating provisions of the treaty of 1837, respect-

---

* James Outram.—*Ed.*

ing an increased military force, would not be carried into effect, the *entire abrogation of it was never communicated to his Majesty*. The effect of this reserve and want of full communication is felt to be embarrassing today. It is the more embarrassing that the cancelled instrument was still included in a volume of treaties which was published in 1845, by the authority of Government."

In the same minute, sec. 17, it is said:

"If the King should allude to the treaty of 1837, and should ask why, if further measures are necessary in relation to the administration of Oudh, the large powers which are given to the British Government by the said treaty should not now be put in force, his Majesty must be informed that the treaty has had no existence since it was communicated to the Court of Directors, by whom it was wholly annulled. His Majesty will be reminded that the Court of Lucknow was informed at the time that certain articles of the treaty of 1837, by which the payment of an additional military force was imposed upon the King, were to be set aside. It must be presumed that it was not thought necessary at that time to make any communication to his Majesty regarding those articles of the treaty which were not of immediate operation, and that the subsequent communication was inadvertently neglected."

But not only was this treaty inserted in the official collection of 1845, it was also officially adverted to as a subsisting treaty in Lord Auckland's notification to the King of Oudh, dated July 8, 1839; in Lord Hardinge's (then Governor-General) remonstrance to the same King, of November 23, 1847, and in Col. Sleeman's (Resident at Lucknow) communication to Lord Dalhousie himself, of the 10th December, 1851. Now, why was Lord Dalhousie so eager to deny the validity of a treaty which all his predecessors, and even his own agents, had acknowledged to be in force in their communications with the King of Oudh? Solely because, by this treaty, whatever pretext the King might give for interference, that interference was limited to an assumption of government by British officers *in the name of the King of Oudh,* who was to receive the surplus revenue. That was the very opposite of what was wanted. Nothing short of annexation would do. This denying the validity of treaties which had formed the acknowledged base of intercourse for twenty years; this seizing violently upon independent territories in open infraction even of the acknowledged treaties; this final confiscation of every acre of land in the whole country; all these treacherous and brutal modes of proceeding of the British toward the natives of India are now beginning to avenge themselves, not only in India, but in England.

Written on May 14, 1858

Published in the
New-York Daily Tribune,
No. 5336, May 28, 1858

Printed according to the text of the newspaper

Karl Marx

LORD CANNING'S PROCLAMATION AND LAND TENURE IN INDIA

Lord Canning's proclamation in relation to Oudh, some important documents in reference to which we published on Saturday, has revived the discussion as to the land tenures of India—a subject upon which there have been great disputes and differences of opinion in times past, and misapprehensions in reference to which have led, so it is alleged, to very serious practical mistakes in the administration of those parts of India directly under British rule. The great point in this controversy is, what is the exact position which the zemindars, talukdars or sirdars, so called, hold in the economical system of India? Are they properly to be considered as landed proprietors or as mere tax-gatherers?

It is agreed that in India, as in most Asiatic countries, the ultimate property in the soil vests the Government; but while one party to this controversy insists that the Government is to be looked upon as a soil proprietor, letting out the land on shares to the cultivators, the other side maintains that in substance the land in India is just as much private property as in any other country whatever—this alleged property in the Government being nothing more than the derivation of title from the sovereign, theoretically acknowledged in all countries, the codes of which are based on the feudal law and substantially acknowledged in all countries whatever in the power of the Government to levy taxes on the land to the extent of the needs of the Government, quite independent of all considerations, except as mere matter of policy, of the convenience of the owners.

Admitting, however, that the lands of India are private property, held by as good and strong a private title as land elsewhere, who shall be regarded as the real owners? There are two parties for whom this claim has been set up. One of these parties is the class known as zemindars and talukdars, who have been considered to occupy a position similar to that of the landed nobility and gentry of Europe; to be, indeed, the real owners of the land, subject to a certain assessment due to the Government, and, as owners, to have the right of displacing at pleasure the actual cultivators, who, in this view of the case, are regarded as standing in the position of mere tenants at will, liable to any payment in the way of rent which the zemindars may see fit to impose. The view of the case which naturally fell in with English ideas, as to the importance and necessity of a landed gentry as the main pillar of the social fabric, was made the foundation of the famous landed settlement of Bengal seventy years ago, under the Governor-Generalship of Lord Conrwallis—a settlement which still remains in force, but which, as it is maintained by many, wrought great injustice alike to the Government and to the actual cultivators. A more thorough study of the institutions of Hindustan, together with the inconveniences, both social and political, resulting from the Bengal settlement, has given currency to the opinion that by the original Hindu institutions, the property of the land was in the village corporations, in which resided the power of allotting it out to individuals for cultivation · while the zemindars and talukdars were in their origin nothing but officers of the Government, appointed to look after, to collect, and to pay over to the prince the assessment due from the village.

This view has influenced to a considerable degree the settlement of the landed tenures and revenue made of late years in the Indian provinces, of which the direct administration has been assumed by the English. The exclusive proprietary rights claimed by the talukdars and zemindars have been regarded as originating in usurpations at once against the Government and the cultivators, and every effort has been made to get rid of them as an incubus on the real cultivators of the soil and the general improvement of the country. As, however, these middlemen, whatever the origin of their rights might be, could claim prescription in their favour, it was impossible not to recognize their claims as to a certain extent legal, however inconvenient, arbitrary and oppressive to the people. In Oudh, under the feeble reign of the native princes, these feudal landholders had gone very far in curtailing alike the claims of the Government and the rights of the cultivators; and when, upon the recent annexation of that Kingdom, this matter came under revision, the Commissioners charged with making the settlement soon got into a very acrimonious controversy with them as to the real extent of their rights. Hence resulted a state of discontent on their part which led them to make common cause with the revolted sepoys.

By those who incline to the policy above indicated—that of a system of village settlement—looking at the actual cultivators as invested with a proprietary right in the land, superior to that of the middlemen, through whom the Government receives its share of the landed produce—the proclamation of Lord Canning is defended as an advantage taken of the position in which the great body of the zemindars and talukdars of Oudh had placed themselves, to open a door for the introduction of much more extensive reforms than otherwise would have been practicable—the proprietary right confiscated by that proclamation being merely zemindari or talukdari right, and affecting only a very small part of the population, and that by no means the actual cultivators.

Independently of any question of justice and humanity, the view taken on the other hand by the Derby Ministry of Lord Canning's proclamation, corresponds sufficiently well with the general principles which the Tory, or Conservative, party maintain on the sacredness of vested rights and the importance of upholding an aristocratic landed interest. In speaking of the landed interest at home, they always refer rather to the landlords and rent-receivers than to the rent-payers and to the actual cultivators; and it is, therefore, not surprising that they should regard the interests of the zemindars and talukdars, however few their actual number, as equivalent to the interests of the great body of the people.

Here indeed is one of the greatest inconveniences and

difficulties in the government of India from England, that views of Indian questions are liable to be influenced by purely English prejudices or sentiments, applied to a state of society and a condition of things to which they have in fact very little real pertinency. The defence which Lord Canning makes in his dispatch, published to-day, of the policy of his proclamation against the objections of Sir James Outram, the Commissioner of Oudh, is very plausible, though it appears that he so far yielded to the representations of the Commissioner as to insert into the proclamation the modifying sentence, not contained in the original draft sent to England, and on which Lord Ellenborough's dispatch was based.

Lord Canning's opinion as to the light in which the conduct of landholders of Oudh in joining in the rebellion ought to be viewed does not appear to differ much from that of Sir James Outram and Lord Ellenborough. He argues that they stand in a very different position not only from the mutinous sepoys, but from that of the inhabitants of rebellious districts in which the British rule had been longer established. He admits that they are entitled to be treated as persons having provocation for the course they took; but at the same time insists that they must be made to understand that rebellion cannot be resorted to without involving serious consequences to themselves. We shall soon learn what the effect of the issue of the proclamation has been, and whether Lord Canning or Sir James Outram was nearer right in his anticipation of its results.

Written on May 25, 1858

Published in the *New-York Daily Tribune*, No. 5344, June 7, 1858

Printed according to the text of the newspaper

Frederick Engels

THE BRITISH ARMY IN INDIA

Our indiscreet friend, Mr. William Russell of *The London Times,* has recently been induced, by his love of the picturesque, to illustrate, for the second time, the sack of Lucknow, to a degree which other people will not think very flattering to the British character. It now appears that Delhi, too, was "looted" to a very considerable extent, and that besides the Kaisarbagh, the city of Lucknow generally contributed to reward the British soldier for his previous privations and heroic efforts. We quote from Mr. Russell:

> "There are companies which can boast of privates with thousands of pounds worth in their ranks. One man I heard of who complacently offered to lend an officer 'whatever sum he wanted if he wished to buy over the Captain'. Others have remitted large sums to their friends. Ere this letter reaches England, many a diamond, emerald and delicate pearl will have told its tale in a very quiet, pleasant way, of the storm and sack of the Kaisarbagh. *It is as well that the fair wearers... saw not how the glittering baubles were won, or the scenes in which the treasure was trove....* Some of these officers have made, literally, *their fortunes....* There are certain small caskets in battered uniform cases which contain *estates in Scotland and Ireland,* and snug fishing and shooting boxes in every game-haunted or salmon-frequented angle of the world."

This, then, accounts for the inactivity of the British army after the conquest of Lucknow. The fortnight devoted to plunder was well spent. Officers and soldiers went into the town poor and debt-ridden, and came out suddenly enriched. They were no longer the same men; yet they were expected to return to their former military duty, to submission, silent obedience, fatigue, privation and battle. But this is out of the question. The army, disbanded for the purpose of plunder, is changed for ever; no word of command, no prestige of the General, can make it again what it once was. Listen again to Mr. Russell:

"It is curious to observe how riches develop disease; how one's liver is affected by loot, and what tremendous ravages in one's family, among the nearest and dearest, can be caused by a few crystals of carbon. . . . The weight of the belt round the private's waist, full of rupees and gold mohurs, assures him that the vision" (of a comfortable independency at home) "can be realized, and it is no wonder he resents the 'fall in, then, fall in!' . . . Two battles, two shares of prize-money, the plunder of two cities, and many pickings by the way, have made some of our men too rich for easy soldiering."

Accordingly, we hear that above 150 officers have sent in their resignations to Sir Colin Campbell—a very singular proceeding indeed in an army before the enemy, which in any other service would be followed up in twenty-four hours by cashiering and severest punishment otherwise, but which, we suppose, is considered in the British army as a very proper act for "an officer and a gentleman" who has suddenly made his fortune. As to the private soldiers, with them the proceeding is different. Loot engenders the desire for more; and if no more Indian treasures are at hand for the purpose, why not loot those of the British Government? Accordingly, says Mr. Russell:

"There has been a suspicious upsetting of two treasure tumbrils under a European guard, in which some few rupees were missing, and *paymasters exhibit a preference for natives in the discharge of the delicate duty of convoy!*"

Very good, indeed. The Hindu or Sikh is better disciplined, less thieving, less rapacious than that incomparable model of a warrior, the British soldier! But so far we have seen the individual Briton only employed. Let us now cast a glance at the British army, "looting" in its collective capacity:

"Every day adds to the prize property, and it is estimated that the sales will produce £600,000. *The town of Cawnpore is said to be full of the plunder of Lucknow;* and if the damage done to public buildings, the destruction of private property, the deterioration in value of houses and land, and the results of depopulation could be estimated, it would be found that *the capital of Oudh has sustained a loss of five or six millions sterling.*"

The Kalmuk hordes of Genghis Khan and Timur, falling upon a city like a swarm of locusts, and devouring everything that came in their way, must have been a blessing to a country, compared with the irruption of these Christian, civilized, chivalrous and gentle British soldiers. The former, at least, soon passed away on their erratic course ; but these methodic Englishmen bring along with them their prize-agents, who convert loot into a system, who register the plunder, sell it by auction, and keep a sharp look-out that British heroism is not defrauded of a title of its reward. We shall watch with curiosity the capabilities of this army, relaxed as its discipline is by the effects of wholesale plunder, at a time when the fatigues of a hot weather campaign require the greatest stringency of discipline.

The Hindus must, however, by this time be still less fit for regular battle than they were at Lucknow, but that is not now the main question. It is far more important to know what shall be done if the insurgents, after a show of resistance, again shift the seat of war, say to Rajputana, which is far from being subdued. Sir Colin Campbell must leave garrisons everywhere; his field army has melted down to less than one-half of the force he had before Lucknow. If he is to occupy Rohilkhand what disposable strength will remain for the field? The hot weather is now upon him; in June the rains must have put a stop to active campaigning, and allowed the insurgents breathing time. The loss of European soldiers through sickness will have increased every day after the middle of April, when the weather became oppressive; and the young men imported into India last winter must succumb to the climate in far greater numbers than the seasoned Indian campaigners who last summer fought under Havelock and Wilson. Rohilkhand is no more the decisive point than Lucknow was, or Delhi. The insurrection, it is true, has lost most of its capacity for pitched battles; but it is far more formidable in its present scattered form, which compels the English to ruin their army by marching and exposure. Look at the many new centres of resistance. There is Rohilkhand, where the mass of the old sepoys are collected; there is north-eastern Oudh beyond the Gogra, where the Oudhians have taken up position; there is Kalpi, which for the present serves as a point of concentration for the insurgents of Bundelkhand. We shall most likely hear in a few weeks, if not sooner, that both Bareilly and Kalpi have fallen. The former will be of little importance, inasmuch as it will serve to absorb nearly all, if not the whole of Campbell's disposable forces. Kalpi, menaced now by General Whitlock, who has led his column from Nagpur to Banda, in Bundelkhand, and by General Rose, who approaches from Jhansi, and has defeated the advanced guard of the Kalpi forces, will be a more important conquest; it will free Campbell's base of operations, Cawnpore, from the only danger menacing it, and thus perhaps enable him to recruit his field forces to some extent by troops set at liberty thereby. But it is very doubtful whether there will be enough to do more than to clear Oudh.

Thus, the strongest army England ever concentrated on one point in India is again scattered in all directions, and has more work cut out than it can conveniently do. The ravages of the climate, during the summer's heat and rains, must be terrible; and whatever the moral superiority of the European over the Hindus, it is very doubtful whether the physical superiority of the Hindus in braving the heat and rains of an Indian summer will not again be the means of destroying the English forces. There are at present but few British troops on the road to India, and it is not intended to send out large reinforcements before July and August. Up to October and November, therefore, Campbell has but that one army, melting down rapidly as it is, to hold his own with. What if in the meantime the insurgent Hindus succeed in raising Rajputana and Mahratta country in rebellion? What if the Sikhs, of whom there are 80,000 in the British service, and who claim all the honour of the victories for themselves, and whose temper is not altogether favourable to the British, were to rise?

Altogether, one more winter's campaign, at least, appears to be in store for the British in India, and that cannot be carried on without another army from England.

Written about June 4, 1858

Published in the *New-York Daily Tribune*, No. 5361, June 26, 1858

Printed according to the text of the newspaper

Karl Marx

THE BRITISH GOVERNMENT AND THE SLAVE-TRADE

London, June 18, 1858

In the sitting of the House of Lords on June 17, the question of the slave-trade was introduced by the Bishop of Oxford, who presented a petition against that trade from the Parish of St. Mary in Jamaica. The impression these debates are sure to produce upon every mind not strongly prejudiced is that of great moderation on the part of the present British Government, and its firm purpose of avoiding any pretext of quarrel with the United States. Lord Malmesbury dropped altogether the "right of visit" as far as ships under the American flag are concerned, by the following declaration:

"The United States say that on no account, for no purpose, and upon no suspicion shall a ship carrying the American flag be boarded except by an American ship, unless at the risk of the officer boarding or detaining her. I have not admitted the international law as laid down by the American Minister for Foreign Affairs, until that statement had been approved and fortified by the law officers of the Crown. But having admitted that, I have put it as strong as possible to the American Government that if it is known that the American flag covers every iniquity, every pirate and slaver on earth will carry it and no other; that this must bring disgrace on that honoured banner, and that instead of vindicating the honour of the country by an obstinate adherence to their present declaration the contrary result will follow; that the American flag will be prostituted to the worst of purposes. I shall continue to urge that it is necessary in these civilized times, with countless vessels navigating the ocean, that there should be a police on the ocean; that there should be, if not a right by international law, an agreement among nations how far they would go to verify the nationality of vessels, and ascertain their right to bear a particular flag. From the language I have used, from the conversations which I had with the American Minister resident in this country, and from the observations contained in a very able paper drawn up by Gen. Cass on this subject, I am not without strong hope that some arrangement of this kind may be made with the United States, which, with the orders given to the officers of both countries, may enable us to verify the flags of all countries, without running the risk of offence to the country to which a ship belongs."

On the Opposition benches there was also no attempt made at vindicating the right of visit on the part of Great Britain against the United States, but, as Earl Grey remarked,

"the English had treaties with Spain and other powers for the prevention of the slave-trade, and if they had reasonable grounds for suspecting that a vessel was engaged in this abominable traffic, and that she had for the time made use of the United States flag, that she was not really an American ship at all, they had a right to overhaul her and to search her. If, however, she produced the American papers, even though she be full of slaves, it was their duty to discharge her, and to leave to the United States the disgrace of that iniquitous traffic. He hoped and trusted that the orders to their cruisers were strict in this respect, and that any excess of that discretion which was allowed their officers under the circumstances would meet with proper punishment."

The question then turns exclusively upon the point, and even this point seems abandoned by Lord Malmesbury, whether or not vessels suspected of usurping the American flag may not be called upon to produce their papers. Lord Aberdeen directly denied that any controversy could arise out of such a practice, since the instructions under which the British officers were to proceed on such an occurrence —instructions drawn up by Dr. Lushington and Sir G. Cockburn—had been communicated at the time to the American Government and acquiesced in by Mr. Webster, on the part of that Government. If, therefore, there had been no change in these instructions, and if the officers had acted within their limits, "the American Government could have no ground of complaint." There seemed, indeed, a strong suspicion hovering in the minds of the hereditary wisdom, that Palmerston had played one of his usual tricks by effecting some arbitrary change in the orders issued to the British cruisers. It is known that Palmerston, while boasting of his zeal in the suppression of the slave-trade, had, during the eleven years of his administration of foreign affairs, ending in 1841, broken up all the existing slave-trade treaties, had ordered acts which the British law authorities pronounced criminal, and which actually subjected one of his instruments to legal procedure and placed a slave-dealer under the protection of the law of England against its own Government. He chose the slave-trade as his field of battle, and converted it into a mere instrument of provoking quarrels between England and other states. Before leaving office in 1841 he had given instructions which, according to the words of Sir Robert Peel, "must have led, had they not been countermanded, to a collision with the United States." In *his own words*, he had enjoined the naval officers "to have no very nice regard to the law of nations." Lord Malmesbury, although in very reserved language, intimated that "by sending the British squadrons to the Cuban waters, instead of leaving them on the coast of Africa," Palmerston removed them from a station where, before the outbreak of the Russian war, they had almost succeeded in extinguishing the slave-trade, to a place where they could be good for little else than picking up a quarrel with the United States. Lord Woodhouse, Palmerston's own late Ambassador to the Court of St. Petersburg, concurring in this view of the case, remarked that,

> "No matter what instructions had been given, if the Government gave authority to the British vessels to go in such numbers into the American waters, a difference would sooner or later arise between us and the United States."

Yet, whatever may have been Palmerston's secret intentions, it is evident that they are baffled by the Tory Government in 1858, as they had been in 1842, and that the war cry so lustily raised in the Congress and in the press is doomed to result in "much ado about nothing."

As to the question of the slave-trade itself, Spain was denounced by the Bishop of Oxford as well as Lord Brougham, as the mainstay of that nefarious traffic. Both of them called upon the British Government to force, by every means in its power, that country into a course of policy consonant to existing treaties. As early as 1814 a general treaty was entered into between Great Britain and Spain, by which the latter passed an unequivocal condemnation of the slave-trade. In 1817 a specific treaty was concluded, by which Spain fixed the abolition of the slave-trade, on the part of her own subjects, for the year 1820, and, by way of compensation for the losses her subjects might suffer by carrying out the contract, received an indemnity of £400,000. The money was pocketed, but no equivalent was tendered for it. In 1835 a new treaty was entered into, by which Spain bound herself formally to bring in a sufficiently stringent penal law to make it impossible for her subjects to continue the traffic. The procrastinating Spanish proverb, "*A la mañana*,"* was again strictly adhered to. It was only ten years later that the penal law was carried; but, by a singular mischance, the principal clause contended for by England was left out, namely, that of making the slave-trade piracy. In one word, nothing was done, save that the Captain-General of Cuba, the Minister at Home, the Camarilla, and, if rumour speaks truth, royal personages themselves, raised a private tax upon the slavers, selling the licence of dealing in human flesh and blood at so many doubloons per head.

"Spain," said the Bishop of Oxford, "had not the excuse that this traffic was a system which her Government was not strong enough to put down, because Gen. Valdés had shown that such a plea could not be urged with any show of truth. On his arrival in the island he called together the principal contractors, and, giving them six months' time to close all their transactions in the slave-trade, told them that he was determined to put it down at the end of that period. What was the result? In 1840, the year previous to the administration of Gen. Valdés, the number of ships which came to Cuba from the coast of Africa with slaves was 56. In 1842, while Gen. Valdés was Captain-General, the number was only 3. In 1840 no less than 14,470 slaves were landed at the island; in 1842 the number was 3,100."

Now what shall England do with Spain? Repeat her protests, multiply her dispatches, renew her negotiations? Lord Malmesbury himself states that they could cover all the waters from the Spanish coast to Cuba with the documents vainly exchanged between the two Governments. Or shall England enforce her claims, sanctioned by so many treaties? Here it is that the shoe pinches. In steps the sinister figure of the "August ally," now the acknowledged guardian angel of the slave-trade. The third Bonaparte, the

* Tomorrow.—*Ed.*

patron of slavery, in all its forms, forbids England to act up to her convictions and her treaties. Lord Malmesbury, it is known, is strongly suspected of an undue intimacy with the hero of Satory.[79] Nevertheless, he denounced him in plain terms as the general slave-dealer of Europe—as the man who had revived the infamous traffic in its worst features under the pretext of "free emigration" of the blacks to the French colonies. Earl Grey completed this denunciation by stating that "wars had been undertaken in Africa for the purpose of making captives, who were to be sold to the agents of the French Government." The Earl of Clarendon added that "both Spain and France were rivals in the African market, offering a certain sum per man; and there was not the least difference in the treatment of these Negroes, whether they were conveyed to Cuba or to a French colony."

Such, then, is the glorious position England finds herself in by having lent her help to that man in overthrowing the Republic. The second Republic, like the first one, had abolished slavery. Bonaparte, who acquired his power solely by truckling to the meanest passions of men, is unable to prolong it save by buying day by day new accomplices. Thus he has not only restored slavery, but has bought the planters by the renewal of the slave-trade. Everything degrading the conscience of the nation, is a new lease of power granted to him. To convert France into a slave-trading nation would be the surest means of enslaving France, who, when herself, had the boldness of proclaiming in the face of the world: Let the colonies perish, but let principles live! One thing at least has been accomplished by Bonaparte. The slave-trade has become a battle-cry between the Imperialist and the Republican camps. If the French Republic be restored today, tomorrow Spain will be *forced* to abandon the infamous traffic.

Published in the
New-York Daily Tribune,
No. 5366, July 2, 1858

Printed according to the text
of the newspaper

Karl Marx

TAXES IN INDIA

According to the London journals, Indian stock and railway securities have of late been distinguished by a downward movement in that market, which is far from testifying to the genuineness of the sanguine convictions which John Bull likes to exhibit in regard to the state of the Indian guerrilla war; and which, at all events, indicates a stubborn distrust in the elasticity of Indian financial resources. As to the latter, two opposite views are propounded. On the one hand, it is affirmed that taxes in India are onerous and oppressive beyond those of any country in the world; that as a rule throughout most of the presidencies, and through those presidencies most where they have been longest under British rule, the cultivators, that is, the great body of the people of India, are in a condition of unmitigated impoverishment and dejection; that, consequently, Indian revenues have been stretched to their utmost possible limit, and Indian finances are therefore past recovery. A rather discomfortable opinion this at a period when, according to Mr. Gladstone, for some years to come, the extraordinary Indian expenditure alone will annually amount to about £20,000,000 sterling. On the other hand, it is asserted—the asseveration being made good by an array of statistical illustrations—that India is the least taxed country in the world; that, if expenditure is going on increasing, revenue may be increased too; and that it is an utter fallacy to imagine that the Indian people will not bear any new taxes. Mr. Bright, who may be considered the most arduous and influential representative of the "discomfortable" doctrine, made, on the occasion of the second reading of the new Government of India bill, the following statement:

"The Indian Government had cost more to govern India than it was possible to extort from the population of India, although the Government had been by no means scrupulous either as to the taxes imposed, or as to the mode in which they had been levied. It cost more than £30,000,000 to govern India, for that was the gross revenue, and there was always a deficit, which had to be made up by loans borrowed at a high rate of interest. The Indian debt now amounted to £60,000,000, and was increasing; while the credit of the Government was falling, partly because they had not treated their creditors very honourably on one or two occasions, and now on account of the calamities which had recently happened in India. He had alluded to the gross revenue; but as that included the opium revenue, which was hardly a tax upon the people of India, he would take the taxation which really pressed upon them at £25,000,000. Now, let not this £25,000,000 be compared with the £60,000,000 that was raised in this country. Let the House recollect that in India it was possible to purchase twelve days' labour for the same amount of gold or silver that would be obtained in payment for one in England. This £25,000,000 expended in the purchase of labour in India would buy as much as an outlay of £300,000,000 would procure in England. He might be asked how much was the labour of an Indian worth? Well, if the labour of an Indian was only worth 2d. a day, it was clear that we could not expect him to pay as much taxation as if it was worth 2s. We had 30,000,000 of population in Great Britain and Ireland; in India there were 150,000,000 inhabitants. We raised here £60,000,000 sterling of taxes; in India, reckoning by the day's labour of the people of India, we raised £300,000,000 of revenue, or five times a greater revenue than was collected at home. Looking at the fact that the population of India was five times greater than that of the British Empire, a man might say that the taxation per head in India and England was about the same, and that therefore there was no greater hardship inflicted. But in England there was an incalculable power of machinery and steam, of means of transit, and of everything that capital and human invention could bring to aid the industry of a people. In India there was nothing of the kind. They had scarcely a decent road throughout India."

Now, it must be admitted that there is something wrong in this method of comparing Indian taxes with British taxes. There is on the one side the Indian population, five times as great as the British one, and there is on the other side the Indian taxation amounting to half the British. But, then, Mr. Bright says, Indian labour is an equivalent for about one-twelfth only of British labour. Consequently

£30,000,000 of taxes in India would represent £300,000,000 of taxes in Great Britain, instead of the £60,000,000 actually there raised. What then is the conclusion he ought to have arrived at? That the people of India in regard to their numerical strength pay the *same* taxation as the people in Great Britain, if allowance is made for the comparative poverty of the people in India, and £30,000,000 is supposed to weigh as heavily upon 150,000,000 Indians as £60,000,000 upon 30,000,000 Britons. Such being his supposition, it is certainly fallacious to turn round and say that a poor people cannot pay so much as a rich one, because the comparative poverty of the Indian people has already been taken into account in making out the statement that the Indian pays as much as the Briton. There might, in fact, another question be raised. It might be asked, whether a man who earns say 12 cents a day can be fairly expected to pay 1 cent with the same ease with which another, earning $12 a day, pays $1? Both would relatively contribute the same aliquot part of their income, but still the tax might bear in quite different proportions upon their respective necessities. Yet, Mr. Bright has not yet put the question in these terms, and, if he had, the comparison between the burden of taxation, borne by the British wages' labourer on the one hand, and the British capitalist on the other, would perhaps have struck nearer home than the comparison between Indian and British taxation. Moreover, he admits himself that from the £30,000,000 of Indian taxes, the £5,000,000 constituting the opium revenue must be subtracted, since this is, properly speaking, no tax pressing upon the Indian people, but rather an export duty charged upon Chinese consumption. Then we are reminded by the apologists of the Anglo-Indian Administration that £16,000,000 of income is derived from the land revenue, or rent, which from times immemorial has belonged to the State in its capacity as supreme landlord, never constituted part of the private fortune of the cultivator, and does, in fact, no more enter into taxation, properly so called, than the rent paid by the British farmers to the British aristocracy can be said to enter British taxation. Indian taxation, according to this point of view, would stand thus:

Aggregate sum raised	£30,000,000
Deduct for opium revenue	5,000,000
Deduct for rent of land	16,000,000
Taxation proper	£9,000,000

Of this £9,000,000, again, it must be admitted that some important items, such as the post-office, the stamp duties, and the custom duties, bear in a very minute proportion on the mass of the people. Accordingly, Mr. Hendricks, in a paper recently laid before the British Statistical Society on the Finances of India, tries to prove, from Parliamentary and other official documents, that of the total revenue paid by the people of India, not more than one-fifth is at present raised by taxation, i.e., from the real income of the people; that in Bengal 27 per cent only, in the Punjab 23 per cent only, in Madras 21 per cent only, in the north-west provinces 17 per cent only, and in Bombay 16 per cent only of the total revenue is derived from taxation proper.

The following comparative view of the average amount of taxation derived from each inhabitant of India and the United Kingdom, during the years 1855-56, is abstracted from Mr. Hendricks's statement:

Bengal, per head, revenue	£0 5 0.....	Taxation proper	£0 1 4
North-west provinces . .	3 5.....	Taxation proper	0 7
Madras	4 7.....	Taxation proper	1 0
Bombay	8 3.....	Taxation proper	1 4
Punjab	3 3.....	Taxation proper	0 9
United Kingdom	.....	Taxation proper	1 10 0

For a different year the following estimate of the average paid by each individual to the national revenue is made by Gen. Briggs:

In England, 1852	£1 19 4
In France	1 12 0
In Prussia	19 3
In India, 1854	3 8½

From these statements it is inferred by the apologists of the British Administration that there is not a single country in Europe, where, even if the comparative poverty of India is taken into account, the people are so lightly taxed. Thus it seems that not only opinions with respect to Indian taxation are conflicting, but that the facts from which they purport to be drawn are themselves contradictory. On the one hand, we must admit the nominal amount of Indian taxation to be relatively small: but on the other, we might heap evidence upon evidence from Parliamentary documents, as well as from the writings of the greatest authorities on Indian affairs, all proving beyond doubt that this apparently light taxation crushes the mass of the Indian people to the dust, and that its exaction necessitates a resort to such infamies as torture, for instance. But is any other proof wanted beyond the constant and rapid increase of the Indian debt and the accumulation of Indian deficits? It will certainly not be contended that the Indian Government prefers increasing debts and deficits because it shrinks from touching too roughly upon the resources of the people. It embarks in debt, because it sees no other way to make both ends meet. In 1805 the Indian debt amounted to £25,626,631; in 1829 it reached about £34,000,000; in 1850, £47,151,018; and at present it amounts to about £60,000,000. By the by, we leave out of the count the East Indian debt contracted in England, which is also chargeable upon the East Indian revenue.

The annual deficit, which in 1805 amounted to about two and a half millions, had, under Lord Dalhousie's administration, reached the average of five millions. Mr. George Campbell of the Bengal Civil Service, and of a mind strongly biased in favour of the Anglo-Indian Administration, was obliged to avow, in 1852, that:

> "Although no Oriental conquerors have ever obtained so complete an ascendancy, so quiet, universal and undisputed possession of India as we have, yet all have enriched themselves from the revenues of the country, and many have out of their abundance laid out considerable sums on works of public improvements.... From doing this we are debarred. ...The quantity of the whole burden is by no means diminished" (under the English rule), "*yet we have no surplus.*"

In estimating the burden of taxation, its nominal amount must not fall heavier into the balance than the method of raising it, and the manner of employing it. The former is detestable in India, and in the branch of the land-tax, for instance, wastes perhaps more produce than it gets. As to the application of the taxes, it will suffice to say that no part of them is returned to the people in works of public utility, more indispensable in Asiatic countries than anywhere else, and that, as Mr. Bright justly remarked, nowhere so extravagant is a provision made for the governing class itself.

Written on June 29, 1858

Published in the
New-York Daily Tribune,
No. 5383; July 23, 1858

Printed according to the text
of the newspaper

Karl Marx

THE INDIAN BILL

The latest Indian bill has passed through its third reading in the House of Commons, and since the Lords, swayed by Derby's influence, are not likely to show fight, the doom of the East India Company appears to be sealed. They do not die like heroes, it must be confessed; but they have bartered away their power, as they crept into it, bit by bit, in a business-like way. In fact, their whole history is one of buying and selling. They commenced by buying sovereignty, and they have ended by selling it. *They have fallen*, not in a pitched battle, but under the hammer of the auctioneer, into the hands of the highest bidder. In 1693 they procured from the Crown a Charter for twenty-one years by paying large sums to the Duke of Leeds and other public officers. In 1767 they prolonged their tenure of power for two years by the promise of annually paying £400,000 into the Imperial Exchequer. In 1769 they struck a similar bargain for five years; but soon after, in return for the Exchequer's forgoing the stipulated annual payment and lending them £1,400,000 at 4 per cent, they alienated some parcels of sovereignty, leaving to Parliament in the first instance the nomination of the Governor-General and four Councillors, altogether surrendering to the Crown the appointment of the Lord Chief Justice and his three Judges, and agreeing to the conversion of the Court of Proprietors from a democratic into an oligarchic body. In 1858, after having solemnly pledged themselves to the Court of Proprietors to resist by all Constitutional "means" the transfer to the Crown of the governing powers of the

East India Company, they have accepted that principle, and agreed to a bill penal as regards the Company, but securing emolument and place to its principal Directors. If the death of a hero, as Schiller says, resembles the setting of the sun,* the exit of the East India Company bears more likeness to the compromise effected by a bankrupt with his creditors.

By this bill the principal functions of administration are entrusted to a Secretary of State in Council, just as at Calcutta the Governor-General in Council manages affairs. But both these functionaries—the Secretary of State in England and the Governor-General in India—are alike authorized to disregard the advice of their assessors and to act upon their own judgement. The new bill also invests the Secretary of State with all the powers at present exercised by the President of the Board of Control, through the agency of the Secret Committee**—the power, that is, in urgent cases, of dispatching orders to India without stopping to ask the advice of his Council. In constituting that Council it has been found necessary, after all, to resort to the East India Company as the only practicable source of appointments to it other than nominations by the Crown. The elective members of the Council are to be elected by the Directors of the East India Company from among their own number.

Thus, after all, the name of the East India Company is to outlive its substance. At the last hour it was confessed by the Derby Cabinet that their bill contains no clause abolishing the East India Company, as represented by a Court of Directors, but that it becomes reduced to its ancient character of a company of stockholders, distributing the dividends guaranteed by different acts of legislation. Pitt's bill of 1784 virtually subjected their government to the sway of the Cabinet under the name of the Board of Control. The act of 1813 stripped them of their monopoly of commerce, save the trade with China. The act of 1834 destroyed their commercial character altogether, and the act of 1854 annihilated their last remnant of power, still leaving them in

* Schiller, *The Robbers*, Act 3, Scene 2.—*Ed.*

** See this collection, p. 64.—*Ed.*

possession of the Indian Administration. By the rotation of history the East India Company, converted in 1612 into a joint-stock company, is again clothed in its primitive garb, only that it represents now a trading partnership without trade, and a joint-stock company which has no funds to administer, but only fixed dividends to draw.

The history of the Indian bill is marked by greater dramatic changes than any other act of modern Parliamentary legislation. When the sepoy insurrection broke out, the cry of Indian Reform rang through all classes of British society. Popular imagination was heated by the torture reports; the Government interference with the native religion was loudly denounced by Indian general officers and civilians of high standing; the rapacious annexation policy of Lord Dalhousie, the mere tool of Downing Street; the fermentation recklessly created in the Asiatic mind by the piratical wars in Persia and China—wars commenced and pursued on Palmerston's private dictation—the weak measures with which he met the outbreak, sailing ships being chosen for transport in preference to steam vessels, and the circuitous navigation around the Cape of Good Hope instead of transportation over the Isthmus of Suez—all these accumulated grievances burst into the cry for Indian Reform—reform of the Company's Indian Administration, reform of the Government's Indian policy. Palmerston caught at the popular cry, but resolved upon turning it to his exclusive profit. Because both the Government and the Company had miserably broken down, the Company was to be killed in sacrifice, and the Government to be rendered omnipotent. The power of the Company was to be simply transferred to the dictator of the day, pretending to represent the Crown as against the Parliament, and to represent Parliament as against the Crown, thus absorbing the privileges of the one and the other in his single person. With the Indian army at his back, the Indian Treasury at his command, and the Indian patronage in his pocket, Palmerston's position would have become impregnable.

His bill passed triumphantly through the first-reading, but his career was cut short by the famous Conspiracy bill, followed by the advent of the Tories to power.

On the very first day of their official reappearance on

the Treasury benches, they declared that, out of deference for the decisive will of the Commons, they would forsake their opposition to the transfer from the Company to the Crown of the Indian Government. Lord Ellenborough's legislative abortion seemed to hasten Palmerston's restoration, when Lord John Russell, in order to force the dictator into a compromise, stepped in, and saved the Government by proposing to proceed with the Indian bill by way of Parliamentary resolution, instead of by a governmental bill. Then Lord Ellenborough's Oudh dispatch, his sudden resignation, and the consequent disorganization in the Ministerial camp, were eagerly seized upon by Palmerston. The Tories were again to be planted in the cold shade of opposition, after they had employed their short lease of power in breaking down the opposition of their own party against the confiscation of the East India Company. Yet it is sufficiently known how these fine calculations were baffled. Instead of rising on the ruins of the East India Company, Palmerston has been buried beneath them. During the whole of the Indian debates, the House seemed to indulge the peculiar satisfaction of humiliating the *Civis Romanus*. All his amendments, great and small, were ignominiously lost; allusions of the most unsavoury kind, relating to the Afghan war, the Persian war, and the Chinese war, were continually flung at his head; and Mr. Gladstone's clause, withdrawing from the Indian Minister the power of originating wars beyond the boundaries of India, intended as a general vote of censure on Palmerston's past foreign policy, was passed by a crushing majority, despite his furious resistance. But although the man has been thrown overboard, his principle, upon the whole, has been accepted. Although somewhat checked by the obstructive attributes of the Board of Council, which, in fact, is but the well-paid spectre of the old Court of Directors, the power of the executive has, by the formal annexation of India, been raised to such a degree that, to counterpoise it, democratic weight must be thrown into the Parliamentary scale.

Written on July 9, 1858

Published in the
New-York Daily Tribune,
No. 5384, July 24, 1858

Printed according to the text
of the newspaper

Karl Marx

THE OPIUM TRADE

The news ot the new treaty wrung from China by the allied Plenipotentiaries[80] has, it would appear, conjured up the same wild vistas of an immense extension of trade which danced before the eyes of the commercial mind in 1845, after the conclusion of the first Chinese war. Supposing the Petersburg wires to have spoken truth, is it quite certain that an increase of the Chinese trade must follow upon the multiplication of its emporiums? Is there any probability that the war of 1857-58 will lead to more splendid results than the war of 1841-42? So much is certain that the treaty of 1843, instead of increasing American and English exports to China, proved instrumental only in precipitating and aggravating the commercial crisis of 1847. In a similar way, by raising dreams of an inexhaustible market and by fostering false speculations, the present treaty may help preparing a new crisis at the very moment when the market of the world is but slowly recovering from the recent universal shock. Beside its negative result, the first opium war succeeded in stimulating the opium trade at the expense of legitimate commerce, and so will this second opium war do, if England be not forced by the general pressure of the civilized world to abandon the compulsory opium cultivation in India and the armed opium propaganda to China. We forbear dwelling on the morality of that trade, described by Montgomery Martin, himself an Englishman, in the following terms:

"Why, the slave-trade was merciful compared with the opium trade: We did not destroy the bodies of the Africans, for it was our immediate interest to keep them alive; we did not debase their nature, corrupt their minds, nor destroy their souls. But the opium seller slays the body after he has corrupted, degraded and annihilated the moral being of unhappy sinners, which every hour is bringing new victims to a Moloch which knows no satiety, and where the English murderer and Chinese suicide vie with each other in offerings at his shrine."

The Chinese cannot take both goods and drug; under actual circumstances, extension of the Chinese trade resolves into extension of the opium trade; the growth of the latter is incompatible with the development of legitimate commerce—these propositions were pretty generally admitted two years ago. A Committee of the House of Commons, appointed in 1847 to take into consideration the state of British commercial intercourse with China, reported thus:

"We regret that the trade with that country has been for some time in a very unsatisfactory condition, and that the *result of our extended intercourse has by no means realized the just expectations* which had naturally been founded in a *free access to so magnificent a market*. We find that the difficulties of the trade do not arise from any want of demand in China for articles of British manufactures, or from the increasing competition of other nations; *the payment for opium* absorbs the silver to the great inconvenience of the general traffic of the Chinese, and tea and silk must in fact pay the rest."

The Friend of China, of July 28, 1849, generalizing the same proposition, says in set terms:

"The opium trade progresses steadily. The increased consumption of teas and silk in Great Britain and the United States would merely result in the increase of the opium trade; the case of the manufacturers is hopeless."

One of the leading American merchants in China reduced, in an article inserted in Hunt's *Merchants' Magazine*, for January, 1850, the whole question of the trade with China to this point:

"Which branch of commerce is to be suppressed, the opium trade or the export trade of American or English produce?"

The Chinese themselves took exactly the same view of the case. Montgomery Martin narrates:

"I inquired of the Taotai* at Shanghai which would be the best means of increasing our commerce with China, and his first answer to

* High official.—*Ed.*

me, in presence of Capt. Balfour, Her Majesty's Consul, was: 'Cease to sent us so much opium and we will be able to take your manufactures.'"

The history of general commerce during the last eight years has, in a new and striking manner, illustrated these positions; but, before analyzing the deleterious effects on legitimate commerce of the opium trade, we propose giving a short review of the rise and progress of that stupendous traffic, which, whether we regard the tragical collisions forming, so to say, the axis round which it turns, or the effects produced by it on the general relations of the Eastern and Western worlds, stands solitary on record in the annals of mankind.

Previous to 1767 the quantity of opium exported from India did not exceed 200 chests, the chest weighing about 133 lbs. Opium was legally admitted in China on the payment of a duty of about $3 per chest, as a medicine; the Portuguese, who brought it from Turkey, being its almost exclusive exporters into the Celestial Empire.

In 1773, Colonel Watson and Vice-President Wheeler—persons deserving to take a place among the Hermentiers, Palmers and other poisoners of world-wide fame—suggested to the East India Company the idea of entering upon the opium traffic with China. Consequently, there was established a depot for opium in vessels anchored in a bay to the south-west of Macao. The speculation proved a failure. In 1781 the Bengal Government sent an armed vessel, laden with opium, to China; and, in 1794, the Company stationed a large opium vessel at Whampoa, the anchorage for the port of Canton. It seems that Whampoa proved a more convenient depot than Macao, because, only two years after its election, the Chinese Government found it necessary to pass a law which threatens Chinese smugglers of opium to be beaten with a bamboo and exposed in the streets with wooden collars around their necks. About 1798, the East India Company ceased to be direct exporters of opium, but they became its producers. The opium monopoly was established in India, while the Company's own ships were hypocritically forbidden from trafficking in the drug, the licences it granted for private ships trading to China contained a provision which attached a penalty to them if freighted with opium of other than the Company's own make.

In 1800, the import into China had reached the number of 2,000 chests. Having, during the 18th century, borne the aspect common to all feuds between the foreign merchant and the national custom-house, the struggle between the East India Company and the Celestial Empire assumed, since the beginning of the nineteenth century, features quite distinct and exceptional; while the Chinese Emperor, in order to check the suicide of his people, prohibited at once the import of the poison by the foreigner, and its consumption by the natives, the East India Company was rapidly converting the cultivation of opium in India, and its contraband sale to China, into internal parts of its own financial system. While the semi-barbarian stood on the principle of morality, the civilized opposed the principle of pelf. That a giant empire, containing almost one-third of the human race, vegetating in the teeth of time, insulated by the forced exclusion of general intercourse, and thus contriving to dupe itself with delusions of Celestial perfection—that such an empire should at last be overtaken by the fate on occasion of a deadly duel, in which the representative of the antiquated world appears prompted by ethical motives, while the representative of overwhelming modern society fights for the privilege of buying in the cheapest and selling in the dearest markets—this, indeed, is a sort of tragical couplet, stranger than any poet would ever have dared to fancy.

Written on August 31, 1858

Published in the
New-York Daily Tribune,
No. 5433, September 20, 1858

Printed according to the text of the newspaper

Karl Marx

THE OPIUM TRADE

It was the assumption of the opium monopoly in India by the British Government, which led to the proscription of the opium trade in China. The cruel punishments inflicted by the Celestial legislator upon his own contumacious subjects, and the stringent prohibition established at the China custom-houses proved alike nugatory. The next effect of the moral resistance of the Chinaman was the demoralization, by the Englishman, of the Imperial authorities, custom-house officers and mandarins generally. The corruption that ate into the heart of the Celestial bureaucracy, and destroyed the bulwark of the patriarchal constitution, was, together with the opium chests, smuggled into the Empire from the English store-ships anchored at Whampoa.

Nurtured by the East India Company, vainly combated by the Central Government at Peking, the opium trade gradually assumed larger proportions, until it absorbed about £2,500,000 in 1816. The throwing open in that year of the Indian commerce, with the single exception of the tea trade, which still continues to be monopolized by the East India Company, gave a new and powerful stimulus to the operations of the English contrabandists. In 1820, the number of chests smuggled into China had increased to 5,147; in 1821, to 7,000, and in 1824, to 12,639. Meanwhile, the Chinese Government, at the same time that it addressed threatening remonstrances to the foreign merchants, punished the Kong merchants, known as their abettors, developed an unwonted activity in its prosecution of the native opium consumers, and, at its custom-houses, put into practice more stringent measures. The final result, like that of similar exertions in 1794, was to drive the opium depots from a precarious to a more convenient basis of operations. Macao and Whampoa were abandoned for the Island of Lingting, at the entrance of the Canton River, there to become permanently established in vessels armed to the teeth, and well manned. In the same way, when the Chinese Government temporarily succeeded in stopping the operations of the old Canton house, the trade only shifted hands, and passed to a lower class of men, prepared to carry it on at all hazards and by whatever means. Thanks to the greater facilities thus afforded, the opium trade increased during the ten years from 1824 to 1834 from 12,639 to 21,785 chests.

Like the years 1800, 1816 and 1824, the year 1834 marks an epoch in the history of the opium trade. The East India Company then lost not only its privilege of trading in Chinese tea, but had to discontinue and abstain from all commercial business whatever. It being thus transformed from a mercantile into a merely government establishment, the trade to China became completely thrown open to English private enterprise, which pushed on with such vigour that, in 1837, 39,000 chests of opium, valued at $25,000,000, were successfully smuggled into China, despite the desperate resistance of the Celestial Government. Two facts here claim our attention: First, that of every step in the progress of the export trade to China since 1816, a disproportionately large part progressively fell upon the opium-smuggling branch; and secondly, that hand in hand with the gradual extinction of the ostensible mercantile interest of the Anglo-Indian Government in the opium trade, grew the importance of its fiscal interest in that illicit traffic. In 1837 the Chinese Government had at last arrived at a point where decisive action could no longer be delayed. The continuous drain of silver, caused by the opium importations, had begun to derange the exchequer, as well as the moneyed circulation of the Celestial Empire. Hsü Nai-chi, one of the most distinguished Chinese statesmen, proposed to legalize the opium trade and make money out of it; but after a full deliberation, in which all the high officers of the Empire shared, and which extended over a period of more than a year's duration, the Chinese Government decided that, "On account of the injuries it inflicted on the people, the nefarious traffic should not be legalized." As early as 1830, a duty of 25 per cent would have yielded a revenue of $3,850,000. In 1837, it would have yielded double that sum, but then the Celestial barbarian declined laying a tax sure to rise in proportion to the degradation of his people. In 1853, Hsien Feng, the present Emperor, under still more distressed circumstances, and with the full knowledge of the futility of all efforts at stopping the increasing import of opium, persevered in the stern policy of his ancestors. Let me remark, *en passant*, that by persecuting the opium consumption as a heresy the Emperor gave its traffic all the advantages of a religious propaganda. The extraordinary measures of the Chinese Government during the years 1837, 1838 and 1839, which culminated in Commissioner Lin's arrival at Canton, and the confiscation and destruction, by his orders, of the smuggled opium, afforded the pretext for the first Anglo-Chinese war, the results of which developed themselves in the Chinese rebellion, the utter exhaustion of the Imperial exchequer, the successful encroachment of Russia from the North, and the gigantic dimensions assumed by the opium trade in the South. Although proscribed in the treaty with which England terminated a war, commenced and carried on in its defence, the opium trade has practically enjoyed perfect impunity since 1843. The importation was estimated, in 1856, at about $35,000,000, while in the same year, the Anglo-Indian Government drew a revenue of $25,000,000, just the sixth part of its total state income, from the opium monopoly. The pretexts on which the second Opium War has been undertaken are of too recent date to need any commentary.

We cannot leave this part of the subject without singling out one flagrant self-contradiction of the Christianity-canting and civilization-mongering British Government. In its imperial capacity it affects to be a thorough stranger to the contraband opium trade, and even to enter into treaties proscribing it. Yet, in its Indian capacity, it forces the opium cultivation upon Bengal, to the great damage of the productive resources of that country; compels one part of the

Indian ryots to engage in the poppy culture; entices another part into the same by dint of money advances; keeps the wholesale manufacture of the deleterious drug a close monopoly in its hands; watches by a whole army of official spies its growth, its delivery at appointed places, its inspissation and preparation for the taste of the Chinese consumers, its formation into packages especially adapted to the conveniency of smuggling, and finally its conveyance to Calcutta, where it is put up at auction at the Government sales, and made over by the state officers to the speculators, thence to pass into the hands of the contrabandists who land it in China. The chest costing the British Government about 250 rupees is sold at the Calcutta auction mart at a price ranging from 1,210 to 1,600 rupees. But not yet satisfied with this matter of fact complicity, the same Government, to this hour, enters into express profit and loss accounts with the merchants and shippers, who embark in the hazardous operation of poisoning an empire.

The Indian finances of the British Government have, in fact, been made to depend not only on the opium trade with China, but on the contraband character of that trade. Were the Chinese Government to legalize the opium trade simultaneously with tolerating the cultivation of the poppy in China, the Anglo-Indian exchequer would experience a serious catastrophe. While openly preaching free trade in poison, it secretly defends the monopoly of its manufacture. Whenever we look closely into the nature of British free trade, monopoly is pretty generally found to lie at the bottom of its "freedom."

Written on September 3, 1858

Published in the *New-York Daily Tribune*, No. 5438, September 25, 1858

Printed according to the text of the newspaper

Karl Marx

THE ANGLO-CHINESE TREATY

The unsuccessful issue, in a commercial point of view, of Sir Henry Pottinger's Chinese treaty,[81] signed on August 29, 1842, and dictated, like the new treaties with China, at the cannon's mouth, is a fact now recollected even by that eminent organ of British Free Trade, *The London Economist.* Having stood forward as one of the staunchest apologists of the late invasion of China, that journal now feels itself obliged to "temper" the sanguine hopes which have been cultivated in other quarters. *The Economist* considers the effects on the British export trade of the treaty of 1842, "a precedent by which to guard ourselves against the result of mistaken operations." This certainly is sound advice. The reasons, however, which Mr. Wilson alleges in explanation of the failure of the first attempt at forcibly enlarging the Chinese market for Western produce, appear far from conclusive.

The first great cause pointed out of the signal failure is the speculative overstocking of the Chinese market, during the first three years following the Pottinger treaty, and the carelessness of the English merchants as to the nature of the Chinese demand. The English exports to China which, in 1836, amounted to £1,326,388, had fallen in 1842 to £960,000. Their rapid and continued rise during the following four years, is shown by these figures:

1842	£969,000	1844	£2,305,000
1843	1,456,000	1845	2,396,000

Yet in 1846 the exports did not only sink below the level of 1836, but the disasters overtaking the China houses at

London during the crisis of 1847 proved the *computed* value of the exports from 1843 to 1846, such as it appears in the official return tables, to have by no means corresponded to the value actually *realized*. If the English exporters thus erred in the quantity, they did not less so in the quality of the articles offered to Chinese consumption. In proof of the latter assertion, *The Economist* quotes from Mr. W. Cooke, the late correspondent of *The London Times* at Shanghai and Canton, the following passages:

"In 1843, 1844 and 1845, when the northern ports had just been opened, the people at home were wild with excitement. An eminent firm at Sheffield sent out a large consignment of knives and forks, and declared themselves prepared to supply all China with cutlery. They were sold at prices which scarcely realized their freight. A London house, of famous fame, sent out a tremendous consignment of pianofortes, which shared the same fate. What happened in the case of cutlery and pianos occurred also, in a less noticeable manner, in the case of worsted and cotton manufactures. Manchester made a great blind effort when the ports were opened, and that effort failed. Since then she has fallen into an apathy, and trusts to the chapter of accidents."

Lastly, to prove the dependence of the reduction, maintenance or improvement of the trade, on the study of the wants of the consumer, *The Economist* reproduces from the same authority the following return for the year 1856:

	1845	*1846*	*1856*
Worsted Stuffs (pieces)	13,569	8,415	7,428
Camlets	13,374	8,034	4,470
Long ells	91,530	75,784	36,642
Woollens	62,731	56,996	88,583
Printed Cottons	100,615	81,150	281,784
Plain Cottons	2,998,126	1,854,740	2,817,624
Cotton Twist, lbs	2,640,098	5,324,050	5,579,600

Now all these arguments and illustrations explain nothing beyond the reaction following the over-trade of 1843-45. It is a phenomenon by no means peculiar to the Chinese trade, that a sudden expansion of commerce should be followed by its violent contractions, or that a new market, at its opening, should be choked by British oversupplies; the articles thrown upon it being not very nicely calculated, in regard either to the actual wants or the paying powers of the consumers. In fact, this is a standing feature in the history of the markets of the world. On Napoleon's fall, after the opening of the European continent, British imports proved so disproportionate to the continental faculties of absorption, that "the transition from war to peace" proved more disastrous than the continental system itself. Canning's recognition of the independence of the Spanish colonies in America, was also instrumental in producing the commercial crisis of 1825. Wares calculated for the meridian of Moscow, were then dispatched to Mexico and Colombia. And in our own day, notwithstanding its elasticity, even Australia has not escaped the fate common to all new markets, of having its powers of consumption as well as its means of payment over-stocked. The phenomenon peculiar to the Chinese market is this, that since its opening by the treaty of 1842, the export to Great Britain of tea and silk of Chinese produce has continually been expanding, while the import trade into China of British manufactures has, on the whole, remained stationary. The continuous and increasing balance of trade in favour of China might be said to bear an analogy to the state of commercial balance between Russia and Great Britain; but, then, in the latter case, everything is explained by the protective policy of Russia, while the Chinese import duties are lower than those of any other country England trades with. The aggregate value of Chinese exports to England, which before 1842 might be rated at about £7,000,000, amounted in 1856 to the sum of about £9,500,000. While the quantity of tea imported into Great Britain never reached more than 50,000,000 lbs. before 1842, it had swollen in 1856 to about 90,000,000 lbs. On the other hand, the importance of the British import of Chinese silks only dates from 1852. Its progress may be computed from the following figures:

	1852	1853	1854	1855	1856
Silk imp'd lbs.	2,418,343	2,838,047	4,576,706	4,436,862	3,723,693
Value £	—	—	3,318,112	3,013,396	3,676,116

Now take, on the other hand, the movement of the

British Exports to China, Valued in Pounds Sterling

1834	£842,852	1836	£1,326,386
1835	1,074,708	1838	1,204,358

For the period following the opening of the market in 1842 and the acquisition of Hongkong by the British, we find the following returns:

1845	£2,359,000	1853	£1,749,597
1846	1,200,000	1854	1,000,716
1848	1,445,950	1855	1,122,241
1852	2,508,599	1856, upward of	2,000,000

The Economist tries to account for the stationary and relatively decreasing imports of British manufacture into the Chinese market by foreign competition, and Mr. Cooke is again quoted to bear witness to this proposition. According to this authority, the English are beaten by fair competition in the Chinese market in many branches of trade. The Americans, he says, beat the English in drills and sheetings. At Shanghai in 1856 the imports were 221,716 pieces of American drills, against 8,745 English, and 14,420 of American sheetings, against 1,240 English. In woollen goods, on the other hand, Germany and Russia are said to press hardly on their English rivals. We want no other proof than this illustration to convince us that Mr. Cooke and *The Economist* are both mistaken in the appreciation of the Chinese market. They consider as limited to the Anglo-Chinese trade features which are exactly reproduced in the trade between the United States and the Celestial Empire. In 1837, the excess of the Chinese exports to the United States over the imports into China was about £860,000. During the period since the treaty of 1842, the United States have received an annual average of £2,000,000 in Chinese produce, for which it paid in American merchandise £900,000. Of the £1,602,849, to which the aggregate imports into Shanghai, exclusive of specie and opium, amounted in 1855, England supplied £1,122,241, America £272,708, and other countries £207,900; while the exports reached a total of £12,603,540, of which £6,405,040 were to England, £5,396,406 to America, and £102,088 to other countries. Compare only the American exports to the value of £272,708, with their imports from Shanghai exceeding £5,000,000. If, nevertheless, American competition has, to any sensible degree, made inroads on British traffic, how limited a field of employment for the aggregate commerce of foreign nations the Chinese market must offer.

The last cause assigned to the trifling importance the Chinese import market has assumed since its opening in 1842, is the Chinese revolution, but notwithstanding that revolution, the exports to China relatively shared, in 1851-52, in the general increase of trade, and, during the whole of the revolutionary epoch, the opium trade, instead of falling off, rapidly obtained colossal dimensions. However that may be this much will be admitted, that all the obstacles to foreign imports originating in the disordered state of the Empire must be increased, instead of being diminished, by the late piratical war, and the fresh humiliations heaped on the ruling dynasty.

It appears to us, after a careful survey of the history of Chinese commerce, that, generally speaking, the consuming and paying powers of the Celestials have been greatly overestimated. With the present economical framework of Chinese society, which turns upon diminutive agriculture and domestic manufactures as its pivots, any large import of foreign produce is out of the question. Still, to the amount of £8,000,000, a sum which may be roughly calculated to form the aggregate balance in favour of China, as against England and the United States, it might gradually absorb a surplus quantity of English and American goods, if the opium trade were suppressed. This conclusion is necessarily arrived at on the analysis of the simple fact, that the Chinese finances and monetary circulation, in spite of the favourable balance of trade, are seriously deranged by an import of opium to the amount of about £7,000,000.

John Bull, however, used to plume himself on his high standard of morality, prefers to bring up his adverse balance of trade by periodical war tributes, extorted from China on piratical pretexts. He only forgets that the Carthaginian and Roman methods of making foreign people pay, are, if combined in the same hands, sure to clash with, and destroy each other.

Written on September 10, 1858

Published in the
New-York Daily Tribune,
No. 5446, October 5, 1858

Printed according to the text
of the newspaper

Karl Marx

QUESTION OF THE IONIAN ISLANDS

London, December 17, 1858

The case of Mr. William Hudson Guernsey, alias Washington Guernsey, criminally prosecuted for stealing from the library of the British Colonial Office two secret dispatches addressed—the one on June 10, 1857, the other on July 18, 1858—to the late Government of Lord Palmerston by Sir John Young, Lord High Commissioner of the Ionian Islands, has just been tried before Baron Martin of the Central Criminal Court, and ended in the acquittal of the accused. The trial was interesting, both in a political and a judicial point of view. It will be remembered that the Homeric Mr. Gladstone had hardly left London, on his extraordinary mission to pacify the Ionian Islands,[82] when, like a Scythian arrow, darted from an unseen hand, Sir John Young's dispatch, which proposes to abandon the protectorate of the islands and surrender them to Greece, but only after having cut off the finest morsel by merging Corfu in the colonial domains of Great Britain, made its appearance in the columns of *The Daily News*. Great and general was the astonishment. The portion of the London press opposed to secret diplomacy congratulated Lord Derby's Cabinet on the bold step of initiating the public into the mystery of diplomatic whisperings; and *The Morning Star*, in its naïve enthusiasm, proclaimed that a new epoch of international policy had dawned upon the United Kingdom. The sweet voice of praise became, however, in no time, overhowled by shrill and angry tones of criticism. The anti-ministerial press eagerly seized upon the "premeditated blunder," as they called it, which, they said, was aimed at nothing else than the destruction, in the first instance, of Mr. Gladstone's political independence and at his temporary removal from the Parliamentary arena; while, at the same time, by an unscrupulous stroke of Machiavellian perfidy, his mission was to be baffled on the part of his own employers by the publication of a document which put him at once in a false position toward the party he had to negotiate with, toward public opinion in England, and toward the public law of Europe. To ruin a too confiding rival, said *The Times, The Globe, The Observer*, and the smaller anti-ministerial fry, the Derby Cabinet had not hesitated to commit an indiscretion which, under existing circumstances, amounted to nothing less than treason. How could Mr. Gladstone negotiate when the Ionians were not only informed that a foregone conclusion was arrived at on the part of Britain, but when the leading Ionian patriots were compromised by the betrayal of their acceptance of a plan resulting in the dismemberment of the seven islands? How could he negotiate in face of the European remonstrances, which were sure to result from such an infringement of the treaty of Vienna,[83] that treaty constituting England not the owner of Corfu, but the protector only of the seven islands, and settling the territorial divisions of the European map forever? These newspaper articles were, in fact, followed by actual remonstrances on the part of Russia and France.

Let me remark, *en passant*, that the treaty of Vienna, the only acknowledged code of international law in Europe, forms one of the most monstrous *fictiones juris publici* ever heard of in the annals of mankind. What is the first article of that treaty? The eternal exclusion of the Bonaparte family from the French throne; yet there sits Louis Napoleon, the founder of the Second Empire, acknowledged and fraternized with, and cajoled and bowed to by all the crowned heads of Europe. Another article runs to the effect that Belgium is forever granted to Holland; while, on the other hand, for eighteen years past, the separation of Belgium from Holland is not only a *fait accompli*, but a legal fact. Then the treaty of Vienna prescribes that Cracow, incorporated with Austria since 1846, shall forever remain an independent republic; and last, not least, that Poland, merged by Nicholas into the Russian Empire, shall be an independent constitutional kingdom, linked with Russia by the personal bond of the Romanoff dynasty only. Thus, leaf after leaf has been torn out of this holy book of the European *jus publicum*, and it is only appealed to when it suits the interests of one party and the weakness of the other.

The Derby Cabinet was evidently wavering, whether to pocket the unmerited praises of one part of the press, or meet the unmerited slanders of the other. Yet; after eight days' vacillation, it decided on the latter step, declared by a public advertisement that it had no hand in the publication of Sir John Young's dispatches, and that an investigation was actually going on as to the performer of the criminal trick. Finally, Mr. William Hudson Guernsey was traced out as the guilty man, tried before the Central Criminal Court, and convicted of having purloined the dispatches. The Derby Cabinet consequently comes out victorious in the contest; and here the political interest of the trial ends. Still, in consequence of this lawsuit, the attention of the world has been again directed to the relations between Great Britain and the Ionian Islands. That the plan of Sir John Young was no private crotchet, is conclusively proved by the following extract from a public address of his predecessor, Sir Henry Ward, to the Ionian Assembly, on the 13th of April, 1850:

> "It is not for me to speak, in the name of the British Crown, of that distant future which the address shadows forth, when the scattered members of the Greek race may be reunited in one mighty empire, with the consent of the European powers. But I have no difficulty in expressing my own opinion" (he spoke in the name of the British Crown) "that, if such an event be within the scope of human contingencies, the Sovereign and the Parliament of England would be equally willing to see the Ionians resume their place as members of the new power that would then take its place in the policy of the world."

Meanwhile, the philanthropic feelings of Great Britain for the islands, gave themselves vent in the truly Austrian ferocity with which Sir Henry Ward crushed the then rebellion in the islands. Out of a population of 200,000 souls, 8,000 were punished by hanging, scourging, imprisonment and exile; women and children being whipped until blood flowed. In order not to be suspected of exaggeration, I will quote a British paper, *The Morning Chronicle*, of April 25, 1850:

"We shudder at the awful measure of retribution which was inflicted by the Court Martials, under the direction of the Lord High Commissioner. Death, transportation and corporal punishments were awarded to the wretched criminals in some cases *without trial*, in another by the rapid *process of martial law*. Of capital executions there were 21, and of other punishments a large number."

But, then, the Britishers boast of having blessed the Ionians with a free Constitution and developed their material resources to a pitch forming a bright contrast with the wretched economical state of Greece proper. Now, as to the Constitution, Lord Grey, at the moment when he was given to constitution-mongering for the whole Colonial Empire of Great Britain, could with no good grace pass over the Ionian Islands; but he only gave them back what England for long years had fraudulently wrested from them.

By a treaty drawn up by Count Capo D'Istria, and signed with Russia at Paris in 1815, the protection of the Ionian Islands was made over to Great Britain, on the express condition of her abiding by the Russian Constitution granted to them in 1803.[84] The first British Lord High Commissioner, Sir Thomas Maitland, abrogated that Constitution, and replaced it by one investing him with absolute power. In 1839, the Chevalier Mustoxidis, an Ionian, states in his *Pro Memoria*, printed by the House of Commons, June 22, 1840:

"The Ionians do not enjoy the privilege which the communities of Greece used to possess even in the days of Turkish tyranny, that of electing their own magistrates, and managing their own affairs, but are under officers imposed upon them by the police. The slight latitude which had been allowed to the municipal bodies of each island of administering their own revenues has been scotched from them, and in order to render them more dependent, these revenues have been thrown into the public exchequer."

As to the development of the material resources, it will suffice to say that England, Free-Trade England, is not ashamed to pester the Ionians with export duties, a barbarous expedient which seemed relegated to the financial code of Turkey. Currants, for instance, the staple product of the islands, are charged with an export duty of $22\frac{1}{2}$ per cent.

"The intervening seas," says an Ionian, "which form, as it were, the highway of the islands, are stopped, after the method of a turnpike gate, at each harbour, by transit duties, which tax the commodities of every name and description *interchanged between island and island.*"

Nor is this all. During the first twenty-three years of British administration, the taxation was increased threefold and the expenditure fivefold. Some reduction took place afterward, but then in 1850 there was a deficiency equal to one half of what was previously the total taxation, as is shown by the following table:

	Annual Taxation	*Expenditure*
1815	£68,459	£48,500
1817*	108,997	87,420
1850	147,482	170,000

Thus, export duties on their own produce, transit duties between the different islands, increase of taxation and waste of expenditure are the economical blessings conferred on the Ionians by John Bull. According to his oracle in Printing-House Square,[85] he grasps after colonies only in order to educate them in the principles of public liberty; but, if we adhere to facts, the Ionian Islands, like India and Ireland, prove only that to be free at home, John Bull must enslave abroad. Thus, at this very moment, while giving vent to his virtuous indignation against Bonaparte's spy system at Paris, he is himself introducing it at Dublin.

The judicial interest of the trial in question hangs upon one point: Guernsey's advocate confessed to the purloining of ten copies of the dispatches, but pleaded not guilty, because they had not been intended to be used for a private purpose. If the crime of larceny depends on the intention only with which foreign property is unlawfully appropriated, the criminal law is brought to a dead stop in that respect. The solid citizens of the jury-box scarcely intended to effect such a revolution in the conditions of property, but only meant to assert, by their verdict, that public documents are the property—not of the Government, but of the public.

Published in the
New-York Daily Tribune,
No. 5526, January 6, 1859

Printed according to the text of the newspaper

* First year of the British Protectorate.

Karl Marx

THE NEW CHINESE WAR[86]

I

London, September 13, 1859

At the time when England was generally congratulated upon the extortion from the Celestials of the treaty of Tientsin,[87] I tried to show that, Russia being in point of fact the only power benefited by the piratical Anglo-Chinese war, the commercial advantages accruing from the treaty to England were rather nugatory, while, in a political point of view, so far from establishing peace, that treaty, on the contrary, rendered resumption of war unavoidable. The march of events has fully confirmed these views. The treaty of Tientsin has become a thing of the past, and the semblance of peace has vanished before the stern realities of war.

Let me first state the facts as reported by the last overland mail.

The Hon. Mr. Bruce, accompanied by M. de Bourboulon, the French Plenipotentiary, set out with a British expedition destined to ascend the Peiho, and to accompany the two ambassadors on their message to Peking. The expedition, under the orders of Admiral Hope, consisted of seven steamships, ten gunboats, two troop and storeships, and several hundred marines and royal engineers. The Chinese, on their part, had objected to the mission taking that particular route. Admiral Hope, consequently, found the entrance of the Peiho barred by booms and stakes, and having stayed for nine days, from the 17th till the 25th June, at the mouth of that river, attempted its forcible passage, the Plenipotentiaries having joined the squadron on the 20th of June. On his arrival off the Peiho River, Admiral Hope had made sure of the Taku forts, razed during the last war, having been rebuilt—a fact which, be it said *en passant,* he ought to have known before, since it had been officially announced in the *Peking Gazette.*

On the 25th of June, while the British attempted to force the Peiho passage, the Taku batteries, supported by a Mongol force of apparently 20,000 men, were unmasked, and opened a destructive fire on the British vessels. An engagement on land and water took place, resulting in the utter discomfiture of the aggressors. The expedition had to withdraw, after the loss of three English vessels of war, the *Cormorant*, the *Lee*, and *Plover,* and with a loss of 464 killed and wounded on the part of the British, while of the 60 Frenchmen present 14 were killed or wounded. Five English officers were killed and 23 wounded, the Admiral himself escaping not unhurt. After this defeat, Mr. Bruce and M. de Bourboulon returned to Shanghai, while the British squadron was to station off Chinhae, Ningpo.

On the receipt in England of these unpleasant tidings, the Palmerstonian press at once bestrode the British lion, and unanimously roared for wholesale revenge. *The London Times,* of course, affected some dignity in its appeals to the bloody instincts of its countrymen; but the lower class of Palmerstonian organs were quite grotesque in acting the part of *Orlando Furioso*. Listen, for instance, to *The London Daily Telegraph*:

> "Great Britain must attack the seaboard of China throughout its whole extent, invade the capital, expel the Emperor from his palace and possess herself of a material guaranty against future aggression.... We must cat-o'-nine-tail any dragon-decorated official who presumes to treat our national symbols with contumely.... Every one of them (the Chinese generals) must be hanged as a pirate and a homicide to the yard-arms of a British man-of-war. It would be a refreshing and salutary spectacle—that of a dozen bebuttoned villains, with the countenances of ogres, and the apparel of buffoons, swinging in the sight of the population. Terror must to struck, by one means or the other; and we have already had more than enough of leniency.... The Chinese must now be taught to value the English, who are their superiors, and ought to be their *masters*.... The least that can be attempted is to capture Peking; while, if a bold policy were adopted, the confiscation in perpetuity of Canton would follow. We might retain Canton as we held Calcutta, make it the centre of our ultra Eastern trade, compensate ourselves for the influence of Russia on the Tartar frontiers of the Empire, and lay the basis of a new dominion."

Now, from these ravings of Palmerston's penmen, let me return to the facts and, as far as it is possible with the present meagre information, try to unravel the true bearings of the untoward event.

The first question to be answered is, whether, on the supposition that the treaty of Tientsin stipulates for the immediate access to Peking of the British Ambassador, the Chinese Government have committed an infraction of that treaty, wrung from them by a piratical war, in withstanding the forcible passage by a British squadron of the Peiho River? As will be seen from the news conveyed by the overland mail, the Chinese authorities had objected, not to the British mission to Peking, but to the British armament ascending the Peiho. They had proposed that Mr. Bruce should travel by land. divested o an armament which, with a fresh recollection of the Canton bombardment, the Celestials could but consider the instrument of invasion. Does the right of the French Ambassador to reside at London involve the right of forcing the river Thames at the head of an armed French expedition? It must certainly be allowed that this interpretation put by the British on the admission to Peking of their Ambassador, sounds at least as strange as the discovery made by them during the last Chinese war, that in bombarding the town of an empire, you are not waging war upon that empire itself, but only exchanging local hostilities with one of its dependencies. In answer to the reclamations of the Celestials, the British had "taken," according to their own statement, "every precaution to force, if necessary, admission to Peking," by ascending the Peiho with a rather formidable squadron. Even if bound to admit their pacific Ambassador, the Chinese were certainly warranted in resisting their armed expedition. In thus acting they did not infringe a treaty, but baffled encroachment.

In the second instance, it may be questioned whether, although the abstract right of legation had been accorded to the British by the treaty of Tientsin, the actual enjoyment of that right had, for the present, at least, not been waived by Lord Elgin? A reference to "*The Correspondence Relating to the Earl of Elgin's Special Mission to China, printed by command of her Majesty*," will convince every impartial inquirer that, first, the admission to Peking of the English Ambassador was to take place not now, but at a *more remote period*; secondly, that his right of residence at Peking was qualified by various clauses; and, finally, that the peremptory article III in the English text of the treaty, relating to the Ambassador's admission, was, on the request of the Chinese envoys, altered in the Chinese text of the treaty. This discrepancy between the two versions of the treaty is admitted by Lord Elgin himself, who, however, was, as he says, "compelled by his instructions to require the Chinese to accept, as the authoritative version of an international agreement, a text of which they did not understand a syllable." Can the Chinese be impeached for acting on the Chinese text of the treaty, instead of the English one, which, according to Lord Elgin's admission, somewhat diverges from "the correct sense of the stipulation"?

In conclusion, I will state that Mr. T. Chisholm Anstey, the late British Attorney-General at Hongkong, formally declares in a letter addressed by him to the editor of *The London Morning Star*:

> "The treaty itself, be it what it may, has been long since abrogated by the violent acts of the British Government and its subordinates, to the extent at least of depriving the Crown of Great Britain of every advantage or privilege conferred by the treaty."

Being on the one hand harassed by the Indian difficulties, and on the other hand arming for the eventuality of a European war, England is likely to incur great dangers from this new Chinese catastrophe, probably of Palmerston's own cooking. The next result must be the break up of the present Administration, whose head was the author of the last Chinese war, while its principal members had passed a vote of censure on their present chief for undertaking that war. At all events, Mr. Milner Gibson and the Manchester School must either withdraw from the present Liberal coalition, or, a thing not very probable, in unison with Lord John Russell, Mr. Gladstone and his Peelite colleagues,[88] compel their chief to submit to their own policy.

Published in the
New-York Daily Tribune,
No. 5750, September 27, 1859

Printed according to the text
of the newspaper

II

London, September 16, 1859

A Cabinet Council is announced for tomorrow in order to decide upon the course to be taken in regard to the Chinese catastrophe. The lucubrations of the French *Moniteur* and *The London Times* leave no doubt as to the resolutions arrived at by Palmerston and Bonaparte. They want another Chinese war. I am informed from an authentic source that at the impending Cabinet Council Mr. Milner Gibson, in the first instance, will contest the validity of the plea for war; in the second instance, will protest against any declaration of war not previously sanctioned by both Houses of Parliament; and if his opinion be overwhelmed by a majority of votes, will secede from the Cabinet, thus again giving the signal for a new onslaught on Palmerston's administration and the break up of the Liberal coalition that led to the ousting of the Derby Cabinet. Palmerston is said to feel somewhat nervous as to the intended proceedings of Mr. Milner Gibson, the only one of his colleagues whom he is afraid of, and whom he has characterized more than once as a man peculiarly able "in picking holes." It is possible that simultaneously with this letter you may receive from Liverpool the news of the results of the Ministerial Council. Meanwhile, the real bearing of the case in question may be best judged, not from what has been printed, but from what has been wilfully suppressed by the Palmerston organs in their first publications of the news conveyed by the last overland mail.

First, then, they suppressed the statement that the Russian treaty had already been ratified, and that the Emperor of China had given instructions to his mandarins to receive and escort the American Embassy to the capital for the exchange of the ratified copies of the American treaty. These acts were suppressed with a view to stifle the suspicion that would naturally arise, that the English and French Envoys, instead of the Court of Peking, are responsible for meeting obstacles in the transaction of their business, which were not encountered either by their Russian or American colleagues. The other, still more important, fact that was at first suppressed by *The Times*, and the other Palmerston organs, but is now avowed on their part, is that the Chinese authorities had given notice of their willingness to conduct the English and French Envoys to Peking; that they were actually in waiting to receive them at one of the mouths of the river, and offered them an escort if they only consented to leave their vessels and troops. Now, as the treaty of Tientsin contains no clause granting to the English and French the right of sending a squadron of men-of-war up the Peiho, it becomes evident that the treaty was violated, not by the Chinese, but by the English, and that on the part of the latter there existed the foregone conclusion to pick a quarrel just before the period appointed for the exchange of the ratifications. Nobody will fancy that the Hon. Mr. Bruce acted on his own responsibility in thus baffling the ostensible end aimed at by the last Chinese war, but that, on the contrary, he only executed secret instructions received from London. Now, it is true that Mr. Bruce was dispatched not by Palmerston, but by Derby; but, then I have only to remind you that during the first administration of Sir Robert Peel when Lord Aberdeen kept the seals of the Foreign Office, Sir Henry Bulwer, the English Ambassador at Madrid, picked a quarrel with the Spanish Court, resulting in his expulsion from Spain, and that, during the debates in the House of Lords on this "untoward event," it was proved that Bulwer, instead of obeying the official instructions of Aberdeen, had acted up to the secret instructions of Palmerston, who then sat on the Opposition benches.

A manoeuvre has also been carried out during these last days in the Palmerstonian press, which leaves no doubt, at least to those acquainted with the secret history of English diplomacy during the last thirty years, as to the real author of the Peiho catastrophe and the impending third Anglo-Chinese war. *The Times* intimates that the guns planted on the forts of Taku which caused such havoc among the British squadron were of Russian origin, and were directed by Russian officers. Another Palmerstonian organ is still more plain spoken. I quote:

> "We now perceive how closely the policy of Russia is interwoven with that of Peking; we detect great movements on the Amur; we discern large Cossack armies manoeuvring far beyond Lake Baikal, in the frozen dreamland on the twilight borders of the Old World; we trace the course of innumerable caravans; we espy a special Russian envoy (Gen. Mouravieff, the Governor of Eastern Siberia) making his way, with secret designs, from the remoteness of Eastern Siberia to the secluded Chinese metropolis; and well may public opinion in this country burn at the thought that foreign influences have had a share in procuring our disgrace and the slaughter of our soldiers and sailors."

Now, this is one of Lord Palmerston's old tricks. When Russia wanted to conclude a treaty of commerce with China, he drove the latter by the opium war into the arms of her northern neighbour. When Russia requested the cession of the Amur, he brought it about by the second Chinese war, and now that Russia wants to consolidate her influence at Peking, he extemporizes the third Chinese war. In all his transactions with the weak Asiatic states, with China, Persia, Central Asia, Turkey, it has always been his invariable and constant rule to ostensibly oppose Russia's designs by picking a quarrel, not with Russia, but with the Asiatic State, to estrange the latter from England by piratical hostilities, and by this roundabout way drive it to the concessions it had been unwilling to yield to Russia. You may be sure that on this occasion the whole past Asiatic policy of Palmerston will be again sifted, and I draw, therefore, your attention to the Afghan papers, ordered by the House of Commons to be printed on the 8th June, 1839. They throw more light on Palmerston's sinister policy, and the diplomatic history of the last thirty years, than any documents ever before printed. The case is, in a few words, this: In 1838 Palmerston commenced a war against Dost Mohammed, the ruler of Kabul, a war that led to the destruction of an English army, and was commenced on the plea of Dost Mohammed having entered into a secret alliance against England with Persia and Russia. In proof of this assertion, Palmerston laid, in 1839, before Parliament, a Blue Book, chiefly consisting of the correspondence of Sir A. Burnes, the British Envoy at Kabul, with the Government at Calcutta. Burnes had been assassinated during an insurrection at Kabul against the English invaders, but, distrustful of the British Foreign Minister, had sent copies of some of his official letters to his brother, Dr. Burnes, at London. On the appearance, in 1839, of the "Afghan papers," prepared by Palmerston, Dr. Burnes accused him of having "garbled and forged the dispatches of the late Sir A. Burnes," and, in corroboration of his statement, had some of the genuine dispatches printed. But it was only last summer that the murder came out. Under the Derby Ministry, on the motion of Mr. Hadfield, the House of Commons ordered all the "Afghan papers" to be published in full, and this order has been executed in such a form as to constitute a demonstration, to the meanest capacity, of the truth of the charge of garbling and forgery, in the *interest of Russia.* On the title-page of the Blue Book appears the following:

"*Note.*—The correspondence, only partially given in former returns, is here given entire, the omitted passages being marked by brackets, [ ]".

The name of the official, which appears as a guaranty for the fidelity of the return, is "J. W. Kaye, Secretary in Political and Secret Departments," Mr. Kaye being the "upright historian of the war in Afghanistan."

Now, to illustrate the real relations of Palmerston with Russia, against which he pretended to have set up the Afghan war, one instance may suffice for the present. The Russian agent, Vicovitch, who came to Kabul in 1837, was the bearer of a letter from the Czar to Dost Mohammed. Sir Alexander Burnes obtained a copy of the letter, and sent it to Lord Auckland, the Governor-General of India. In his own dispatches, and various documents enclosed by him, this circumstance is referred to over and over again. But the copy of the Czar's letter was expunged altogether from the papers presented by Palmerston in 1839, and in every dispatch in which it is referred to, such alterations were made as were necessary to suppress the circumstance of the connection of the "Emperor of Russia" with the mission to Kabul. This forgery was committed in order to suppress the evidence of the Autocrat's connection with Vicovitch, whom, on his return to St. Petersburg, it suited Nicholas to formally disavow. For instance, at page 82 of the Blue Book will be found the translation of a letter to Dost Mohammed, which reads now as follows, the brackets showing the words originally suppressed by Palmerston:

> "The Ambassador on the part of [the] Russia [or Emperor] came [from Moscow] to Teheran, and has been appointed to wait on the Sindars at Kandahar, and thence to proceed to the presence of the Ameer. He is the bearer of [confidential messages from the Emperor and of the] letters from the Russian Ambassador at Teheran. The Russian Ambassador recommends this man to be a most trusty individual, and to possess full authority to make any negotiations [on the part of the Emperor and himself], etc., etc."

These, and similar forgeries committed by Palmerston in order to protect the honour of the Czar, are not the only curiosity exhibited by the "Afghan papers." The invasion of Afghanistan was justified by Palmerston on the ground that Sir Alexander Burnes had advised it as a proper means for baffling Russian intrigues in Central Asia. Now Sir A. Burnes did quite the contrary, and consequently all his appeals in behalf of Dost Mohammed were altogether suppressed in Palmerston's edition of the "Blue Book"; the correspondence being, by dint of garbling and forgery, turned quite to the reverse of its original meaning.

Such is the man now about to enter on a third Chinese war, on the ostensible plea of thwarting Russia's designs in that quarter.

Published in the *New-York Daily Tribune*, No. 5754, October 1, 1859

Printed according to the text of the newspaper

III

London, September 20, 1859

That there is to be another civilization war against the Celestials seems a matter now pretty generally settled with the English press. Still, since the meeting of the Cabinet Council on Saturday last, a remarkable change has come over those very papers that were foremost in the howl for blood. At first *The London Times*, in an apparent trance of patriotic fury, thundered at the double treachery committed—by cowardly Mongols who lured on the *bonhomme** of the British Admiral by studiously falsifying appearances and screening their artillery—by the Court of Peking, which, with deeper Machiavellism, had set those Mongol ogres to their damnable practical jokes. Curiously to say, although tossed on a sea of passion, *The Times* had, in its reprints, contrived to carefully expunge from the original reports all points favourable to the doomed Chinaman. To confound things may be the work of passion, but to garble them seems rather the operation of a cool head. However that be, on September 16, just one day before the meeting of the Ministers, *The Times* veered round, and, without much ado, cut one head off its Janus-headed impeachment. "*We fear,*" it said, "that we cannot accuse the *Mongols* who resisted our attack on the forts of the Peiho of treachery;" but then, to make up for that awkward concession, it clung the more desperately to "the deliberate and perfidious violation of a solemn treaty by the *Court of Peking*." Three days later, after the Cabinet Council had been held, *The*

* Simple-minded person.—*Ed.*

Times, on further consideration, even "found *no room for doubt* that if Mr. Bruce and M. de Bourboulon had solicited the mandarins to conduct them to Peking, they would have been permitted to effect the ratification of the treaty." What, then, remains there of the treachery of the Court of Peking? Not a shadow even, but in its place there remain two doubts on the mind of *The Times.* "It is," says it, "perhaps *doubtful* whether, as a *military* measure, it was wise to try with such a squadron, our way to Peking. It is *still more doubtful* whether, as a *diplomatic* measure, it was desirable to use force at all." Such is the lame conclusion of all the indignation-bluster indulged in by the "leading organ," but, with a logic of its own, it drops the reasons for war without dropping the war itself. Another semi-governmental paper, *The Economist,* which had distinguished itself by its fervent apology for the Canton bombardment, seems to take a more economical and less rhetorical view of things now that Mr. J. Wilson has got his appointment of Chancellor of the Exchequer for India. *The Economist* brings two articles on the subject, the one political, the other economical; the first one winding up with the following sentences:

"Now, all these things considered, it is obvious that the article of the treaty, which gave our Ambassador a right of visiting or residing at Peking, was one literally *forced* upon the Chinese Government; and if it were thought absolutely essential to our interests that it should be observed, we think there was much room for the display of consideration and patience in exacting its fulfilment. No doubt it may be said that with such a government as the Chinese, delay and patience are interpreted as signs of fatal weakness, and therefore the most unsound policy we could pursue. But how far are we entitled, on this plea, to vary the principles on which we should assuredly act toward any civilized nation in our treatment of these Oriental Governments? When we have wrung out an unwelcome concession from their fears, it may be perhaps the most consistent policy to wring out, also from their fears, the immediate execution of the bargain in the way most convenient to ourselves. But if we fail in so doing—if, in the meantime, the Chinese overcome their fears, and insist, with a suitable display of force, on our consulting them as to the mode to be taken for giving our treaty effect—can we justly accuse them of treachery? Are they not rather practising upon us our own methods of persuasion? The Chinese Government may—and it is very likely that it is so—have intended to entrap us into this murderous snare, and never have purposed to execute the treaty at all. If this should prove to be so, we must and ought to exact reparation. But it may also prove that the intention to defend the mouth of the Peiho against the recurrence of such a violent entry as was made good by Lord Elgin in the previous year, was not accompanied by any desire to break faith on the general articles of the treaty. As the hostile initiative came entirely from our side, and it was, of course, at any moment competent to our commanders to retire from the murderous fire, opened only for the defence of the forts, we cannot certainly prove any intention of breaking faith on the part of China. And, till proof of a deliberate intention to break the treaty reaches us—we think we have some reason to suspend our judgement, and ponder whether we may not have been applying to our treatment of barbarians a code of principles not very widely different from that which they have practised toward ourselves."

In a second article, on the same subject, *The Economist* dwells on the importance, direct and indirect, of the English trade to China. In the year 1858, the British exports to China had risen to £2,876,000, while the value of the British imports from China had averaged upward of £9,000,000 for each of the last three years, so that the aggregate direct trade of England with China may be put down at about £12,000,000. But beside these direct transactions there are three other important trades with which, less or more, England is intimately connected in the circle of exchanges, the trade between India and China, the trade between China and Australia, and the trade between China and the United States.

"Australia," says *The Economist,* "takes from China large quantities of tea annually, and has nothing to give in exchange which finds a market in China. America also takes large quantities of tea and some silk of a value far exceeding that of their direct exports to China."

Both these balances in favour of China have to be made good by England, who is paid for this equalization of exchanges by the gold of Australia and the cotton of the United States. England, therefore, independent of the balance due by herself to China, has also to pay to that country large sums in respect to gold imported from Australia and cotton from America. Now this balance due to China by England, Australia, and the United States is, to a great extent, transferred from China to India, as a set-off against the amount due by China to India, on account of opium and cotton. Be it remarked, *en passant*, that the imports from China to India have never yet reached the amount of £1,000,000 sterling, while the exports to China from

India realize the sum of nearly £10,000,000. The inference *The Economist* draws from these economical observations is, that any serious interruption of the British trade with China would "be a calamity of greater magnitude than the mere figures of exports and imports might at first sight suggest," and that the embarrassment consequent upon such a disturbance would not be felt in the direct British tea and silk trade only, but must also "affect" the British transactions with Australia and the United States. *The Economist* is, of course, aware of the fact that during the last Chinese war, the trade was not so much interfered with by the war as had been apprehended; and that, at the port of Shanghai, it was even not affected at all. But then, *The Economist* calls attention upon "two novel features in the present dispute" which might essentially modify the effects of a new Chinese war upon trade—these two novel features being the "Imperial" not "local" character of the present conflict, and the "signal success" which, for the first time, the Chinese have effected against European forces.

How very different sounds this language from the war cry *The Economist* so lustily shouted at the time of the lorcha affair.

The Ministerial Council, as I anticipated in my last letter,* witnessed Mr. Milner Gibson's protest against the war, and his menace of seceding from the Cabinet, should Palmerston act up to the foregone conclusions betrayed in the columns of the French *Moniteur*. For the moment Palmerston prevented any rupture of the Cabinet, and the Liberal Coalition, by the statement that the force indispensable for the protection of British trade should be gathered in the Chinese waters, while before the arrival of more explicit reports on the part of the British Envoy, no resolution should be taken as to the war question. Thus the burning question was put off. Palmerston's real intention, however, transpires through the columns of his mob-organ, *The Daily Telegraph*, which in one of its recent numbers says:

"Should any event lead to a vote unfavourable to the Government, in the course of next year, an appeal will certainly be made to the constituencies.... The House of Commons will test the result of their

* See this collection, pp. 236-40.—*Ed.*

activity by a verdict on the Chinese question, seeing that to the professional malignants, headed by Mr. Disraeli, must be added the Cosmopolitans, who declare that the Mongols were thoroughly in the right."

The fix in which the Tories are hemmed up, by having allowed themselves to become inveigled into the responsible editorship of events planned by Palmerston and enacted by two of his agents, Lord Elgin and Mr. Bruce (Lord Elgin's brother), I shall, perhaps, find another occasion of remarking upon.

Published in the
New-York Daily Tribune,
No. 5761, October 10, 1859

Printed according to the text
of the newspaper

IV

London, September 30, 1859

In a former letter* I asserted that the Peiho conflict had not sprung from accident, but, on the contrary, been beforehand prepared by Lord Elgin, acting upon Palmerston's secret instructions, and fastening upon Lord Malmesbury, the Tory Foreign Minister, the project of the noble Viscount, then seated at the head of the Opposition benches. Now, first, the idea of the "accidents" in China arising from "instructions" drawn up by the present British Premier is so far from being new, that, during the debates on the lorcha war, it was suggested to the House of Commons, by so well informed a personage as Mr. Disraeli, and, curious to say, confirmed by no less an authority than Lord Palmerston himself. On February 3, 1857, Mr. Disraeli warned the House of Commons in the following terms:

"I cannot resist the conviction that what has taken place in China has not been in consequence of the alleged pretext, but is, in fact, in consequence of *instructions received from home*, some considerable time ago. If that be the case, I think the time has arrived when this House would not be doing its duty unless it earnestly considered whether it has any means of controlling a *system*, which if pursued, will be one, in my mind, fatal to the interests of this country."

And Lord Palmerston most coolly replied:

"The right hon. gentleman says the course of events appeared to be the result of *some system predetermined by the Government at home*. Undoubtedly it was."

---

* See this collection, pp. 232-35.—*Ed.*

In the present instance, a cursory glance at the Blue Book, entitled: "*Correspondence Relative to the Earl of Elgin's special missions to China and Japan, 1857-59,*" will show, how the event, that occurred at the Peiho, on the 25th June, was already receded by Lord Elgin on the 2d of March. Page 484 of the said correspondence, we find the following two dispatches:

The Earl of Elgin to Rear-Admiral Sir Michael Seymour
Furious, March 2, 1859

"Sir: With reference to my dispatch to your Excellency of the 17th ult., I would beg leave to state that I entertain some hope that the decision come to by her Majesty's Government on the subject of the permanent residence of a British Ambassador at Peking, which I communicated to your Excellency in a conversation yesterday, may induce the Chinese Government to receive, in a becoming manner, the representative of her Majesty, when he proceeds to Peking for the exchange of ratifications of the treaty of Tientsin. At the same time, it is no doubt possible that this hope may not be realized, and, at any rate, I apprehend *that her Majesty's Government will desire* that our Ambassador, *when he proceeds to Tientsin*, be accompanied by an *imposing force*. Under these circumstances, I would venture to submit, for your Excellency's consideration, whether it would not be expedient to concentrate at Shanghai, at the earliest convenient period, a *sufficient* fleet of gunboats *for this service*, as Mr. Bruce's arrival in China cannot long be delayed. I have, etc.

"*Elgin* and *Kincardine*"

The Earl of Malmesbury to the Earl of Elgin
Foreign Office, May 2, 1859

"My Lord: I have received your Excellency's dispatch of the 7th of March, 1859, and I have to inform you that her Majesty's Government approve of the note, of which a copy is therein enclosed, and in which your Excellency announced to the Imperial Commissioner that her Majesty's Government would not insist upon the residence of her Majesty's Minister being permanently fixed at Peking.

"Her Majesty's Government also approve of *your having suggested* to Rear-Admiral Seymour that a fleet of gunboats should be collected at Shanghai in order to accompany Mr. Bruce *up the Peiho*.

I am, *Malmesbury*"

Lord Elgin, then, knows beforehand that the British Government "will desire" that his brother, Mr. Bruce, be accompanied by "an imposing force" of "gunboats" up the Peiho, and he orders Admiral Seymour to make ready "for this service." The Earl of Malmesbury, in his dispatch dated May 2, approves of the suggestion intimated by Lord

Elgin to the Admiral. The whole correspondence exhibits Lord Elgin as the master, and Lord Malmesbury as the man. While the former constantly takes the initiative and acts upon the instructions originally received from Palmerston, without even waiting for new instructions from Downing Street, Lord Malmesbury contents himself with indulging "the desires" which his imperious subaltern anticipates him to feel. He nods assent, when Elgin states that the treaty being not yet ratified, they had not the right to ascend any Chinese river; he nods assent, when Elgin thinks they ought to show much forbearance toward the Chinese in regard to the execution of the article of the treaty relating to the embassy to Peking; and, nothing daunted, he nods assent when in direct contradiction to his own former statements, Elgin claims the right to enforce the passage of the Peiho by an "imposing fleet of gunboats." He nods assent in the same way that Dogberry nodded assent to the suggestions of the sexton.*

The sorry figure cut by the Earl of Malmesbury, and the humility of his attitude, are easily understood if one calls to mind the cry raised on the advent of the Tory Cabinet, by *The London Times* and other influential papers, as to the great peril threatening the brilliant success which Lord Elgin, under the instructions of Palmerston, was about to secure in China, but which the Tory Administration, if for pique only, and in order to justify their vote of censure on Palmerston's Canton bombardment, were likely to baffle. Malmesbury allowed himself to be intimidated by that cry. He had, moreover, before his eyes and in his heart the fate of Lord Ellenborough, who had dared openly to counteract the Indian policy of the noble Viscount, and in reward for his patriotic courage, was sacrificed by his own colleagues of the Derby Cabinet. Consequently, Malmesbury resigned the whole initiative into the hands of Elgin, and thus enabled the latter to execute Palmerston's plan on the responsibility of his official antagonists, the Tories. It is this same circumstance which for the present has put the Tories in a very dismal alternative as to the course to be taken in

* Shakespeare, *Much Ado About Nothing*, Act IV, Scene 2, Act V, Scene 1.—*Ed.*

regard to the Peiho affair. Either they must sound the war-trumpet with Palmerston, and thus keep him in office, or they must turn their backs on Malmesbury, upon whom they heaped such sickening flatteries during the last Italian war.

The alternative is the more trying since the impending third China war is anything but popular with the British mercantile classes. In 1857 they bestrode the British lion, because they expected great commercial profits from a forcible opening of the Chinese market. At this moment, they feel, on the contrary, rather angry at seeing the fruits of the treaty obtained, all at once snapped away from their hold. They know that affairs look menacing enough in Europe and India, without the further complication of a Chinese war on a grand scale. They have not forgotten that in 1857, the imports of tea fell by upward of 24 millions of pounds, that being the article almost exclusively exported from Canton, which was then the exclusively theatre of war, and they apprehend that this interruption of trade by war may now be extended to Shanghai, and the other trading ports of the Celestial Empire. After a first Chinese war undertaken by the English in the interest of opium smuggling, and a second war carried on for the defence of the lorcha of a pirate, nothing was wanted for a climax but a war extemporized for the purpose of pestering China with the nuisance of permanent Embassies at its capital.

Published in the
New-York Daily Tribune,
No. 5768, October 18, 1859

Printed according to the text
of the newspaper

Karl Marx

THE BRITISH COTTON TRADE

(Excerpt)

From the outbreak of the American war[89] the prices of cotton were steadily rising, but the ruinous disproportion between the prices of the raw material and the prices of yarns and cloth was not declared until the last weeks of August. Till then, any serious decline in the prices of cotton manufactures, which might have been anticipated from the considerable decrease of the American demand, had been balanced by an accumulation of stocks in first hands, and by speculative consignments to China and India. Those Asiatic markets, however, were soon overdone.

"Stocks," says *The Calcutta Price Current* of Aug. 7, 1861, "are accumulating, the arrivals since our last being no less than 24,000,000 yards of plain cottons. Home advices show a continuation of shipments in excess of our requirements, and so long as this is the case, improvement cannot be looked for. . . . The Bombay market, also, has been greatly over-supplied."

Some other circumstances contributed to contract the Indian market. The late famine in the north-western provinces has been succeeded by the ravages of the cholera, while throughout Lower Bengal an excessive fall of rain, laying the country under water, seriously damaged the rice crops. In letters from Calcutta, which reached England last week, sales were reported giving a net return of $9^{1}/_{4}$d. per pound for 40s twist, which cannot be bought at Manchester for less than $11^{3}/_{8}$d., while sales of 40-inch shirtings, compared with present rates at Manchester, yield losses at $7^{1}/_{2}$d., 9d., and 12d. per piece. In the China market, prices were also forced down by the accumulation of the stocks imported.

Under these circumstances, the demand for the British cotton manufactures decreasing, their prices can, of course, not keep pace with the progressive rise in the price of the raw material; but, on the contrary, the spinning, weaving, and printing of cotton must, in many instances, cease to pay the costs of production. Take, as an example, the following case, stated by one of the greatest Manchester manufacturers, in reference to coarse spinning:

Sept. 17, 1860	Per lb.	Margin	Cost of spinning per lb.
Cost of cotton	$6^1/_4$ d.	4 d.	3 d.
16s warp sold for	$10^1/_4$ d.	—	—
Profit, 1d. per lb.			
Sept. 17, 1861			
Cost of cotton	9 d.	2d.	$3^1/_2$ d.
16s warp sold for	11 d.	—	—
Loss, $1^1/_2$ d. per lb.			

The consumption of Indian cotton is rapidly growing, and with a further rise in prices, the Indian supply will come forward at increasing ratios; but still it remains impossible to change, at a few months' notice, all the conditions of production and turn the current of commerce. England pays now, in fact, the penalty for her protracted misrule of that vast Indian Empire. The two main obstacles she has now to grapple with in her attempts at supplanting American cotton by Indian cotton, is the want of means of communication and transport throughout India, and the miserable state of the Indian peasant, disabling him from improving favourable circumstances. Both these difficulties the English have themselves to thank for. English modern industry, in general, relied upon two pivots equally monstrous. The one was the *potato* as the only means of feeding Ireland and a great part of the English working class. This pivot was swept away by the potato disease and the subsequent Irish catastrophe.[90] A larger basis for the reproduction and maintenance of the toiling millions had then to be adopted. The second pivot of English industry was the slave-grown cotton of the United States. The present American crisis forces them to enlarge their field of supply and emancipate cotton from slave-breeding and slave-consuming oligarchies. As long as the English cotton manufactures depended on slave-grown cotton, it could be truthfully asserted that they rested on a twofold slavery, the indirect slavery of the white men in England and the direct slavery of the black men on the other side of the Atlantic.

Written on September 21, 1861

Published in the *New-York Daily Tribune*, No. 6405, October 14, 1861

Printed according to the text of the newspaper

Karl Marx

THE BRITISH GOVERNMENT AND THE FENIAN PRISONERS[91]

London, February 21, 1870

The silence observed by the European press about the infamies committed by the British oligarchic bourgeois government is due to several reasons. To begin with, the British Government is *rich*, and the press, as you know, is *incorruptible*. Furthermore, the British Government is a model government, recognized as such by the landlords, by the capitalists of the Continent, and even by Garibaldi (see his book): hence, one should not speak ill of that ideal government. Finally, the French republicans are so narrow-minded and egoistic in spirit that they reserve all their wrath for the Empire. It would be a crime against freedom of speech to inform their compatriots that *in a country of bourgeois freedom* people are sentenced to 20 years of hard labour for things punishable with 6 months' imprisonment *in the country of cantonments*. Here follow a few details taken from English dailies about the treatment of Fenian prisoners:

Mulcahy, sub-editor of *The Irish People*, condemned for having taken part in a Fenian conspiracy, had an iron collar put round his neck at Dartmoor and was hitched to a cart loaded with stones.

O'Donovan Rossa, proprietor of *The Irish People*, was for 35 days kept in a dungeon with his arms chained behind his back night and day. He was not even unshackled to take his food—the meagre brew that was left for him on the prison floor.

Although Kickham, one of the editors of *The Irish People*, did not have the use of his right hand owing to an abscess, he was made to sit with his companions on a pile of rubbish in the fog and cold of November and to break stones and bricks with his left hand. For the night he was taken back to his cell, and had nothing more to sustain him than six ounces of bread and a pint of warm water.

O'Leary, an old man of sixty or seventy, was while in prison put on bread and water for three weeks because he did no want to renounce his *paganism* (that, evidently, is what the gaoler calls free thinking) and to become either papist, protestant, presbyterian, or even Quaker, or embrace one of the numerous religions which the governor of the prison offered for the Irish pagan's choice.

Martin H. Carey is incarcerated in an insane asylum at Mill-Bank; the silence that was imposed on him and other ill treatment made him lose his reason.

Colonel Richard Burke is in no better condition. One of his friends writes that his reason is affected, that he has lost his memory and that his ways, his manners and his speech indicate insanity.

Political prisoners are transferred from one prison to another as though they were wild beasts. The company of the vilest rogues is imposed on them; they are obliged to scour utensils which were used by these miserables, to wear the shirts and flannels of these criminals, many of whom are afflicted with the most disgusting diseases, and to wash in water which these latter had already used. All these criminals were allowed to speak with visitors until the arrival of the Fenians to Portland. A visiting cage was installed for the Fenian prisoners. It consisted of three compartments separated by thick iron bars; the gaoler occupies the central compartment, and the prisoner and his friends cannot see each other but through this double row of bars.

There are prisoners in the docks who eat all the snails, and frogs are considered a delicacy at Chatham. General Thomas Burke declares that he was not surprised to see a dead mouse floating in the soup. The condemned say that it was an unhappy day for them when the Fenians were brought to the prisons. (The routine has become much stricter.)

I shall add a few words to the above:

Last year Mr. Bruce, Minister for the Interior, grand

Liberal, grand policeman, grand proprietor of mines in Wales, and a fierce exploiter of labour, was interpellated on the bad treatment of Fenian prisoners and especially O'Donovan Rossa. At first he denied everything; later he was compelled to admit it. Then Mr. Moore, Irish member of the House of Commons, demanded an investigation. It was flatly refused by that *radical ministry* of which that demi-saint (he has been publicly compared to Jesus Christ) Mr. Gladstone is head and the old bourgeois demagogue John Bright is one of the most influential members.

Lately, after the rumours of bad treatment were renewed, a few M.P.s demanded permission from Minister Bruce to visit the prisoners, in order *to be able to state the falsity of these rumours.* Mr. Bruce refused the permission because, he said, the governors of the prisons feared that the prisoners would be excited by visits of that kind.

Last week the Minister for the Interior was again interpellated. He was asked whether it was true that after his nomination as deputy for Tipperary O'Donovan Rossa received corporal punishment (i.e., was whipped); the Minister declared that this did not happen after 1868 (which goes to say that in the course of two to three years the political prisoner was indeed whipped).

I am also sending you extracts concerning Michael Terbert, a Fenian who was sentenced like all the others to hard labour and who served his sentence at Spike Island Convict Prison, Cork County, Ireland. You will see that the coroner himself attributes his death to tortures. The inquest took place last week.

In the course of two years *more than twenty* Fenian workers died or lost their reason by grace of the philanthropy of these good bourgeois, supported by those good landlords.

You probably know that the English press professes a chaste horror of the abominable general emergency laws which embellish beautiful France. But it is general emergency laws that—brief intervals excepted—make up the Irish Charter. Ever since 1793 the English Government has for every possible reason regularly and periodically suspended the operation of the Habeas Corpus Bill (the law which guarantees freedom of person) in Ireland and, in effect, every law save that of brutal force. In this manner thousands of people *suspected of being Fenian supporters* were taken into custody in Ireland without trial or judgement, without even being formally charged. Not content with depriving them of their liberty, the English Government subjected them to most savage tortures. Here is an example:

One of the prisons where suspected Fenians were buried alive is Mountjoy Prison in Dublin. The inspector of that prison, Murray, is a wild beast. He has maltreated prisoners in a manner so savage that a few of them went out of their minds. The prison doctor, O'Donnell, an excellent man (who has played an honourable part in the inquest of Michael Terbert's death), wrote letters of protest for some months, which he at first addressed to Murray himself. Since Murray did not reply to them, he addressed his reports to the superior authorities, but Murray, an expert gaoler, intercepted them.

Finally O'Donnell addressed himself directly to Lord Mayo, then Viceroy of Ireland. This was at the time when the Tories (Derby-Disraeli) were in power. What were the results of these actions? The documents related to the affair were published by order of Parliament and ... Doctor O'Donnell was dismissed from his post! As for Murray, he kept his.

Then came the so-called radical ministry of Gladstone, that delicate, that unctuous, that magnanimous Gladstone who shed such hot and sincere tears over the lot of Poerio and the other bourgeois maltreated by King Bomba.[92] What did this idol of the progressive bourgeoisie do? While insulting the Irish with his insolent rejection of their amnesty demands, he not only confirmed the Monster Murray in his functions, but in gratitude added a fat sinecure to his post of chief gaoler! Such is the apostle of bourgeois philanthropy!

But dust had to be thrown in the eyes of the public; one had to create the impression that something was being done for Ireland, and with grand fanfare he announced a law to regulate the land question (the Land Bill). But all this is nothing but deceit with the ultimate object of creating an impression in Europe, of enticing the Irish judges and barristers with prospects of endless litigations between landlords and farmers, attracting the landlords with promises of subventions, and luring the richer farmers with some half-concessions.

In the lengthy introduction to his grandiloquent and confused discourse, Gladstone confessed that even the "benevolent" laws which Liberal England had granted Ireland in the last hundred years have unfailingly led to that country's deterioration. And after that naïve confession the selfsame Gladstone persists in torturing the men who want to end this wrongful and imbecile legislation.

Published in
L'Internationale,
No. 59, February 27, 1870

Printed according to the text
of the newspaper
Translated from the French

Karl Marx

CONFIDENTIAL COMMUNICATION

(Excerpt)

5) *Question of the General Council Resolution on the Irish Amnesty.*[93]

If England is the bulwark of landlordism and European capitalism, the only point where one can hit official England really hard *is Ireland.*

In the first place, Ireland is the *bulwark* of English landlordism. If it fell in Ireland it would fall in England. In Ireland this is a hundred times easier since *the economic struggle there is concentrated exclusively on landed property*, since this struggle is at the same time national, and since the people there are more revolutionary and exasperated than in England. Landlordism in Ireland is maintained solely by the *English army*. The moment the *forced union* between the two countries ends, a social revolution will immediately break out in Ireland, though in outmoded forms. English landlordism would not only lose a great source of wealth, but also its *greatest moral force*, i.e., that of *representing the domination of England over Ireland.* On the other hand, by maintaining the power of their landlords in Ireland, the English proletariat makes them invulnerable in England itself.

In the second place, the English bourgeoisie has not only exploited the Irish poverty to keep down the working class in England by *forced immigration* of poor Irishmen, but it has also divided the proletariat into two hostile camps. The revolutionary fire of the Celtic worker does not go well with the nature of the Anglo-Saxon worker, solid, but slow. On the contrary, in all *the big industrial centres in England* there is profound antagonism between the Irish proletariat and the English proletariat. The average English worker hates the Irish worker as a competitor who lowers wages and the *standard of life*. He feels national and religious antipathies for him. He regards him somewhat like the *poor whites* of the Southern States of North America regard their black slaves. This antagonism among the proletarians of England is artificially nourished and supported by the bourgeoisie. It knows that this scission is the true secret of maintaining its power.

This antagonism is reproduced on the other side of the Atlantic. The Irish, chased from their native soil by the bulls and the sheep, reassemble in North America where they constitute a huge, ever-growing section of the population. Their only thought, their only passion, is hatred for England. The English and American governments (or the classes they represent) play on these feelings in order to perpetuate the covert struggle between the United States and England. They thereby prevent a sincere and lasting alliance between the workers on both sides of the Atlantic, and consequently, their emancipation.

Furthermore, Ireland is the only pretext the English Government has for retaining a *big standing army*, which, if need be, as has happened before, can be used against the English workers after having done its military training in Ireland.

Lastly, England today is seeing a repetition of what happened on a monstrous scale in ancient Rome. Any nation that oppresses another forges its own chains.

Thus, the attitude of the International Association to the Irish question is very clear. Its first need is to encourage the social revolution in England. To this end a great blow must be struck in Ireland.

The General Council's resolutions on the Irish amnesty serve only as an introduction to other resolutions which will affirm that, quite apart from international justice, it is a *precondition to the emancipation of the English work-*

ing class to transform the present *forced union* (i.e., the enslavement of Ireland) into *equal and free confederation* if possible, into *complete separation* if need be.

Written about March 28, 1870

First published in *Die Neue Zeit*, Vol. 2, No. 15, 1902

Printed according to the text of the document "The General Council to the Federal Council of Romance Switzerland" in *The General Council of the First International, 1868-1870, Minutes*, Moscow

Frederick Engels

From Excerpts to the Work:
HISTORY OF IRELAND

...The English proved to be able to reconcile peoples of the most diverse races to their domination. The inhabitants of Wales, who clung so tenaciously to their nationality and language, have fused completely with the British Empire. The Scottish Celts, despite the rebellious spirit displayed by them until 1745 and despite their almost complete extermination first by the Government and then by their own aristocracy, do not even think of rebellion. The French from the Normandes Isles, even during the Great Revolution, fought bitterly against France. And even the Heligoland Frisians, sold to England by the Danish, are satisfied with their lot, and a long time passed before the laurels of Sadowa and the conquests of the North German Federation wrenched from their throats a pained wail about unification with the "great fatherland." But the English were never able to cope with the Irish, the reason for this being the enormous flexibility of the Irish nation. After the most savage suppression, after every attempt at extermination, the Irish would, following a short interval of time, rise once more in revolt that eclipsed all their preceding rebellions; it seemed that they drew their main strength from the foreign garrison hung round their necks in order to oppress them. The second and, frequently, the first generation of these foreigners became more Irish than the Irish themselves (*Hiberniores ipsis Hibernicis*) and the latter became more Irish the more they learned the English language and forgot their own....

Written in May-early in July, 1870
First published in Russian in *The Archives of Marx and Engels*, Vol. X, 1948

Translated from the German

Frederick Engels

ABOUT THE IRISH QUESTION

There are two trends in the Irish movement. The first, the earliest one, is the *agrarian* trend, which has gradually developed from the brigandage supported by the peasants and organised by the clan chiefs dispossessed by the English and the major Catholic landowners (in the 17th century these brigands were called *Tories*, and it is from them that the present-day Tories take their name) into a spontaneous peasant resistance in the districts and provinces against the uninvited English landlords. The names—Ribbonmen, Whiteboys, Captain Rock, Captain Moonlight, etc.—have changed, but the form of resistance—the shooting not only of the more obnoxious landlords and their agents (collectors), but also of peasants who occupy farms from which others have been forcibly evicted, boycotts, threatening letters, night raids, etc.—all this is as old as the contemporary English land tenure in Ireland; that is, it began at the latest at the close of the 17th century. This form of resistance is not to be suppressed, force can do little against it, and it will disappear when its causes disappear. But by its nature it is *local and isolated* and can never become a general form of *political* struggle.

The *liberal national* opposition of the *urban bourgeoisie*, which, as is the case in all agrarian countries with declining townships (Denmark, for example), has its natural leaders in the *lawyers*, came to the fore soon after the Union (1800).[94] This also stands in need of peasant support, and has therefore had to search for slogans that would appeal to the peasants. Thus, O'Connell found one first in

Catholic emancipation and later in the *repeal of the Union*. Lately this trend has, in view of the landlords' infamies, been compelled to choose a different path. While the *Land League* pursues more revolutionary (and here feasible) aims in the *social* sphere: the total removal of the uninvited landlords, it acts fairly timidly in the *political* sphere and only demands home rule, i.e., a local Irish parliament alongside and under the general all-British Parliament. This too is certainly attainable in a constitutional manner. The frightened landlords are already clamouring (and even the Tories propose it) for the earliest redemption of peasant land in order to save what can still be saved. On the other hand, *Gladstone* says that greater self-government for Ireland is quite admissible.

After the American Civil War, *Fenianism* wedged itself in between these two trends. Hundreds of thousands of Irish soldiers and officers who took part in that war did so with the secret intent of building up an army to liberate Ireland. The differences between America and Britain after the war became the principal motive lever of the Fenians. If it had come to a war, Ireland would in a few months have become a member of the United States or at least a republic under its protectorate. The sum which England so readily undertook and paid in the Alabama case by decision of the Geneva arbitration was its price for *buying off the American intervention in Ireland*.

That was the moment when the chief danger was removed. The police sufficed to settle with the Fenians. As in every conspiracy it was the inevitable betrayal that lent a hand in this, and yet it was only the *leaders* who betrayed and then became *direct* spies and false witnesses. The leaders who escaped to America dabbled there in emigrant revolution and mostly went to seed, like O'Donovan Rossa. Whoever has witnessed the European emigration of 1849-52 will find all this familiar, with the sole difference, of course, that it all went on in a typically American excessive degree.

By now many of the Fenians have doubtlessly returned and revived their old armed organisation. They make up an important element in the movement and compel the Liberals to more resolute action. But aside from this, they can achieve nothing save frightening John Bull. The latter is admittedly weakening somewhat in the outskirts of his Empire, but here, close to his own home, he is still able to suppress any Irish revolt. Firstly, there are in Ireland 14,000 men of the constabulary, the gendarmery, armed with rifles and bayonets and drilled militarily, and then nearly 30,000 troops of the line, which can easily be reinforced with just as many more and with the English militia. Then there is the navy. And in quelling revolts John Bull is known for his unmatched brutality. *An Irish revolt has not the slightest hope of success unless there is a war or danger of a war externally*; and just *two powers* might become dangerous: *France* and, still more so, the *United States*. Yet France is out of the question. And in America the parties are playing coy with the Irish votes, making many promises and keeping none. They would not think of getting involved in a war over Ireland. What is more, they stand to profit by such conditions in Ireland as would cause an intensive Irish migration to America. And it is only natural that a country which is to become the most populated, the wealthiest and most powerful country in the world within 20 years, has no particular wish to involve itself in adventures that might, and inevitably would, impede its gigantic internal growth. In 20 years it will speak an entirely different language.

But if there were a danger of war with America the English would readily grant Ireland all that it demands, short of complete independence, which is in no case desirable in view of its geographic location.

For this reason the Irish have only the constitutional way open to them of gradually winning one position after another; in this, however, the mysterious background of Fenian armed conspiracy may remain a very effective element. But the Fenians themselves are being drawn increasingly to a type of Bakuninism; the assassination of Burke and Cavendish[95] could have pursued the sole aim of thwarting the compromise between the Land League and Gladstone. Yet this compromise would have been the best possible way out for Ireland in the present circumstances. The landlords are driving tenants off the land by the tens of thousands for being in arrears with their rent, sometimes even with military assistance. To curb this systematic depopulation of Ireland (the dispossessed must either starve or emigrate to America) is the cardinal demand of the day. Gladstone is prepared to introduce a bill under which the arrears would be settled much as the redemption of feudal imposts was in Austria in 1848: one third by the peasant, another third by the government, with the remainder lost by the landlord. That is the proposal of the Land League. In this light the "heroic deed" in Phoenix Park appears as a purely Bakuninist, boastful and senseless "*propagande par le fait*" (propaganda by deed), if not as crass foolishness. If it did not have the same consequences as the similar foolishness of *Hödel* and *Nobiling*, this is merely due to the fact that Ireland is not part of Prussia. It should be left to the Bakuninists and revolutionary phrase-mongers to place these childish things on the same footing as the assassination of Alexander II and to threaten with an "Irish revolution" that does not come.

There is another thing to be borne in mind about Ireland: never praise any Irish "*politician*" unconditionally, never declare yourself at one with him, until he is dead. Their Celtic credulity and customary exploitation of peasants (all "educated" classes, and particularly the juristic profession, live by it in Ireland) make the professional Irish politicians an easy prey to corruption. O'Connell let the peasants pay him a full £30,000 annually for his agitation.

When the Union was established, which England is known to have bought at the cost of a million pounds in bribes, one of the bribed was rebuked: "You have sold your fatherland," to which he replied with a laugh: "And damned glad I was that I had a fatherland to sell."

Published in
Der Sozialdemokrat,
No. 29, July 13 1882

Printed according to the text
of the newspaper
Translated from the German

Frederick Engels

ENGLAND IN 1845 AND 1885

(Excerpt)

Free Trade meant the re-adjustment of the whole home and foreign, commercial and financial policy of England in accordance with the interests of the manufacturing capitalists—the class which now represented the nation. And they set about this task with a will. Every obstacle to industrial production was mercilessly removed. The tariff and the whole system of taxation were revolutionized. Everything was made subordinate to one end, but that end of the utmost importance to the manufacturing capitalist: the cheapening of all raw produce, and especially of the means of living of the working-class; the reduction of the cost of raw material, and the keeping down—if not as yet the *bringing down*—of wages. England was to become the "workshop of the world"; all other countries were to become for England what Ireland already was—markets for her manufactured goods, supplying her in return with raw materials and food. England, the great manufacturing centre of an agricultural world, with an ever-increasing number of corn and cotton-growing Irelands revolving around her, the industrial sun. What a glorious prospect!

Written in mid-February 1885

Printed in the magazine *The Commonweal*, No. 2, March 1, 1885

Printed according to the text in Karl Marx and Frederick Engels, *On Britain*, Moscow, 1962

Frederick Engels

PROTECTION AND FREE TRADE

(Excerpt)

It was under the fostering wing of protection that the system of modern industry—production by steam-moved machinery—was hatched and developed in England during the last third of the 18th century. And, as if tariff-protection was not sufficient, the wars against the French Revolution helped to secure to England the monopoly of the new industrial methods. For more than twenty years English men-of-war cut off the industrial rivals of England from their respective colonial markets, while they forcibly opened these markets to English commerce. The secession of the South American colonies from the rule of their European mother countries, the conquest by England of all French and Dutch colonies worth having, the progressive subjugation of India, turned the people of all these immense territories into customers for English goods. England thus supplemented the protection she practised at home, by the Free Trade she forced upon her possible customers abroad; and, thanks to this happy mixture of both systems, at the end of the wars, in 1815, she found herself, with regard to all important branches of industry, in possession of the virtual monopoly of the trade of the world.

This monopoly was further extended and strengthened during the ensuing years of peace. The start which England had obtained during the war, was increased from year to year; she seemed to distance more and more all her possible rivals. The exports of manufactured goods in ever growing quantities became indeed a question of life and death to that country. And there seemed but two obstacles in the way: the prohibitive or protective legislation of other countries, and the taxes upon the import of raw materials and articles of food in England.

Then the Free Trade doctrines of classical political economy—of the French physiocrats and their English successors, Adam Smith and Ricardo—became popular in the land of John Bull. Protection at home was needless to manufacturers who beat all their foreign rivals, and whose very existence was staked on the expansion of their exports. Protection at home was of advantage to none but the producers of articles of food and other raw materials, to the agricultural interest, which, under then existing circumstances in England, meant the receivers of rent, the landed aristocracy. And this kind of protection was hurtful to the manufacturers. By taxing raw materials it raised the price of the articles manufactured from them; by taxing food, it raised the price of labour; in both ways, it placed the British manufacturer at a disadvantage as compared with his foreign competitor. And, as all other countries sent to England chiefly agricultural products, and drew from England chiefly manufactured goods, repeal of the English protective duties on corn and raw materials generally, was at the same time an appeal to foreign countries, to do away with, or at least, to reduce, in return, the import duties levied by them on English manufactures.

After a long and violent struggle, the English industrial capitalists, already in reality the leading class of the nation, that class whose interests were then the chief national interests, were victorious. The landed aristocracy had to give in. The duties on corn and other raw materials were repealed. Free Trade became the watchword of the day. To convert all other countries to the gospel of Free Trade, and thus to create a world in which England was the great manufacturing centre, with all other countries for its dependent agricultural districts, that was the next task before the English manufacturers and their mouthpieces, the political economists.

That was the time of the Brussels Congress, the time when Marx prepared the speech in question.[96] While recognizing that protection may still, under certain circumstances, for instance in the Germany of 1847, be of advantage to the manufacturing capitalists; while proving that Free Trade was not the panacea for all the evils under which the working class suffered, and might even aggravate them; he pronounces, ultimately and on principle, in favour of Free Trade. To him, Free Trade is the normal condition of modern capitalist production. Only under Free Trade can the immense productive powers of steam, of electricity, of machinery, be fully developed; and the quicker the pace of this development, the sooner and the more fully will be realized its inevitable results: society splits up into two classes, capitalists here, wage-labourers there; hereditary wealth on one side, hereditary poverty on the other; supply outstripping demand, the markets being unable to absorb the ever growing mass of the productions of industry; an ever recurring cycle of prosperity, glut, crisis, panic, chronic depression and gradual revival of trade, the harbinger not of permanent improvement but of renewed overproduction and crisis; in short, productive forces expanding to such a degree that they rebel, as against unbearable fetters, against the social institutions under which they are put in motion; the only possible solution: a social revolution, freeing the social productive forces from the fetters of an antiquated social order, and the actual producers, the great mass of the people, from wage-slavery. And because Free Trade is the natural, the normal atmosphere for this historical evolution, the economic medium in which the conditions for the inevitable social revolution will be the soonest created,—for this reason, and for this alone, did Marx declare in favour of Free Trade.

Anyhow, the years immediately following the victory of Free Trade in England seemed to verify the most extravagant expectations of prosperity founded upon that event. British commerce rose to a fabulous amount; the industrial monopoly of England on the market of the world seemed more firmly established than ever; new iron works, new textile factories arose by wholesale; new branches of industry grew up on every side. There was, indeed, a severe crisis in 1857, but that was overcome, and the onward movement in trade and manufactures soon was in full swing again, until in 1866 a fresh panic occurred, a panic, this time, which seems to mark a new departure in the economic history of the world.

The unparalleled expansion of British manufactures and commerce between 1848 and 1866 was no doubt due, to a great extent, to the removal of the protective duties on food and raw materials. But not entirely. Other important changes took place simultaneously and helped it on. The above years comprise the discovery and working of the Californian and Australian gold fields which increased so immensely the circulating medium of the world; they mark the final victory of steam over all other means of transport; on the ocean, steamers now superseded sailing vessels; on land, in all civilized countries, the railroad took the first place, the macadamized road the second, transport now became four times quicker and four times cheaper. No wonder that under such favourable circumstances British manufactures worked by steam should extend their sway at the expense of foreign domestic industries based upon manual labour. But were the other countries to sit still and to submit in humility to this change, which degraded them to be mere agricultural appendages of England, the "workshop of the world"?

Published in *Neue Zeit* in July 1888 and in the American edition of Marx's speech on Free Trade, 1889

Printed according to the text of Marx's speech on Free Trade, published in America

FROM MARX'S *CAPITAL*

Karl Marx

IRELAND

(Excerpt from *Capital*, Volume I, Chapter XXV, "The General Law of Capitalist Accumulation")

In concluding this section, we must travel for a moment to Ireland. First, the main facts of the case.

The population of Ireland had, in 1841, reached 8,222,664; in 1851, it had dwindled to 6,623,985; in 1861, to 5,850,309; in 1866, to $5^1/_2$ millions, nearly to its level in 1801. The diminution began with the famine year, 1846, so that Ireland, in less than twenty years, lost more than $^5/_{16}$ths of its people.* Its total emigration from May, 1851, to July, 1865, numbered 1,591,487: the emigration during the years 1861-1865 was more than half-a-million. The number of inhabited houses fell, from 1851-1861, by 52,990. From 1851-1861, the number of holdings of 15 to 30 acres increased 61,000, that of holdings over 30 acres, 109,000, whilst the total number of all farms fell 120,000, a fall, therefore, solely due to the suppression of farms under 15 acres—*i.e.*, to their centralisation.

The decrease of the population was naturally accompanied by a decrease in the mass of products. For our purpose, it suffices to consider the 5 years from 1861-1865 during which over half-a-million emigrated, and the absolute number of people sank by more than $^1/_3$ of a million.

Let us now turn to agriculture, which yields the means of subsistence for cattle and for men. In the following table is calculated the decrease or increase for each separate year, as compared with its immediate predecessor. The Cereal Crops include wheat, oats, barley, rye, beans, and

---

* Population of Ireland, 1801, 5,319,867 persons; 1811, 6,084,996; 1821, 6,869,544; 1831, 7,828,347; 1841, 8,222,664.

Table A

LIVE STOCK

Year	Horses		Cattle		
	Total Number	Decrease	Total Number	Decrease	Increase
1860	619,811		3,606,374		
1861	614,232	5,579	3,471,688	138,316	
1862	602,894	11,338	3,254,890	216,798	
1863	579,978	22,916	3,144,231	110,695	
1864	562,158	17,820	3,262,294		118,063
1865	547,867	14,291	3,493,414		231,120

Year	Sheep			Pigs		
	Total Number	Decrease	Increase	Total Number	Decrease	Increase
1860	3,542,080			1,271,072		
1861	3,556,050		13,970	1,102,042	169,030	
1862	3,456,132	99,918		1,154,324		52,282
1863	3,308,204	147,982		1,067,458	86,866	
1864	3,366,941		58,737	1,058,480	8,978	
1865	3,688,742		321,801	1,299,893		241,413

From the above table it results:

Horses	Cattle	Sheep	Pigs
Absolute Decrease	Absolute Decrease	Absolute Increase	Absolute Increase
71,944	112,960	146,662	28,821*

peas; the Green Crops, potatoes, turnips, mangolds, beet-root, cabbages, carrots, parsnips, vetches, &c.

* The result would be found yet more unfavourable if we went further back. Thus: Sheep in 1865, 3,688,742, but in 1856, 3,694,294. Pigs in 1865, 1,299,893, but in 1858, 1,409,883.

Table B

INCREASE OR DECREASE IN THE AREA UNDER CROPS AND GRASS IN ACREAGE

Year	Cereal Crops	Green Crops		Grass and Clover		Flax		Total Cultivated Land	
	Decrease	Decrease	Increase	Decrease	Increase	Decrease	Increase	Decrease	Increase
	Acres	Acres	Acres	Acres	Acres	Acres	Acres	Acres	Acres
1861	15,701	36,974		47,969			19,271	81,873	
1862	72,734	74,785			6,623		2,055	138,841	
1863	144,719	19,358			7,724		63,922	92,431	
1864	122,437	2,317			47,486		87,761		10,493
1865	72,450		25,241		68,970	50,159		28,398	
1861-65	428,041	108,193			82,834		122,850	330,850	

INCREASE OR DECREASE IN THE AREA UNDER CULTIVATION.

Product	Acres of Cultivated Land		Increase or Decrease, 1865		Product per Acre		
	1864	1865				1864	1865
Wheat	276,483	266,989		9,494	Wheat, cwt.	13.3	13.0
Oats	1,814,886	1,745,228		69,658	Oats "	12.1	12.3
Barley	172,700	177,102	4,402		Barley "	15.9	14.9
Bere } Rye }	8,894	10,091	1,197		Bere	16.4	14.8
					Rye	8.5	10.4
Potatoes	1,039,724	1,066,260	26,536		Potatoes, tons	4.1	3.6
Turnips	337,355	334,212		3,143	Turnips, tons	10.3	9.9
Mangold-wurzel	14,073	14,389	316		Mangold-wurzel	10.5	13.3
Cabbages	31,821	33,622	1,801		Cabbages	9.3	10.4
Flax	301,693	251,433		50,260	Flax, st (14 lb.)	34.2	25.2
Hay	1,609,569	1,678,493	68,924		Hay, tons	1.6	1.8

In the year 1865, 127,470 additional acres came under the heading "grass land," chiefly because the area under the heading of "bog and waste unoccupied," decreased by 101,543 acres. If we compare 1865 with 1864, there is a decrease in cereals of 246,667 qrs., of which 48,999 were wheat, 166,605 oats, 29,892 barley, &c.: the decrease in potatoes was 446,398 tons, although the area of their cultivation increased in 1865. (See Table C above.)

From the movement of population and the agricultural produce of Ireland, we pass to the movement in the purse of its landlords, larger farmers, and industrial capitalists. It is reflected in the rise and fall of the Income-tax. It may be remembered that Schedule D. (profits with the exception of those of farmers), includes also the so-called "professional" profits—*i.e.*, the incomes of lawyers, doctors, &c.; and the Schedules C. and E., in which no special details are given, include the incomes of employés, officers, State sinecurists, State fundholders, &c. (Table D.)

Table C

PRODUCT PER ACRE AND TOTAL PRODUCT OF 1865 COMPARED WITH 1864

Increase or Decrease, 1865		Total Product			
		1864	1865	Increase or Decrease. 1865	
	0.3	875,782 Qrs.	826,783 Qrs.		48,999 Qrs.
0.2		7,826,332 "	7,659,727 "		166,605 "
	1.0	761,909 "	732,017 "		29,892 "
	1.6	15,160 "	13,989 "		1,171 "
1.9		12,680 "	18,364 "	5,684 Qrs.	
	0.5	4,312,388 ts.	3,865,990 ts.		446,398 ts.
	0.4	3,467,659 "	3,301,683 "		165,976 "
2.8		147,284 "	191,937 "	44,653 ts.	
1.1		297,375 "	350,252 "	52,877 "	
	9.0	64,506 st.	39,561 st.		24,945 st.*
0.2		2,607,153 ts.	3,068,707 ts.	461,554 "	

Under Schedule D. the average annual increase of income from 1853-1864 was only 0.93; whilst, in the same period, in Great Britain, it was 4.58. The following table shows the distribution of the profits (with the exception of those of farmers) for the years 1864-1865 (Table E).

* The data of the text are put together from the materials of the "Agricultural Statistics, Ireland, General Abstracts, Dublin," for the years 1860, *et seq.*, and "Agricultural Statistics, Ireland. Tables showing the estimated average produce, &c., Dublin, 1866." These statistics are official, and laid before Parliament annually. [Note to 2nd edition. The official statistics for the year 1872 show, as compared with 1871, a decrease in area under cultivation of 134,915 acres. An increase occurred in the cultivation of green crops, turnips, mangold-wurzel, and the like; a decrease in the area under cultivation for wheat of 16,000 acres; oats, 14,000; barley and rye, 4,000; potatoes, 66,632; flax, 34,667; grass, clover, vetches, rape-seed, 30,000. The soil under cultivation for wheat shows for the last 5 years the following stages of decrease:—1868, 285,000 acres; 1869, 280,000; 1870, 259,000; 1871, 244,000; 1872, 228,000. For 1872 we find, in round numbers, an increase of 2,600 horses, 80,000 horned cattle, 68,609 sheep, and a decrease of 236,000 pigs.]

Table D

THE INCOME-TAX ON THE SUBJOINED INCOMES IN POUNDS STERLING

	1860	1861	1862	1863	1864	1865
Schedule A.						
Rent of Land	13,893,829	13,003,554	13,398,938	13,494,091	13,470,700	13,801,616
Schedule B.						
Farmers' Profits	2,765,387	2,773,644	2,937,899	2,938,823	2,930,874	2,946,072
Schedule D.						
Industrial, &c., Profits	4,891,652	4,836,203	4,858,800	4,846,497	4,546,147	4,850,199
Total Schedules A. to E.	22,962,885	22,998,394	23,597,574	23,658,631	23,236,298	23,930,340*

* Tenth Report of the Commissioners of Inland Revenue. Lond. 1866.

Table E

SCHEDULE D. INCOME FROM PROFITS (OVER £60) IN IRELAND

	1864 £	1865 £
Total yearly income of	4,368,610 divided among 17,467 persons	4,669,979 divided among 18,081 persons
Yearly income over £60 and under £100	238,626 divided among 5,015 persons	222,575 divided among 4,703 persons
Of the yearly total income	1,979,066 divided among 11,321 persons	2,028,471 divided among 12,184 persons
Remainder of the total yearly income	2,150,818 divided among 1,131 persons	2,418,933 divided among 1,194 persons
Of these	1,073,906 divided among 1,010 persons	1,097,927 divided among 1,044 persons
	1,076,912 divided among 121 persons	1,320,906 divided among 150 persons
	430,535 divided among 95 persons	584,458 divided among 122 persons
	646,377 divided among 26 persons	736,448 divided among 28 persons
	262,819 divided among 3 persons	274,528 divided among 3 persons*

England, a country with fully developed capitalist production, and pre-eminently industrial, would have bled to death with such a drain of population as Ireland has suffered. But Ireland is at present only an agricultural district of England, marked off by a wide channel from the country to which it yields corn, wool, cattle, industrial and military recruits.

The depopulation of Ireland has thrown much of the land out of cultivation, has greatly diminished the pro-

* The total yearly income under Schedule D. is different in this table from that which appears in the preceding ones, because of certain deductions allowed by law.

duce of the soil,* and, in spite of the greater area devoted to cattle-breeding, has brought about, in some of its branches, an absolute diminution, in others, an advance scarcely worthy of mention, and constantly interrupted by retrogressions. Nevertheless, with the fall in numbers of the population, rents and farmers' profits rose, although the latter not as steadily as the former. The reason of this is easily comprehensible. On the one hand, with the throwing of small holdings into large ones, and the change of arable into pasture land, a larger part of the whole produce was transformed into surplus-produce. The surplus-produce increased, although the total produce, of which it formed a fraction, decreased. On the other hand, the money-value of this surplus-produce increased yet more rapidly than its mass, in consequence of the rise in the English market-price of meat, wool, &c., during the last 20, and especially during the last 10, years.

The scattered means of production that serve the producers themselves as means of employment and of subsistence, without expanding their own value by the incorporation of the labour of others, are no more capital than a product consumed by its own producer is a commodity. If, with the mass of the population, that of the means of production employed in agriculture also diminished, the mass of the capital employed in agriculture increased, because a part of the means of production that were formerly scattered, was concentrated and turned into capital.

The total capital of Ireland outside agriculture, employed in industry and trade, accumulated during the last two decades slowly, and with great and constantly recurring fluctuations; so much the more rapidly did the concentration of its individual constituents develop. And, however small its absolute increase, in proportion to the dwindling population it had increased largely.

Here, then, under our own eyes and on a large scale, a process is revealed, than which nothing more excellent

* If the product also diminishes relatively per acre, it must not be forgotten that for a century and a half England has indirectly exported the soil of Ireland, without as much as allowing its cultivators the means for making up the constituents of the soil that had been exhausted.

could be wished for by orthodox economy for the support of its dogma: that misery springs from absolute surplus-population, and that equilibrium is re-established by depopulation. This is a far more important experiment than was the plague in the middle of the 14th century so belauded of Malthusians.[97] Note further: If only the naïveté of the schoolmaster could apply, to the conditions of production and population of the 19th century, the standard of the 14th, this naïveté, into the bargain, overlooked the fact that whilst, after the plague and the decimation that accompanied it, followed on this side of the Channel, in England, enfranchisement and enrichment of the agricultural population, on that side, in France, followed greater servitude and more misery.*

The Irish famine of 1846 killed more than 1,000,000 people, but it killed poor devils only. To the wealth of the country it did not the slightest damage. The exodus of the next 20 years, an exodus still constantly increasing, did not, as, *e.g.*, the Thirty Years' War, decimate, along with the human beings, their means of production. Irish genius discovered an altogether new way of spiriting a poor people thousands of miles away from the scene of its misery. The exiles transplanted to the United States, send home sums of money every year as travelling expenses for those left behind. Every troop that emigrates one year, draws another after it the next. Thus, instead of costing Ireland anything, emigration forms one of the most lucrative branches of its export trade. Finally, it is a systematic process, which does not simply make a passing gap in the population, but sucks out of it every year more people than are replaced by the births, so that the absolute level of the population falls year by year.**

---

* As Ireland is regarded as the promised land of the "principle of population," Th. Sadler, before the publication of his work on population, issued his famous book, "Ireland, Its Evils and Their Remedies." 2nd edition, London, 1829. Here, by comparison of the statistics of the individual provinces, and of the individual counties in each province, he proves that the misery there is not, as Malthus would have it, in proportion to the number of the population, but in inverse ratio to this.

** Between 1851 and 1874, the total number of emigrants amounted to 2,325,922.

What were the consequences for the Irish labourers left behind and freed from the surplus-population? That the relative surplus-population is to-day as great as before 1846; that wages are just as low, that the oppression of the labourers has increased, that misery is forcing the country towards a new crisis. The facts are simple. The revolution in agriculture has kept pace with emigration. The production of relative surplus-population has more than kept pace with the absolute depopulation. A glance at Table C shows that the change of arable to pasture land must work yet more acutely in Ireland than in England. In England the cultivation of green crops increases with the breeding of cattle; in Ireland, it decreases. Whilst a large number of acres, that were formerly tilled, lie idle or are turned permanently into grass-land, a great part of the waste land and peat bogs that were unused formerly become of service for the extension of cattle-breeding. The smaller and medium farmers—I reckon among these all who do not cultivate more than 100 acres—still make up about $^{8}/_{10}$ths of the whole number.* They are, one after the other, and with a degree of force unknown before, crushed by the competition of an agriculture managed by capital, and therefore they continually furnish new recruits to the class of wage-labourers. The one great industry of Ireland, linen-manufacture, requires relatively few adult men and only employs altogether, in spite of its expansion since the price of cotton rose in 1861-1866, a comparatively insignificant part of the population. Like all other great modern industries, it constantly produces, by incessant fluctuations, a relative surplus-population within its own sphere, even with an absolute increase in the mass of human beings absorbed by it. The misery of the agricultural population forms the pedestal for gigantic shirt-factories, whose armies of labourers are, for the most part, scattered over the country. Here, we encounter again the system described above of domestic industry, which in underpayment and overwork, possesses its own systematic means for creating supernumerary labourers. Finally, although the depopulation has not

* According to a table in Murphy's "Ireland Industrial, Political and Social," 1870, 94.6 per cent of the holdings do not reach 100 acres, 5.4 exceed 100 acres.

such destructive consequences as would result in a country with fully developed capitalistic production, it does not go on without constant reaction upon the home-market. The gap which emigration causes here, limits not only the local demand for labour, but also the incomes of small shopkeepers, artisans, tradespeople generally. Hence the diminution in incomes between £60 and £100 in Table E.

A clear statement of the condition of the agricultural labourers in Ireland is to be found in the Report of the Irish Poor Law Inspectors (1870).* Officials of a government which is maintained only by bayonets and by a state of siege, now open, now disguised, they have to observe all the precautions of language that their colleagues in England disdain. In spite of this, however, they do not let their government cradle itself in illusions. According to them the rate of wages in the country, still very low, has within the last 20 years risen 50-60 per cent, and stands now, on the average, at 6s. to 9s. per week. But behind this apparent rise, is hidden an actual fall in wages, for it does not correspond at all to the rise in price of the necessary means of subsistence that has taken place in the meantime. For proof, the following extract from the official accounts of an Irish

AVERAGE WEEKLY COST PER HEAD

Year ended	Provisions and Necessaries	Clothing	Total
29th Sept., 1849	1s. 3¼ d.	3d.	1s. 6¼ d.
" " 1869	2s. 7¼ d.	6d.	3s. 1¼ d.

workhouse. The price of the necessary means of subsistence is therefore fully twice, and that of clothing exactly twice, as much as they were 20 years before.

Even apart from this disproportion, the mere comparison of the rate of wages expressed in gold would give a result far from accurate. Before the famine, the great mass of agricultural wages were paid in kind, only the smallest part in

* "Reports from the Poor Law Inspectors on the Wages of Agricultural Labourers in Dublin," 1870. See also "Agricultural Labourers (Ireland). Return, etc." 8 March, 1861, London, 1862.

money; to-day, payment in money is the rule. From this it follows that, whatever the amount of the real wage, its money rate must rise. "Previous to the famine, the labourer enjoyed his cabin ... with a rood, or half-acre or acre of land, and facilities for ... a crop of potatoes. He was able to rear his pig and keep fowl.... But they now have to buy bread, and they have no refuse upon which they can feed a pig or fowl, and they have consequently no benefit from the sale of a pig, fowl, or eggs."* In fact, formerly, the agricultural labourers were but the smallest of the small farmers, and formed for the most part a kind of rear-guard of the medium and large farms on which they found employment. Only since the catastrophe of 1846 have they begun to form a fraction of the class of purely wage-labourers, a special class, connected with its wage-masters only by monetary relations.

We know what were the conditions of their dwellings in 1846. Since then they have grown yet worse. A part of the agricultural labourers, which, however, grows less day by day, dwells still on the holdings of the farmers in overcrowded huts, whose hideousness far surpasses the worst that the English agricultural labourers offered us in this way. And this holds generally with the exception of certain tracts of Ulster; in the south, in the counties of Cork, Limerick, Kilkenny, &c.; in the east, in Wicklow, Wexford, &c.; in the centre of Ireland, in King's and Queen's County, Dublin, &c.; in the west, in Sligo, Roscommon, Mayo, Galway, &c. "The agricultural labourers' huts," an inspector cries out, "are a disgrace to the Christianity and to the civilisation of this country."** In order to increase the attractions of these holes for the labourers, the pieces of land belonging thereto from time immemorial, are systematically confiscated. "The mere sense that they exist subject to this species of ban, on the part of the landlords and their agents, has ... given birth in the minds of the labourers to corresponding sentiments of antagonism and dissatisfaction towards those by whom they are thus led to regard themselves as being treated as ... a proscribed race."***

* l.c., pp. 29, 1.
** l.c., p. 12.
*** l.c., p. 12.

The first act of the agricultural revolution was to sweep away the huts situated on the field of labour. This was done on the largest scale, and as if in obedience to a command from on high. Thus many labourers were compelled to seek shelter in villages and towns. There they were thrown like refuse into garrets, hotels, cellars and corners, in the worst back slums. Thousands of Irish families, who, according to the testimony of the English, eaten up as these are with national prejudice, are notable for their rare attachment to the domestic hearth, for their gaiety and the purity of their home-life, found themselves suddenly transplanted into hotbeds of vice. The men are now obliged to seek work of the neighbouring farmers and are only hired by the day, and therefore under the most precarious form of wage. Hence "they sometimes have long distances to go to and from work, often get wet, and suffer much hardship, not unfrequently ending in sickness, disease and want."*

"The towns have had to receive from year to year what was deemed to be the surplus-labour of the rural division;"** and then people still wonder "there is still a surplus of labour in the towns and villages, and either a scarcity or a threatened scarcity in some of the country divisions."*** The truth is that this want only becomes perceptible "in harvest-time, or during spring, or at such times as agricultural operations are carried on with activity; at other periods of the year many hands are idle;"**** that "from the digging out of the main crop of potatoes in October until the early spring following ... there is no employment for them;"***** and further, that during the active times they "are subject to broken days and to all kinds of interruption."******

These results of the agricultural revolution—*i.e.*, the change of arable into pasture land, the use of machinery, the most rigorous economy of labour, &c., are still further aggravated by the model landlords, who, instead of spending their rents in other countries, condescend to live in Ireland

* l.c., p. 25.
** l.c., p. 27.
*** l.c., p. 25.
**** l.c., p. 1.
***** l.c., pp. 31, 32.
****** l.c., p. 25.

on their demesnes. In order that the law of supply and demand may not be broken, these gentlemen draw their "labour-supply ... chiefly from their small tenants, who are obliged to attend when required to do the landlord's work, at rates of wages, in many instances, considerably under the current rates paid to ordinary labourers, and without regard to the inconvenience or loss to the tenant of being obliged to neglect his own business at critical periods of sowing or reaping."*

The uncertainty and irregularity of employment, the constant return and long duration of gluts of labour, all these symptoms of a relative surplus-population, figure therefore in the reports of the Poor Law administration, as so many hardships of the agricultural proletariat. It will be remembered that we met, in the English agricultural proletariat, with a similar spectacle. But the difference is that in England, an industrial country, the industrial reserve recruits itself from the country districts, whilst in Ireland, an agricultural country, the agricultural reserve recruits itself from the towns, the cities of refuge of the expelled agricultural labourers. In the former, the supernumeraries of agriculture are transformed into factory operatives; in the latter, those forced into the towns, whilst at the same time they press on the wages in towns, remain agricultural labourers, and are constantly sent back to the country districts in search of work.

The official inspectors sum up the material condition of the agricultural labourer as follows: "Though living with the strictest frugality, his own wages are barely sufficient to provide food for an ordinary family and pay his rent, and he depends upon other sources for the means of clothing himself, his wife, and children.... The atmosphere of these cabins, combined with the other privations they are subjected to, has made this class particularly susceptible to low fever and pulmonary consumption."** After this, it is no wonder that, according to the unanimous testimony of the inspectors, a sombre discontent runs through the ranks of this class, that they long for the return of the past, loathe the present, despair of the future, give themselves up "to

---

* l.c., p. 30.
** l.c., pp. 21, 13.

the evil influence of agitators," and have only one fixed idea, to emigrate to America. This is the land of Cockaigne, into which the great Malthusian panacea, depopulation, has transformed green Erin.

What a happy life the Irish factory operative leads, one example will show: "On my recent visit to the North of Ireland," says the English Factory Inspector, Robert Baker, "I met with the following evidence of effort in an Irish skilled workman to afford education to his children; and I give his evidence verbatim, as I took it from his mouth. That he was a skilled factory hand, may be understood when I say that he was employed on goods for the Manchester market. 'Johnson.—I am a beetler and work from 6 in the morning till 11 at night, from Monday to Friday. Saturday we leave off at 6 p.m., and get three hours of it (for meals and rest). I have five children in all. For this work I get 10s. 6d. a week; my wife works here also, and gets 5s. a week. The oldest girl who is 12, minds the house. She is also cook, and all the servant we have. She gets the young ones ready for school. A girl going past the house wakes me at half past five in the morning. My wife gets up and goes along with me. We get nothing (to eat) before we come to work. The child of 12 takes care of the little children all the day, and we get nothing till breakfast at eight. At eight we go home. We get tea once a week; at other times we get stirabout, sometimes of oat-meal, sometimes of Indian meal, as we are able to get it. In the winter we get a little sugar and water to our Indian meal. In the summer we get a few potatoes, planting a small patch ourselves; and when they are done we get back to stirabout. Sometimes we get a little milk as it may be. So we go on from day to day, Sunday and week day, always the same the year round. I am always very much tired when I have done at night. We may see a bit of flesh meat sometimes, but very seldom. Three of our children attend school, for whom we pay 1d. a week a head. Our rent is 9d. a week. Peat for firing costs 1s. 6d. a fortnight at the very lowest.' "* Such are Irish wages, such is Irish life!

In fact the misery of Ireland is again the topic of the day

* "Rept. of Insp. of Fact., 31st Oct., 1866", p. 96.

in England. At the end of 1866 and the beginning of 1867, one of the Irish land magnates, Lord Dufferin, set about its solution in *The Times*. "Wie menschlich von solch grossem Herrn!"

From Table E we saw that, during 1864, of £4,368,610 of total profits, three surplus-value makers pocketed only £262,819; that in 1865, however, out of £4,669,979 total profits, the same three virtuosi of "abstinence" pocketed £274,528; in 1864, 26 surplus-value makers reached to £646,377; in 1865, 28 surplus-value makers reached to £736,448; in 1864, 121 surplus-value makers, £1,076,912; in 1865, 150 surplus-value makers, £1,320,906; in 1864, 1,131 surplus-value makers, £2,150,818, nearly half of the total annual profit; in 1865, 1,194 surplus-value makers, £2,418,833, more than half of the total annual profit. But the lion's share, which an inconceivably small number of land magnates in England, Scotland and Ireland swallow up of the yearly national rental, is so monstrous that the wisdom of the English State does not think fit to afford the same statistical materials about the distribution of rents as about the distribution of profits. Lord Dufferin is one of those land magnates. That rent-rolls and profits can ever be "excessive," or that their plethora is in any way connected with plethora of the people's misery is, of course, an idea as "disreputable" as "unsound." He keeps to facts. The fact is that, as the Irish population diminishes, the Irish rent-rolls swell; that depopulation benefits the landlords, therefore also benefits the soil, and, therefore, the people, that mere accessory of the soil. He declares, therefore, that Ireland is still over-populated, and the stream of emigration still flows too lazily. To be perfectly happy, Ireland must get rid of at least one-third of a million of labouring men. Let no man imagine that this lord, poetic into the bargain, is a physician of the school of Sangrado, who as often as he did not find his patient better, ordered phlebotomy and again phlebotomy, until the patient lost his sickness at the same time as his blood. Lord Dufferin demands a new blood-letting of one-third of a million only, instead of about two millions; in fact, without the getting rid of these, the millennium in Erin is not to be. The proof is easily given.

NUMBER AND EXTENT OF FARMS IN IRELAND IN 1864

(1) Farms not over 1 acre		(2) Farms over 1, not over 5 acres		(3) Farms over 5, not over 15 acres		(4) Farms over 15, not over 30 acres		(5) Farms over 30, not over 50 acres		(6) Farms over 50, not over 100 acres		(7) Farms over 100 acres		(8) Total area
No.	Acres	No.	Acres	No.	Acres	No.	Acres	No.	Acres	No.	Acres	No.	Acres	Acres
48,653	25,394	82,037	288,916	176,368	1,836,310	136,578	3,051,343	71,961	2,906,274	54,247	3,983,880	31,927	8,227,807	26,319,924*

Centralisation has from 1851 to 1861 destroyed principally farms of the first three categories, under 1 and not over 15 acres. These above all must disappear. This gives 307,058 "supernumerary" farmers, and reckoning the families the low average of 4 persons, 1,228,232 persons. On the extravagant supposition that, after the agricultural revolution is complete, one-fourth of these are again absorbable, there remain for emigration 921,174 persons. Categories 4, 5, 6, of over 15 and not over 100 acres, are; as was known long since in England, too small for capitalistic cultivation of corn, and for sheep-breeding are almost vanishing quantities. On the same supposition as before, therefore, there are further 788,761 persons to emigrate; total, 1,709,532. And as l'appétit vient en mangeant, Rentroll's eyes will soon discover that Ireland, with $3^1/_2$ millions, is still always miserable, and miserable because she is overpopulated. Therefore her depopulation must go yet further, that thus she may fulfil her true destiny, that of an English sheep-walk and cattle-pasture.**

* The total area includes also peat, bogs, and waste land.

** How the famine and its consequences have been deliberately made the most of, both by the individual landlords and by the English legislature, to forcibly carry out the agricultural revolution and to thin the population of Ireland down to the proportion satisfactory to the landlords, I shall show more fully in Vol. III of this work, in the section on landed property. There also I return to the condition of

Like all good things in this bad world, this profitable method has its drawbacks. With the accumulation of rents in Ireland, the accumulation of the Irish in America keeps pace. The Irishman, banished by sheep and ox, re-appears on the other side of the ocean as a Fenian, and face to face with the old queen of the seas rises, threatening and more threatening, the young giant Republic:

Acerba fata Romanos agunt
*Scelusque fraternae necis.**

Published according
to the English text of *Capital*,
Vol. I, Moscow, 1958

---

the small farmers and the agricultural labourers. At present, only one quotation. Nassau W. Senior says, with other things, in his posthumous work, "Journals, Conversations and Essays Relating to Ireland." 2 vols. London, 1868; Vol. II, p. 282. "Well," said Dr. G., "we have got our Poor Law and it is a great instrument for giving the victory to the landlords. Another, and a still more powerful instrument is emigration.... No friend to Ireland can wish the war to be prolonged [between the landlords and the small Celtic farmers]—still less, that it should end by the victory of the tenants. The sooner it is over—the sooner Ireland becomes a grazing country, with the comparatively thin population which a grazing country requires, the better for all classes." The English Corn Laws of 1815 secured Ireland the monopoly of the free importation of corn into Great Britain. They favoured artificially, therefore, the cultivation of corn. With the abolition of the Corn Laws in 1846, this monopoly was suddenly removed. Apart from all other circumstances, this event alone was sufficient to give a great impulse to the turning of Irish arable into pasture land, to the concentration of farms, and to the eviction of small cultivators. After the fruitfulness of the Irish soil had been praised from 1815 to 1846, and proclaimed loudly as by Nature herself destined for the cultivation of wheat, English agronomists, economists, politicians, discover suddenly that it is good for nothing but to produce forage. M. Léonce de Lavergne has hastened to repeat this on the other side of the Channel. It takes a "serious" man, à la Lavergne, to be caught by such childishness.

* A grievous fate and dastardly fratricide hounds the Romans.—*Ed.*

Karl Marx

GENESIS OF THE INDUSTRIAL CAPITALIST
(Chapter XXXI of *Capital*, Volume I)

The genesis of the industrial* capitalist did not proceed in such a gradual way as that of the farmer. Doubtless many small guild-masters, and yet more independent small artisans, or even wage-labourers, transformed themselves into small capitalists, and (by gradually extending exploitation of wage-labour and corresponding accumulation) into full-blown capitalists. In the infancy of capitalist production, things often happened as in the infancy of mediaeval towns, where the question, which of the escaped serfs should be master and which servant, was in great part decided by the earlier or later date of their flight. The snail's pace of this method corresponded in no wise with the commercial requirements of the new world-market that the great discoveries of the end of the 15th century created. But the Middle Ages had handed down two distinct forms of capital, which mature in the most different economic social formations, and which, before the era of the capitalist mode of production, are considered as capital quand même—usurer's capital and merchant's capital.

"At present, all the wealth of society goes first into the possession of the capitalist ... he pays the landowner his rent, the labourer his wages, the tax and tithe gatherer their claims, and keeps a large, indeed the largest, and a continually augmenting share, of the annual produce of labour for himself. The capitalist may now be said to be the first owner of all the wealth of the community, though

* Industrial here in contradistinction to agricultural. In the "categoric" sense the farmer is an industrial capitalist as much as the manufacturer.

no law has conferred on him the right to this property... this change has been effected by the taking of interest on capital... and it is not a little curious that all the lawgivers of Europe endeavoured to prevent this by statutes, viz., statutes against usury.... The power of the capitalist over all the wealth of the country is a complete change in the right of property, and by what law, or series of laws, was it effected?"* The author should have remembered that revolutions are not made by laws.

The money capital formed by means of usury and commerce was prevented from turning into industrial capital, in the country by the feudal constitution, in the towns by the guild organisation.** These fetters vanished with the dissolution of feudal society, with the expropriation and partial eviction of the country population. The new manufactures were established at seaports, or at inland points beyond the control of the old municipalities and their guilds. Hence in England an embittered struggle of the corporate towns against these new industrial nurseries.

The discovery of gold and silver in America, the extirpation, enslavement and entombment in mines of the aboriginal population, the beginning of the conquest and looting of the East Indies, the turning of Africa into a warren for the commercial hunting of black-skins, signalised the rosy dawn of the era of capitalist production. These idyllic proceedings are the chief momenta of primitive accumulation. On their heels treads the commercial war of the European nations, with the globe for a theatre. It begins with the revolt of the Netherlands from Spain, assumes giant dimensions in England's Anti-Jacobin War, and is still going on in the opium wars against China, &c.

The different momenta of primitive accumulation distribute themselves now, more or less in chronological order, particularly over Spain, Portugal, Holland, France, and

* "The Natural and Artificial Rights of Property Contrasted." Lond., 1832, pp. 98-99. Author of the anonymous work: "Th. Hodgskin."

** Even as late as 1794, the small cloth-makers of Leeds sent a deputation to Parliament, with a petition for a law to forbid any merchant from becoming a manufacturer. (Dr. Aikin, "Description of the Country from Thirty to Forty Miles Round Manchester." London, 1795.)

England. In England at the end of the 17th century, they arrive at a systematical combination, embracing the colonies, the national debt, the modern mode of taxation, and the protectionist system. These methods depend in part on brute force, *e.g.*, the colonial system. But they all employ the power of the State, the concentrated and organised force of society, to hasten, hothouse fashion, the process of transformation of the feudal mode of production into the capitalist mode, and to shorten the transition. Force is the midwife of every old society pregnant with a new one. It is itself an economic power.

Of the Christian colonial system, W. Howitt, a man who makes a speciality of Christianity, says: "The barbarities and desperate outrages of the so-called Christian race, throughout every region of the world, and upon every people they have been able to subdue, are not to be paralleled by those of any other race, however fierce, however untaught, and however reckless of mercy and of shame, in any age of the earth."* The history of the colonial administration of Holland—and Holland was the head capitalistic nation of the 17th century—"is one of the most extraordinary relations of treachery, bribery, massacre, and meanness."** Nothing is more characteristic than their system of stealing men, to get slaves for Java. The men stealers were trained for this purpose. The thief, the interpreter, and the seller, were the chief agents in this trade, native princes the chief sellers. The young people stolen, were thrown into the secret dungeons of Celebes, until they were ready for sending to the slave-ships. An official report says: "This one town of Macassar, *e.g.*, is full of secret prisons, one more horrible than the other, crammed with unfortunates, victims of greed and tyranny fettered in chains, forcibly torn from their families." To secure Malacca, the Dutch corrupted the

* William Howitt: "Colonisation and Christianity: A Popular History of the Treatment of the Natives by the Europeans in all their Colonies." London, 1838, p. 9. On the treatment of the slaves there is a good compilation in Charles Comte, "Traité de la Législation". 3me éd. Bruxelles, 1837. This subject one must study in detail, to see what the bourgeoisie makes of itself and of the labourer, wherever it can, without restraint, model the world after its own image.

** Thomas Stamford Raffles, late Lieut.-Gov. of that island: "The History of Java," Lond., 1817.

Portuguese Governor. He let them into the town in 1641. They hurried at once to his house and assassinated him, to "abstain" from the payment of £21,875, the price of his treason. Wherever they set foot, devastation and depopulation followed. Banjuwangi, a province of Java, in 1750 numbered over 80,000 inhabitants, in 1811 only 18,000. Sweet commerce!

The English East India Company, as is well known, obtained, besides the political rule in India, the exclusive monopoly of the tea-trade, as well as of the Chinese trade in general, and of the transport of goods to and from Europe. But the coasting trade of India and between the islands, as well as the internal trade of India, were the monopoly of the higher employés of the Company. The monopolies of salt, opium, betel and other commodities, were inexhaustible mines of wealth. The employés themselves fixed the price and plundered at will the unhappy Hindus. The Governor-General took part in this private traffic. His favourites received contracts under conditions whereby they, cleverer than the alchemists, made gold out of nothing. Great fortunes sprang up like mushrooms in a day; primitive accumulation went on without the advance of a shilling. The trial of Warren Hastings swarms with such cases. Here is an instance. A contract for opium was given to a certain Sullivan at the moment of his departure on an official mission to a part of India far removed from the opium district. Sullivan sold his contract to one Binn for £40,000; Binn sold it the same day for £60,000, and the ultimate purchaser who carried out the contract declared that after all he realised an enormous gain. According to one of the lists laid before Parliament, the Company and its employés from 1757-1766 got £6,000,000 from the Indians as gifts. Between 1769 and 1770, the English manufactured a famine by buying up all the rice and refusing to sell it again, except at fabulous prices.*

The treatment of the aborigines was, naturally, most frightful in plantation-colonies destined for export trade only, such as the West Indies, and in rich and well-populated

* In the year 1866 more than a million Hindus died of hunger in the province of Orissa alone. Nevertheless, the attempt was made to enrich the Indian treasury by the price at which the necessaries of life were sold to the starving people.

countries, such as Mexico and India, that were given over to plunder. But even in the colonies properly so-called, the Christian character of primitive accumulation did not belie itself. Those sober virtuosi of Protestantism, the Puritans of New England, in 1703, by decrees of their Assembly set a premium of £40 on every Indian scalp and every captured red-skin: in 1720 a premium of £100 on every scalp; in 1744, after Massachusetts-Bay had proclaimed a certain tribe as rebels, the following prices: for a male scalp of 12 years and upwards £100 (new currency), for a male prisoner £105, for women and children prisoners £50, for scalps of women and children £50. Some decades later, the colonial system took its revenge on the descendants of the pious pilgrim fathers, who had grown seditious in the meantime. At English instigation and for English pay they were tomahawked by red-skins. The British Parliament proclaimed bloodhounds and scalping as "means that God and Nature had given into its hand."

The colonial system ripened, like a hot-house, trade and navigation. The "societies Monopolia"* of Luther were powerful levers for concentration of capital. The colonies secured a market for the budding manufactures, and, through the monopoly of the market, an increased accumulation. The treasures captured outside Europe by undisguised looting, enslavement, and murder, floated back to the mother-country and were there turned into capital. Holland, which first fully developed the colonial system, in 1648 stood already in the acme of its commercial greatness. It was "in almost exclusive possession of the East Indian trade and the commerce between the south-east and north-west of Europe. Its fisheries, marine, manufactures, surpassed those of any other country. The total capital of the Republic was probably more important than that of all the rest of Europe put together."** Gülich forgets to add that by 1648, the people of Holland were more over-worked, poorer and more brutally oppressed than those of all the rest of Europe put together.

To-day industrial supremacy implies commercial suprem-

* "Gesellschaften Monopolia."—*Ed.*

** G. Gülich: "Geschichtliche Darstellung, etc.," Jena 1830, Vol. I, p. 371.—*Ed.*

acy. In the period of manufacture properly so-called, it is, on the other hand, the commercial supremacy that gives industrial predominance. Hence the preponderant rôle that the colonial system plays at that time. It was "the strange God" who perched himself on the altar cheek by jowl with the old Gods of Europe, and one fine day with a shove and a kick chucked them all of a heap. It proclaimed surplus-value making as the sole end and aim of humanity.

The system of public credit, *i.e.*, of national debts, whose origin we discover in Genoa and Venice as early as the middle ages, took possession of Europe generally during the manufacturing period. The colonial system with its maritime trade and commercial wars served as a forcing-house for it. Thus it first took root in Holland. National debts, *i.e.*, the alienation of the state—whether despotic, constitutional or republican—marked with its stamp the capitalistic era. The only part of the so-called national wealth that actually enters into the collective possessions of modern peoples is—their national debt.* Hence, as a necessary consequence, the modern doctrine that a nation becomes the richer the more deeply it is in debt. Public credit becomes the *credo* of capital. And with the rise of national debt-making, want of faith in the national debt takes the place of the blasphemy against the Holy Ghost, which may not be forgiven.

The public debt becomes one of the most powerful levers of primitive accumulation. As with the stroke of an enchanter's wand, it endows barren money with the power of breeding and thus turns it into capital, without the necessity of its exposing itself to the troubles and risks inseparable from its employment in industry or even in usury. The state-creditors actually give nothing away, for the sum lent is transformed into public bonds, easily negotiable, which go on functioning in their hands just as so much hard cash would. But further, apart from the class of lazy annuitants thus created, and from the improvised wealth of the financiers, middlemen between the government and the nation—as also apart from the tax-farmers, merchants, private manufacturers, to whom

* William Cobbett remarks that in England all public institutions are designated "royal"; as compensation for this, however, there is the "national" debt.

a good part of every national loan renders the service of a capital fallen from heaven—the national debt has given rise to joint-stock companies, to dealings in negotiable effects of all kinds, and to agiotage, in a word to stock-exchange gambling and the modern bankocracy.

At their birth the great banks, decorated with national titles, were only associations of private speculators, who placed themselves by the side of governments, and, thanks to the privileges they received, were in a position to advance money to the State. Hence the accumulation of the national debt has no more infallible measure than the successive rise in the stock of these banks, whose full development dates from the founding of the Bank of England in 1694. The Bank of England began with lending its money to the Government at 8%; at the same time it was empowered by Parliament to coin money out of the same capital, by lending it again to the public in the form of banknotes. It was allowed to use these notes for discounting bills, making advances on commodities, and for buying the precious metals. It was not long ere this credit-money, made by the bank itself, became the coin in which the Bank of England made its loans to the State, and paid, on account of the State, the interest on the public debt. It was not enough that the bank gave with one hand and took back more with the other; it remained, even whilst receiving, the eternal creditor of the nation down to the last shilling advanced. Gradually it became inevitably the receptacle of the metallic hoard of the country, and the centre of gravity of all commercial credit. What effect was produced on their contemporaries by the sudden uprising of this brood of bankocrats, financiers, rentiers, brokers, stock-jobbers, &c., is proved by the writings of that time, *e.g.*, by Bolingbroke's.*

With the national debt arose an international credit system, which often conceals one of the sources of primitive accumulation in this or that people. Thus the vil-

* "Si les Tartares inondaient l'Europe aujourd'hui, il faudrait bien des affaires pour leur faire entendre ce que c'est qu'un financier parmi nous." Montesquieu, "Esprit des lois," t. IV., p. 33, éd. Londres, 1769. ("If the Tartars were to invade Europe today, we would have our hands full to make it clear to them what a financier is among us."—*Ed.*)

lainies of the Venetian thieving system formed one of the secret bases of the capital-wealth of Holland to whom Venice in her decadence lent large sums of money. So also was it with Holland and England. By the beginning of the 18th century the Dutch manufactures were far outstripped. Holland had ceased to be the nation preponderant in commerce and industry. One of its main lines of business, therefore, from 1701-1776, is the lending out of enormous amounts of capital, especially to its great rival England. The same thing is going on to-day between England and the United States. A great deal of capital, which appears to-day in the United States without any certificate of birth, was yesterday, in England, the capitalised blood of children.

As the national debt finds its support in the public revenue, which must cover the yearly payments for interest, &c., the modern system of taxation was the necessary complement of the system of national loans. The loans enable the government to meet extraordinary expenses, without the tax-payers feeling it immediately, but they necessitate, as a consequence, increased taxes. On the other hand, the raising of taxation caused by the accumulation of debts contracted one after another, compels the government always to have recourse to new loans for new extraordinary expenses. Modern fiscality, whose pivot is formed by taxes on the most necessary means of subsistence (thereby increasing their price), thus contains within itself the germ of automatic progression. Over-taxation is not an incident, but rather a principle. In Holland, therefore, where this system was first inaugurated, the great patriot, De Witt, has in his "Maxims" extolled it as the best system for making the wage-labourer submissive, frugal, industrious, and overburdened with labour. The destructive influence that it exercises on the condition of the wage-labourer concerns us less however, here, than the forcible expropriation, resulting from it, of peasants, artisans, and in a word, all elements of the lower middle-class. On this there are not two opinions, even among the bourgeois economists. Its expropriating efficacy is still further heightened by the system of protection, which forms one of its integral parts.

The great part that the public debt, and the fiscal system corresponding with it, has played in the capitalisation of wealth and the expropriation of the masses, has led many writers, like Cobbett, Doubleday and others, to seek in this, incorrectly, the fundamental cause of the misery of the modern peoples.

The system of protection was an artificial means of manufacturing manufacturers, of expropriating independent labourers, of capitalising the national means of production and subsistence, of forcibly abbreviating the transition from the mediaeval to the modern mode of production. The European states tore one another to pieces about the patent of this invention, and, once entered into the service of the surplus-value makers, did not merely lay under contribution in the pursuit of this purpose their own people, indirectly through protective duties, directly through export premiums. They also forcibly rooted out, in their dependent countries, all industry, as, *e.g.*, England did with the Irish woollen manufacture. On the continent of Europe, after Colbert's example, the process was much simplified. The primitive industrial capital, here, came in part directly out of the state treasury. "Why," cries Mirabeau, "why go so far to seek the cause of the manufacturing glory of Saxony before the war? 180,000,000 of debts contracted by the sovereigns!"*

Colonial system, public debts, heavy taxes, protection, commercial wars, &c., these children of the true manufacturing period, increase gigantically during the infancy of Modern Industry. The birth of the latter is heralded by a great slaughter of the innocents. Like the royal navy, the factories were recruited by means of the press-gang. Blasé as Sir F. M. Eden is as to the horrors of the expropriation of the agricultural population from the soil, from the last third of the 15th century to his own time; with all the self-satisfaction with which he rejoices in this process, "essential" for establishing capitalistic agriculture and "the due proportion between arable and pasture land"—he does not show, however, the same economic insight in respect to the necessity of child-stealing and child-slavery

* Mirabeau, "De la Monarchie Prussienne sous Frédéric le Grand," Londres 1788, t. VI, p. 101.

for the transformation of manufacturing exploitation into factory exploitation, and the establishment of the "true relation" between capital and labour-power. He says: "It may, perhaps, be worthy the attention of the public to consider, whether any manufacture, which, in order to be carried on successfully, requires that cottages and work-houses should be ransacked for poor children; that they should be employed by turns during the greater part of the night and robbed of that rest which, though indispensable to all, is most required by the young; and that numbers of both sexes, of different ages and dispositions, should be collected together in such a manner that the contagion of example cannot but lead to profligacy and debauchery; will add to the sum of individual or national felicity?"*

"In the counties of Derbyshire, Nottinghamshire, and more particularly in Lancashire," says Fielden, "the newly-invented machinery was used in large factories built on the sides of streams capable of turning the water-wheel. Thousands of hands were suddenly required in these places, remote from towns; and Lancashire, in particular, being, till then, comparatively thinly populated and barren, a population was all that she now wanted. The small and nimble fingers of little children being by very far the most in request, the custom instantly sprang up of procuring *apprentices* from the different parish workhouses of London, Birmingham, and elsewhere. Many, many thousands of these little, hapless creatures were sent down into the north, being from the age of 7 to the age of 13 or 14 years old. The custom was for the master to clothe his apprentices and to feed and lodge them in an "apprentice house" near the factory; overseers were appointed to see to the works, whose interest it was to work the children to the utmost, because their pay was in proportion to the quantity of work that they could exact. Cruelty was, of course, the consequence. . . . In many of the manufacturing districts, but particularly, I am afraid, in the guilty county to which I belong [Lancashire], cruelties the most heartrending were practised upon the unoffending and friendless creatures who were thus con-

* Eden, "The State of the Poor: or an History of the Labouring Classes in England, from the Conquest to the Present Period," Vol. I, Book II, Ch. I, p. 421.

signed to the charge of master-manufacturers; they were harassed to the brink of death by excess of labour ... were flogged, fettered and tortured in the most exquisite refinement of cruelty; ... they were in many cases starved to the bone while flogged to their work and ... even in some instances ... were driven to commit suicide.... The beautiful and romantic valleys of Derbyshire, Nottinghamshire and Lancashire, secluded from the public eye, became the dismal solitudes of torture, and of many a murder. The profits of manufacturers were enormous; but this only whetted the appetite that it should have satisfied, and therefore the manufacturers had recourse to an expedient that seemed to secure to them those profits without any possibility of limit; they began the practice of what is termed 'night-working,' that is, having tired one set of hands, by working them throughout the day, they had another set ready to go on working throughout the night; the day-set getting into the beds that the night-set had just quitted, and in their turn again, the night-set getting into the beds that the day-set quitted in the morning. It is a common tradition in Lancashire, that the beds *never get cold.*"*

With the development of capitalist production during

* John Fielden, "The Curse of the Factory System: or, a short account of the origin of factory cruelties, etc." London 1836, pp. 5, 6. On the earlier infamies of the factory system, cf. Dr. Aikin (1795), l.c., p. 219, and Gisborne: "Enquiry into the Duties of Men," 1795, Vol. II. When the steam-engine transplanted the factories from the country waterfalls to the middle of towns, the "abstemious" surplus-value maker found the child-material ready to his hand, without being forced to seek slaves from the work-houses. When Sir R. Peel (father of the "minister of plausibility") brought in his bill for the protection of children, in 1815, Francis Horner, lumen of the Bullion Committee and intimate friend of Ricardo, said in the House of Commons: "It is notorious, that with a bankrupt's effects, a gang, if he might use the word, of these children had been put up to sale, and were advertised publicly as part of the property. A most atrocious instance had been brought before the Court of King's Bench two years before, in which a number of these boys, apprenticed by a parish in London to one manufacturer, had been transferred to another, and had been found by some benevolent persons in a state of absolute famine. Another case more horrible had come to his knowledge while on a [Parliamentary] Committee ... that not many years ago, an agreement had been made between a London parish and a Lancashire manufacturer, by which it was stipulated, that with every 20 sound children one idiot should be taken."

the manufacturing period, the public opinion of Europe had lost the last remnant of shame and conscience. The nations bragged cynically of every infamy that served them as a means to capitalistic accumulation. Read, *e.g.*, the naïve Annals of Commerce of the worthy A. Anderson. Here it is trumpeted forth as a triumph of English statecraft that at the Peace of Utrecht, England extorted from the Spaniards by the Asiento Treaty the privilege of being allowed to ply the negro-trade, until then only carried on between Africa and the English West Indies, between Africa and Spanish America as well. England thereby acquired the right of supplying Spanish America until 1743 with 4,800 negroes yearly. This threw, at the same time, an official cloak over British smuggling. Liverpool waxed fat on the slave-trade. This was its method of primitive accumulation. And, even to the present day, Liverpool "respectability" is the Pindar of the slave-trade which—compare the work of Aikin (1795) already quoted—"has coincided with that spirit of bold adventure which has characterised the trade of Liverpool and rapidly carried it to its present state of prosperity; has occasioned vast employment for shipping and sailors, and greatly augmented the demand for the manufactures of the country" (p. 339). Liverpool employed in the slave-trade, in 1730, 15 ships; in 1751, 53; in 1760, 74; in 1770, 96; and in 1792, 132.

Whilst the cotton industry introduced child-slavery in England, it gave in the United States a stimulus to the transformation of the earlier, more or less patriarchal slavery, into a system of commercial exploitation. In fact, the veiled slavery of the wage-workers in Europe needed, for its pedestal, slavery pure and simple in the new world.*

Tantae molis erat,** to establish the "eternal laws of Nature" of the capitalist mode of production, to complete the process of separation between labourers and conditions of labour, to transform, at one pole, the social means of production and subsistence into capital, at the opposite pole, the mass of the population into wage-labourers, into "free

* In 1790, there were in the English West Indies ten slaves for one free man, in the French fourteen for one, in the Dutch twenty-three for one. (Henry Broughman: "An Inquiry into the Colonial Policy of the European Powers," Edin, 1803, Vol. II, p. 74.)

** It took so much effort.—*Ed.*

labouring poor," that artificial product of modern society.* If money, according to Augier,** "comes into the world with a congenital blood-stain on one cheek," capital comes dripping from head to foot, from every pore, with blood and dirt.***

Published according
to the English text of *Capital*,
Vol. I, Moscow, 1958

---

* The phrase, "labouring poor", is found in English legislation from the moment when the class of wage-labourers becomes noticeable. This term is used in opposition, on the one hand, to the "idle poor," beggars, etc., on the other to those labourers, who, pigeons not yet plucked, are still possessors of their own means of labour. From the Statute Book it passed into Political Economy, and was handed down by Culpeper, J. Child, etc., to Adam Smith and Eden. After this, one can judge of the good faith of the "execrable political cant-monger," Edmund Burke, when he called the expression, "labouring poor,"—"execrable political cant." This sycophant who, in the pay of the English oligarchy, played the romantic laudator temporis acti against the French Revolution, just as, in the pay of the North American Colonies, at the beginning of the American troubles, he had played the Liberal against the English oligarchy, was an out and out vulgar bourgeois. "The laws of commerce are the laws of Nature, and therefore the laws of God." (E. Burke, "Thoughts and Details on Scarcity, Originally Presented to the Rt. Hon. W. Pitt in the month of November 1795." London 1800, pp. 31, 32.) No wonder that, true to the laws of God and of Nature, he always sold himself in the best market. A very good portrait of this Edmund Burke, during his liberal time, is to be found in the writings of the Rev. Mr. Tucker. Tucker was a parson and a Tory, but, for the rest, an honourable man and a competent political economist. In face of the infamous cowardice of character that reigns to-day, and believes most devoutly in "the laws of commerce," it is our bounden duty again and again to brand the Burkes, who only differ from their successors in one thing—talent.

** Marie Augier: "Du Crédit Public." Paris, 1842.

*** "Capital is said by a Quarterly Reviewer to fly turbulence and strife, and to be timid, which is very true; but this is very incompletely stating the question. Capital eschews no profit, or very small profit, just as Nature was formerly said to abhor a vacuum. With adequate profit, capital is very bold. A certain 10 per cent will ensure its employment anywhere; 20 per cent, certain will produce eagerness: 50 per cent., positive audacity; 100 per cent, will make it ready to trample on all human laws; 300 per cent., and there is not a crime at which it will scruple, nor a risk it will not run, even to the chance of its owner being hanged. If turbulence and strife will bring a profit, it will freely encourage both. Smuggling and the slave-trade have amply proved all that is here stated." (T. J. Dunning, "Trades' Unions and Strikes: Their Philosophy and Intention." London 1860, pp. 35, 36.)

Karl Marx

HISTORICAL FACTS ABOUT MERCHANT'S CAPITAL
(Excerpt from Chapter XX of *Capital*, Volume III)

There is no doubt—and it is precisely this fact which has led to wholly erroneous conceptions—that in the 16th and 17th centuries the great revolutions, which took place in commerce with the geographical discoveries and speeded the development of merchant's capital, constitute one of the principal elements in furthering the transition from feudal to capitalist mode of production. The sudden expansion of the world-market, the multiplication of circulating commodities, the competitive zeal of the European nations to possess themselves of the products of Asia and the treasures of America, and the colonial system—all contributed materially toward destroying the feudal fetters on production. However, in its first period—the manufacturing period—the modern mode of production developed only where the conditions for it had taken shape within the Middle Ages. Compare, for instance, Holland with Portugal.* And when in the 16th, and partially still in the 17th, century the sudden expansion of commerce and emergence of a new world-

* How predominant fishery, manufacture and agriculture, aside from other circumstances, were as the basis for Holland's development, has already been explained by 18th-century writers, such as Massie. In contradistinction to the former view, which underrated the volume and importance of commerce in Asia, in Antiquity, and in the Middle Ages, it has now come to be the custom to extremely overrate it. The best antidote against this conception is to study the imports and exports of England in the early 18th century and to compare them with modern imports and exports. And yet they were incomparably greater than those of any former trading nation. (See Anderson, *History of Commerce*.)

market overwhelmingly contributed to the fall of the old mode of production and the rise of capitalist production, this was accomplished conversely on the basis of the already existing capitalist mode of production. The world-market itself forms the basis for this mode of production. On the other hand, the immanent necessity of this mode of production to produce on an ever-enlarged scale tends to extend the world-market continually, so that it is not commerce in this case which revolutionises industry, but industry which constantly revolutionises commerce. Commercial supremacy itself is now linked with the prevalence to a greater or lesser degree of conditions for a large industry. Compare, for instance, England and Holland. The history of the decline of Holland as the ruling trading nation is the history of the subordination of merchant's capital to industrial capital. The obstacles presented by the internal solidity and organization of pre-capitalistic, national modes of production to the corrosive influence of commerce are strikingly illustrated in the intercourse of the English with India and China. The broad basis of the mode of production here is formed by the unity of small-scale agriculture and home industry, to which in India we should add the form of village communities built upon the common ownership of land, which, incidentally, was the original form in China as well. In India the English lost no time in exercising their direct political and economic power, as rulers and landlords, to disrupt these small economic communities.* English commerce exerted a revolutionary influence on these communities and tore them apart only insofar as the low prices of its goods served to destroy the spinning and weaving industries, which were an ancient integrating element of this unity of industrial and agricultural production. And even so this work of dissolution proceeds very gradually. And still more slowly in China, where it is not reinforced by direct political power. The substan-

* If any nation's history, then the history of the English in India is a string of futile and really absurd (in practice infamous) economic experiments. In Bengal they created a caricature of large-scale English landed estates; in south-eastern India a caricature of small parcelled property; in the north-west they did all they could to transform the Indian economic community with common ownership of the soil into a caricature of itself.

tial economy and saving in time afforded by the association of agriculture with manufacture put up a stubborn resistance to the products of the big industries, whose prices include the *faux frais* of the circulation process which pervades them. Unlike the English, Russian commerce, on the other hand, leaves the economic groundwork of Asiatic production untouched.*

Published according to the English text of *Capital*, Vol. III, Moscow 1959

Translated from the German

---

* Since Russia has been making frantic exertions to develop its own capitalist production, which is exclusively dependent upon its domestic and the neighbouring Asiatic market, this is also beginning to change.—*F.E.*

Karl Marx

ENGLAND'S BALANCE OF TRADE

(Excerpt from *Capital*, Volume III, Chapter XXXV, "Precious Metal and Rate of Exchange." II. The Rate of Exchange)

India alone has to pay 5 million in tribute for "good government," interest and dividends on British capital, etc., not counting the sums sent home annually by officials as savings from their salaries, or by English merchants as part of their profit to be invested in England. Every British colony continually has to make large remittances for the same reason. Most of the banks in Australia, the West Indies, and Canada, have been founded with English capital, and the dividends are payable in England. In the same way, England owns many foreign securities—European, North American and South American—on which it draws interest. In addition to this it has interests in foreign railways, canals, mines, etc., with corresponding dividends. Remittance on all these items is made almost exclusively in products over and above the amount of English exports. On the other hand what is sent from England to owners of English securities abroad and for consumption by Englishmen abroad, is insignificant in comparison.

Published according
to the English text of *Capital*,
Vol. III, Moscow 1959

Frederick Engels

SUPPLEMENT TO *CAPITAL*, VOLUME III

II. THE STOCK EXCHANGE

(Excerpt)

7. Then colonisation. Today this is purely a subsidiary of the stock exchange, in whose interests the European powers divided Africa a few years ago, and the French conquered Tunis and Tonkin. Africa leased directly to companies (Niger, South Africa, German South-West and German East Africa), and Mashonaland and Natal seized by Rhodes for the stock exchange.

Published according to the English text of *Capital*, Vol. III, Moscow 1959

Translated from the German

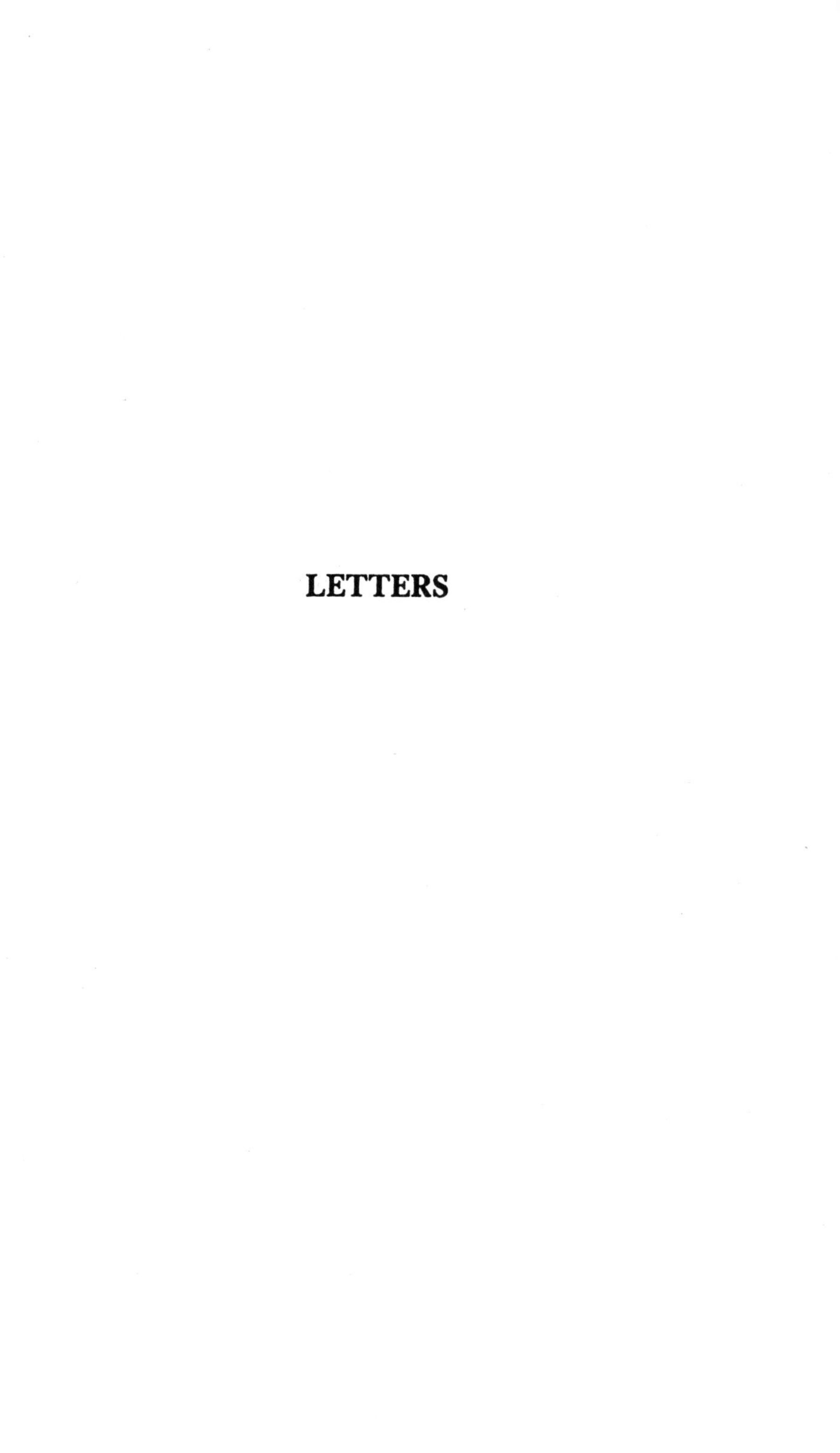

LETTERS

MARX TO ENGELS

London, June 2, 1853

...Bernier rightly considered the basis of all phenomena in the East—he refers to Turkey, Persia, Hindustan—to be the *absence of private property in land*. This is the real key, even to the Oriental heaven....

ENGELS TO MARX

Manchester, June 6, 1853

...The absence of property in land is indeed the key to the whole of the East. Herein lies its political and religious history. But how does it come about that the Orientals did not arrive at landed property, even in its feudal form? I think it is mainly due to the climate, taken in connection with the nature of the soil, especially with the great stretches of desert which extend from the Sahara straight across Arabia, Persia, India and Tartary up to the highest Asiatic plateau. Artificial irrigation is here the first condition of agriculture and this is a matter either for the communes, the provinces or the central government. An Oriental government never had more than three departments: finance (plunder at home), war (plunder at home and abroad), and public works (provision for reproduction). The British Government in India has administered Nos. 1 and 2 in a rather narrow-minded spirit and dropped No. 3 entirely, so that Indian agriculture is being ruined. Free competition discredits itself there completely. This artificial fertilisation of the land, which immediately ceased when the irrigation system fell into decay, explains the otherwise curious fact that whole stretches which were once brilliantly cultivated are now waste and bare (Palmyra, Petra, the ruins in the Yemen, districts in Egypt, Persia and Hindustan); it explains the fact that one single devastating war could depopulate a country for centuries and strip it of its whole civilisation....

MARX TO ENGELS

London, June 14, 1853

...Your article on Switzerland was of course a direct smack at the leading articles in the *Tribune* (against centralization, etc.), and *its* Carey. I have continued this hidden warfare in a first article on India,[98] in which the destruction of the native industry by England is described as *revolutionary*. This will be very shocking to them. As for the rest, the whole rule of Britain in India was swinish, and is to this day.

The stationary character of this part of Asia—despite all the aimless movements on the political surface—is fully explained by two circumstances which supplement each other: 1) the public works were the business of the central government; 2) besides this the whole empire, not counting the few larger towns, was divided into *villages*, each of which possessed a completely separate organisation and formed a little world in itself. In a Parliamentary report these villages are described as follows:

"A village, geographically considered, is a tract of country comprising some 100 or 1,000 acres of arable and waste lands; politically viewed, it resembles a corporation or township. Every village is, and appears always to have been, in fact, a separate community, or republic. Officials: 1) The *Potail*, Goud, Mundil, etc., as he is termed in different languages, is the head inhabitant, who has generally the superintendence of the affairs of the village, settles the disputes of the inhabitants, attends to the police, and performs the duty of collecting the revenue within the village.... 2) The *Curnum*, Shanboag, or Putwaree, is the register. 3) The *Tali-*

ary, or *Sthulwar* and 4) the *Totie,* are severally the watchmen of the village and of the crops. 5) The *Neerguntee* distributes the water of the streams or reservoirs in just proportion to the several fields. 6) The *Joshee,* or astrologer, announces the seed-times and harvests, and the lucky or unlucky days or hours for all the operations of farming. 7) The *smith* and 8) the *carpenter* frame the rude instruments of husbandry, and the ruder dwelling of the farmer. 9) The *potter* fabricates the only utensils of the village. 10) The *washerman* keeps clean the few garments.... 11) The *barber* and 12) the *silversmith,* who often at the same time is also poet and *schoolmaster* of the village—all in one person. Then comes the *Brahmin* for worship. Under this simple form of municipal government, the inhabitants of the country have lived from time immemorial. The boundaries of the villages have been but seldom altered; and although the villages themselves have been sometimes injured, and even desolated, by war, famine and disease, the same name, the same limits, the same interests, and even the same families have continued for ages. The inhabitants give themselves no trouble about the breaking up and division of kingdoms; while the village remains entire, they care not to what power it is transferred, or to what sovereign it devolves; its internal economy remains unchanged."

The Potail is usually hereditary. In some of these communities the lands of the village are cultivated in common, in most cases each occupant tills his own field. Within them there is slavery and the caste system. The waste lands are for common pasture. Domestic weaving and spinning is done by wives and daughters. These idyllic republics, which only jealously guard the *boundaries of their village* against the neighbouring village, still exist in a fairly perfect form in the North-Western parts of India, which were recent English accessions. I do not think anyone could imagine a more solid foundation for stagnant Asiatic despotism. And however much the English may have hibernicised the country, the breaking up of those stereotyped primitive forms was the *sine qua non* for Europeanisation. Alone the tax-gatherer was not the man to achieve this. The destruction of their archaic industry was necessary to deprive the villages of their self-supporting character.

In Bali, an island off the east coast of Java, this Hindu organization, together with Hindu religion, is still intact—its traces, moreover, like those of Hindu influence, are to be found throughout Java. As to the *question of property*, this is a very *controversial* one among the English writers on India. In the broken hill-country south of Krishna, property in land does seem to have existed. In Java on the other hand Sir Stamford Raffles, former *English* Governor of Java, observes in his *History of Java* that "the sovereign was absolute landlord" of the whole surface of the land "where rent to any considerable amount was attainable." In any case it seems to have been the Mohammedans who first established the principle of "no property in land" throughout the whole of Asia.

About the villages mentioned above I must also note that they already figure in Manu* and that the basis of the whole organisation is, according to him: ten villages under a superior collector, then a hundred and then a thousand....

* Ancient Hindu law.—*Ed.*

ENGELS TO MARX

Manchester, May 23, 1856

Dear Marx,

During our tour in Ireland we came from Dublin to Galway on the west coast, then twenty miles north inland, then to Limerick, down the Shannon to Tarbert, Tralee, Killarney and back to Dublin—a total of about 450 to 500 English miles inside the country itself, so that we have seen about two-thirds of the whole of it. With the exception of Dublin, which bears the same relation to London as Düsseldorf does to Berlin and has quite the character of a small one-time capital, all English-built, too, the look of the entire country, and especially of the towns, is as if one were in France or Northern Italy. Gendarmes, priests, lawyers, bureaucrats, country squires in pleasing profusion and a total absence of any industry at all, so that it would be difficult to understand what all these parasitic growths live on if the distress of the peasants did not supply the other half of the picture. "Strong measures" are visible in every corner of the country, the government meddles with everything, of so-called self-government there is not a trace. Ireland may be regarded as the first English colony and as one which because of its proximity is still governed exactly in the old way, and one can already notice here that the so-called liberty of English citizens is based on the oppression of the colonies. I have never seen so many gendarmes in any country, and the sodden look of the bibulous Prussian gendarme is developed to its highest perfection here among the constabulary, who are armed with carbines, bayonets and handcuffs.

Characteristic of this country are its ruins, the oldest dating from the fifth and sixth centuries, the latest from the nineteenth—with every intervening period. The most ancient are all churches: after 1100, churches and castles; after 1800, houses of peasants. The whole of the west, especially in the neighbourhood of Galway, is covered with ruined peasant houses, most of which have only been deserted since 1846. I never thought that famine could have such tangible reality. Whole villages are devastated, and there among them lie the splendid parks of the lesser landlords, who are almost the only people still living there, mostly lawyers.

Famine, emigration and clearances[99] together have accomplished this. There are not even cattle to be seen in the fields. The land is an utter desert which nobody wants. In County Clare, south of Galway, it is somewhat better. Here there are at least cattle, and the hills towards Limerick are excellently cultivated, mostly by Scottish farmers, the ruins have been cleared away and the country has a bourgeois appearance. In the South-West there are a lot of mountains and bogs but there is also wonderfully luxuriant forest land; beyond that again fine pastures, especially in Tipperary, and towards Dublin there is land which, one can see, is gradually coming into the hands of big farmers.

The country was completely ruined by the English wars of conquest from 1100 to 1850 (for in reality both the wars and the state of siege lasted as long as that). It has been established as a fact that most of the ruins were produced by destruction during the wars. The people itself has got its peculiar character from this, and for all their national Irish fanaticism the fellows feel that they are no longer at home in their own country. Ireland for the Saxon! That is now being realized. The Irishman knows that he cannot compete with the Englishman, who comes equipped with means superior in every respect; emigration will go on until the predominantly, indeed almost exclusively, Celtic character of the population is gone to the dogs. How often have the Irish started out to achieve something, and every time they have been crushed, politically and industrially. By consistent oppression they have been artificially converted into an utterly impoverished nation and now, as everyone knows, fulfil the function of supplying England, America, Australia, etc., with prostitutes, casual labourers, pimps, pickpockets, swindlers, beggars and other rabble. Impoverishment characterizes the aristocracy too. The landowners, who everywhere else have become bourgeoisified, are here reduced to complete poverty. Their country-seats are surrounded by enormous, amazingly beautiful parks, but all around is waste land, and where the money is to come from it is impossible to see. These fellows are droll enough to make your sides burst with laughing. Of mixed blood, mostly tall, strong, handsome chaps, they all wear enormous moustaches under colossal Roman noses, give themselves the false military airs of retired colonels, travel around the country after all sorts of pleasures, and if one makes an inquiry, they haven't a penny, are laden with debts, and live in dread of the Encumbered Estates Court.

Concerning the ways and means by which England rules this country—repression and corruption—long before Bonaparte attempted this, I shall write shortly if you won't come over soon. How about it?

Yours,

F. E.

MARX TO ENGELS

January 14, 1858

...Your article is splendid in style and manner and reminiscent of the best days of the *Neue Rheinische Zeitung*. As for Windham, he may be a very bad general, but this time the chap had the misfortune—which was his luck at Redan—of leading recruits into battle. I am generally of the opinion that this second army dedicated by the English to the Indians—and not a single man of it will return—can in no way match the first, which appears to have been wiped out almost entirely, in bravery, self-reliance and steadiness. As for the effect of the climate on the troops, I have shown by means of accurate calculations in various articles—so long as I ran the military department provisionally—that the death rate was disproportionately greater than the official English reports intimated. With the drain of men and bullion which it must cost the English, India is now our best ally....

MARX TO ENGELS

London, [October 8,] 1858

. . . We cannot deny that bourgeois society has experienced its sixteenth century a second time—a sixteenth century which will, I hope, sound the death-knell of bourgeois society just as the first one thrust it into existence. The specific task of bourgeois society is the establishment of a world market, at least in outline, and of production based upon this world market. As the world is round, this seems to have been completed by the colonization of California and Australia and the opening up of China and Japan. The difficult question for us is this: on the Continent the revolution is imminent and will immediately assume a socialist character. Is it not bound to be crushed in this little corner, considering that in a far greater territory the movement of bourgeois society is still in the ascendant?

As to what specially concerns China, I have assured myself by an exact analysis of the movement of trade since 1836, *first*, that the increase of English and American exports (1844-46) proved in 1847 to be a pure fraud and that also in the following ten years the average remained nearly stationary, while the imports into England and America from China grew enormously; *second*, that the opening up of the five ports and the seizure of Hong-Kong only resulted in the trade passing from Canton to Shanghai. The other "emporiums" do not count. The chief reason for the failure of this market appears to be the opium trade, to which in fact any increase in the export trade to China is continually confined; but added to this is the internal economic organisation of the country, its minute agriculture, etc., which it will take an enormous time to break down. England's present treaty with China, which in my opinion was worked out by Palmerston in conjunction with the Petersburg Cabinet and given to Lord Elgin on his journey, is a mockery from beginning to end....

MARX TO ENGELS

November 20, 1865

...The Jamaica affair[100] is typical of the meanness of "true Englishmen." Those chaps have no business rebuking the Russians. But, says the brave *Times,* these damned rogues enjoyed "all the liberties of an Anglo-Saxon Constitution." That is, they enjoyed the liberty, among other things, to be taxed to their ears so as to provide the planters with the means to import coolies and thus to reduce their own labour market to a minimum. And it is these squeamish English dogs who shouted about the "beast Butler" for having hanged *one* man and not permitting the yellow, diamond-hung planter wenches to spit in the faces of the Federal soldiers.[101] For a fuller exposure of English hypocrisy after the American war we only lacked the Irish affair and the Jamaica butcheries....

ENGELS TO MARX

December 1, 1865

...Each successive mail brings ever more startling news of the Jamaica infamies. The letters of English officers about their heroic exploits against unarmed Niggers are priceless. The spirit of the British army has at last emerged unblushingly. "The soldiers enjoy it." Even the *Manchester Guardian* has been compelled this time to come out against the officials in Jamaica....

MARX TO ENGELS

November 2, 1867

...The proceedings against the Fenians in Manchester were every inch what could be expected. You will have seen what a row "our people" kicked up in the Reform League. I have sought in every way to provoke this manifestation of the English workers in support of Fenianism....

Previously I thought Ireland's separation from Britain impossible. Now I think it inevitable, although after separation may come *federation.* How the English carry on is evidenced by the agricultural statistics for the current year, which appeared a few days ago. Furthermore, the form of these evictions. The Irish viceroy, Lord Abicorn (that seems to be his name), "cleared" his estate in the last few weeks by forcibly evicting thousands of people. Among them were prosperous tenants, whose improvements and investments were thus confiscated! In no other European country did foreign rule adopt this form of direct expropriation of the stock population. The Russians confiscate solely on political grounds; the Prussians in Western Prussia buy up....

MARX TO ENGELS

London, November 30, 1867

...What the English do not yet know is that since 1846 the economic content and therefore also the political aim of English domination in Ireland have entered into an entirely new phase, and that, precisely because of this, Fenianism is characterized by a socialist tendency (in a negative sense, directed against the appropriation of the soil) and by being a lower orders movement. What can be more ridiculous than to confuse the barbarities of Elizabeth or Cromwell, who wanted to supplant the Irish by English colonists (in the Roman sense), with the present system, which wants to supplant them by sheep, pigs and oxen! The system of 1801-46, with its rackrents and middlemen, collapsed in 1846. (During that period evictions were exceptional, occurring mainly in Leinster where the land is especially good for cattle raising.) The repeal of the Corn Laws, partly the result of or at any rate hastened by the Irish famine, deprived Ireland of its *monopoly* of England's corn supply in normal times. Wool and meat became the slogan, hence conversion of tillage into pasture. Hence from then onwards systematic consolidation of farms. The Encumbered Estates Act, which turned a mass of previously enriched middlemen into landlords, hastened the process. *Clearing of the Estate of Ireland!* is now the one purpose of English rule in Ireland. The *stupid* English Government in London knows nothing of course itself of this immense change since 1846. But the Irish know it. From *Meagher's Proclamation* (1848) down to the election manifesto of *Hennessy* (Tory and Ur quhartite) (1866), the Irish have expressed their consciousness of it in the clearest and most forcible manner.

The question now is, what shall *we* advise the *English* workers? In my opinion they must make the *repeal of the Union* (in short, the affair of 1783, only democratised and adapted to the conditions of the time) an article of their *pronunziamento*. This is the only *legal* and therefore only possible form of Irish emancipation which can be admitted in the programme of an *English* party. Experience must show later whether a mere personal union can continue to subsist between the two countries. I half think it can if it takes place in time.

What the Irish need is:

1) Self-government and independence from England.

2) An agrarian revolution. With the best intentions in the world the English cannot accomplish this for them, but they can give them the legal means of accomplishing it for themselves.

3) *Protective tariffs against England.* Between 1783 and 1801 every branch of Irish industry flourished. The Union, which overthrew the protective tariffs established by the Irish Parliament, destroyed all industrial life in Ireland. The bit of linen industry is no compensation whatever. The Union of 1801 had just the same effect on Irish industry as the measures for the suppression of the Irish woollen industry, etc., taken by the English Parliament under Anne, George II, and others. Once the Irish are independent, necessity will turn them into protectionists, as it did Canada, Australia, etc. Before I present my views in the Central Council[102] (next Tuesday, this time fortunately *without* reporters), I would like you to give me your opinion in a few lines....

MARX TO L. KUGELMANN

London, April 6, 1868

. . . The Irish question predominates here just now. It has been exploited by Gladstone and company, of course, only in order to get into office again, and, above all, to have an *electoral cry* at the next elections, which will be based on household suffrage. *For the moment* this turn of affairs is bad for the workers' party; the intriguers among the workers, such as Odger and Potter, who want to get into the next Parliament, have now a new *excuse* for attaching themselves to the bourgeois Liberals.

However, this is only a *penalty* which England—and consequently also the English working class—is paying for the great crime it has been committing for many centuries against Ireland. And in the long run it will benefit the English working class itself. You see, the *English* Established *Church in Ireland*[103]—or what they call here the *Irish Church*—is the religious bulwark of *English landlordism* in Ireland, and at the same time the outpost of the Established Church in England itself. (I am speaking here of the Established Church as a *landowner*.) The overthrow of the Established Church in Ireland will mean its downfall in England and the two will be followed by the doom of landlordism—first in Ireland and then in England. I have, however, been convinced from the first that the social revolution must begin *seriously* from the bottom, that is, from landownership.*

---

* In the German a play on words: von *Grund* aus—from the bottom; *Grund*- und Bodeneigentum—landownership. *Grund* means both bottom and land.—*Ed.*

Apart from that, the whole thing will have the very useful result that, once the Irish Church is dead, the *Protestant* Irish tenants in the province of Ulster will make common cause with the Catholic tenants in the three other provinces of Ireland, whereas up to the present landlordism has been able to exploit this *religious* antagonism....

ENGELS TO MARX

Manchester, October 24, 1869

. . . Irish history shows one what a misfortune it is for a nation to have subjugated another nation. All the abominations of the English have their origin in the Irish Pale.[104] I have still to plough my way through the Cromwellian period, but this much seems certain to me, that things would have taken another turn in England, too, but for the necessity of military rule in Ireland and the creation of a new aristocracy there. . . .

MARX TO L. KUGELMANN

[London,] November 29, 1869

...Nevertheless, both my utterance on this Irish amnesty question and my further proposal to the General Council to discuss the attitude of the English working class to Ireland and to pass resolutions on it have of course other objects besides that of speaking out loudly and decidedly for the oppressed Irish against their oppressors.

I have become more and more convinced—and the only question is to drive this conviction home to the English working class—that it can never do anything decisive here in England until it separates its policy with regard to Ireland most definitely from the policy of the ruling classes, until it not only makes common cause with the Irish but actually takes the initiative in dissolving the Union established in 1801 and replacing it by a free federal relationship. And this must be done, not as a matter of sympathy with Ireland but as a demand made in the interests of the English proletariat. If not, the English people will remain tied to the leading-strings of the ruling classes, because it will have to join with them in a common front against Ireland. Every one of its movements in England itself is crippled by the strife with the Irish, who form a very important section of the working class in England. *The prime condition* of emancipation here—the overthrow of the English landed oligarchy —remains impossible because its position here cannot be stormed so long as it maintains its strongly entrenched outposts in Ireland. But there, once affairs are in the hands of the Irish people itself, once it is made its own legislator and ruler, once it becomes autonomous, the abolition of the landed aristocracy (to a large extent the *same persons* as the English landlords) will be infinitely easier than here, because in Ireland it is not merely a simple economic question but at the same time a *national* question, since the landlords there are not, like those in England, the traditional dignitaries and representatives of the nation, but its mortally hated oppressors. And not only does England's internal social development remain crippled by her present relations with Ireland; her foreign policy, and particularly her policy with regard to Russia and the United States of America, suffers the same fate.

But since the English working class undoubtedly throws the decisive weight into the scale of social emancipation generally, the lever has to be applied here. As a matter of fact, the English republic under Cromwell met shipwreck in—Ireland.[105] Non bis in idem!* But the Irish have played a capital joke on the English government by electing the "convict felon" O'Donovan Rossa to Parliament. The government papers are already threatening a renewed suspension of the Habeas Corpus Act, a renewed system of terror. In fact, England never has and never *can*—so long as the present relations last—rule Ireland otherwise than by the most abominable reign of terror and the most reprehensible corruption....

---

* Not twice the same thing!—*Ed.*

MARX TO ENGELS

[London,] December 10, 1869

...The way I shall put forward the matter next Tuesday is this: that quite apart from all phrases about "international" and "humane" *justice for Ireland*—which are taken for granted in the *International Council—it is in the direct and absolute interest of the English working class to get rid of their present connection with Ireland.* And this is my fullest conviction, and for reasons which in part I can *not* tell the English workers themselves. For a long time I believed that it would be possible to overthrow the Irish regime by English working-class ascendancy. I always expressed this point of view in the *New-York Tribune.* Deeper study has now convinced me of the opposite. The English working class will *never accomplish anything* until it has got rid of Ireland. The lever must be applied in Ireland. That is why the Irish question is so important for the social movement in general.

I have read a lot of *Davies* in extracts. The book itself* I had only glanced through superficially in the Museum. So you would do me a great favour if you would copy out for me the passages relating to *common property.* You *must* get *"Curran's Speeches" edited by Davies (London: James Duffy, 22, Paternoster Row).* I meant to give it to you when you were in London. It is now circulating among the English members of the Central Council and God knows when I shall see it again. For the period 1779-1800 (Union) it is of decisive importance, not only because of *Curran's speeches*

* Sir John Davies, *Historical Tracts.—Ed.*

(especially those held in courts; I consider Curran the *only great lawyer* (people's advocate) of the eighteenth century and the *noblest personality,* while *Grattan* was a parliamentary rogue), but because you will find quoted there *all the sources* for the *United Irishmen.*[106] This period is of the highest interest, scientifically and dramatically. Firstly, the deeds of the English in 1588-89 repeated (and perhaps even intensified) in 1788-89. Secondly, a class movement can easily be traced in the Irish movement itself. Thirdly, the infamous policy of Pitt. Fourthly, and that will be very irksome to the English gentlemen, the proof that Ireland came to grief because, in fact, from a revolutionary standpoint, *the Irish were too far advanced for the English King and Church mob,* while on the other hand the English reaction in England had its roots (as in Cromwell's time) in the subjugation of Ireland. *This period* must be described in at least one chapter. Put John Bull in the pillory!...

ENGELS TO MARX

January 19, 1870

... I have finally discovered a copy of Prendergast in a local library and hope that I shall be able to obtain it. To my good or bad fortune, the old Irish laws are also to appear soon, and I shall thus have to wade through those as well. The more I study the subject the clearer it is to me that Ireland has been stunted in its development by the English invasion and thrown centuries back. And this as of the 12th century; furthermore, it should be borne in mind, of course, that three centuries of Danish invasion and plunder had by then substantially drained the country. But these latter had ceased over a hundred years before the English invasion....

MARX TO S. MEYER AND A. VOGT

London, April 9, 1870

...Among the material sent you will also find some of the resolutions of the General Council of *November 30* on the *Irish amnesty,* resolutions that you know about and that were written by me; likewise an Irish pamphlet on the treatment of the Fenian convicts.

I had intended to introduce additional resolutions on the necessary transformation of the present Union (i.e., enslavement of Ireland) into a free and equal federation with Great Britain. For the time being, further progress in this matter, as far as public resolutions go, has been suspended because of my enforced absence from the General Council. No other member of it has sufficient knowledge of Irish affairs, and adequate prestige with its *English* members to be able to replace me here.

Meanwhile time has not been spent idly and I ask you to pay particular attention to the following:

After occupying myself with the Irish question for many years I have come to the conclusion that the decisive blow against the English ruling classes (and it will be decisive for the workers' movement all over the world) *cannot* be delivered *in England* but *only in Ireland.*

On January 1, 1870, the General Council issued a confidential circular drawn up by me in French (for the reaction upon England only the French, not the German, papers are important) on the relation of the Irish national struggle to the emancipation of the working class, and therefore on the attitude which the International Association should take in regard to the Irish question.

I shall give you here only quite briefly the decisive points.

Ireland is the bulwark of the *English landed aristocracy.* The exploitation of that country is not only one of the main sources of this aristocracy's material welfare; it is its greatest *moral* strength. It, in fact, represents the *domination of England over Ireland.* Ireland is therefore the great means by which the English aristocracy maintains *its domination in England itself.*

If, on the other hand, the English army and police were to withdraw from Ireland tomorrow, you would at once have an agrarian revolution there. But the overthrow of the English aristocracy in Ireland involves as a necessary consequence its overthrow in England. And this would fulfil the preliminary condition for the proletarian revolution in England. The destruction of the English landed aristocracy in Ireland is an infinitely easier operation than in England itself, because in Ireland *the land question* has hitherto been the *exclusive form* of the social question, because it is a question of existence, of *life and death,* for the immense majority of the Irish people, and because it is at the same time inseparable from the *national* question. This quite apart from the Irish being more passionate and revolutionary in character than the English.

As for the English *bourgeoisie,* it has in the first place a common interest with the English aristocracy in turning Ireland into mere pasture land which provides the English market with meat and wool at the cheapest possible prices. It is equally interested in reducing, by eviction and forcible emigration, the Irish population to such a small number that *English capital* (capital invested in land leased for farming) can function there with "security." It has the same interest in *clearing the estate of Ireland* as it had in the clearing of the agricultural districts of England and Scotland. The £6,000-10,000 absentee-landlord and other Irish revenues which at present flow annually to London have also to be taken into account.

But the English bourgeoisie has, besides, much more important interests in Ireland's present-day economy.

Owing to the constantly increasing concentration of tenant farming, Ireland steadily supplies its own surplus to the English labour market, and thus forces down wages and lowers the moral and material condition of the English working class.

And most important of all! Every industrial and commercial centre in England now possesses a working class *divided* into two *hostile* camps, English proletarians and Irish proletarians. The ordinary English worker hates the Irish worker as a competitor who lowers his standard of life. In relation to the Irish worker he feels himself a member of the *ruling* nation and so turns himself into a tool of the aristocrats and capitalists of his country *against Ireland,* thus strengthening their domination *over himself.* He cherishes religious, social, and national prejudices against the Irish worker. His attitude towards him is much the same as that of the "poor whites" to the "niggers" in the former slave states of the U.S.A. The Irishman pays him back with interest in his own money. He sees in the English worker at once the accomplice and the stupid tool of the *English rule in Ireland.*

This antagonism is artificially kept alive and intensified by the press, the pulpit, the comic papers, in short, by all the means at the disposal of the ruling classes. This *antagonism* is the *secret of the impotence of the English working class,* despite its organisation. It is the secret by which the capitalist class maintains its power. And that class is fully aware of it.

But the evil does not stop here. It continues across the ocean. The antagonism between English and Irish is the hidden basis of the conflict between the United States and England. It makes any honest and serious co-operation between the working classes of the two countries impossible. It enables the governments of both countries, whenever they think fit, to break the edge off the social conflict by their mutual bullying, and, in case of need, by war with one another.

England, being the metropolis of capital, the power which has hitherto ruled the world market, is for the present the most important country for the workers' revolution, and moreover the *only* country in which the material conditions for this revolution have developed up to a certain degree of maturity. Therefore to hasten the social revolution in England is the most important object of the International Workingmen's Association. The sole means of hastening it is to make Ireland independent.

Hence it is the task of the International everywhere to put the conflict between England and Ireland in the foreground, and everywhere to side openly with Ireland. And it is the special task of the Central Council in London to awaken a consciousness in the English workers that *for them* the *national emancipation of Ireland* is no question of abstract justice or humanitarian sentiment but *the first condition of their own social emancipation.*

These roughly are the main points of the circular letter, which thereby at the same time gave the *raisons d'être* of the resolutions of the Central Council on the Irish amnesty. Shortly afterwards I sent a strong anonymous article on the treatment of the Fenians by the English, etc., against Gladstone, etc., to the *Internationale* (organ of our Belgian Central Committee in Brussels). In this article I at the same time made the charge against the French Republicans (the *Marseillaise* had printed some nonsense on Ireland written here by the wretched Talandier) that in their national egoism they were saving all their wrath for the Empire.

That worked. My daughter Jenny wrote a series of articles to the *Marseillaise* signing them J. Williams (she had called herself Jenny Williams in her private letter to the editorial board), and published, among other things, O'Donovan Rossa's letter. Hence immense noise.

After many years of cynical refusal *Gladstone* was thus finally compelled to agree to a *parliamentary enquiry* into the treatment of the Fenian prisoners. Jenny is now the regular correspondent on Irish affairs for the *Marseillaise. (This is naturally to be a secret between us.)* The British Government and press are fiercely annoyed by the fact that the Irish question has thus now come *to the forefront* in France and that these rogues are now being watched and exposed via Paris on the whole Continent.

We hit another bird with the same stone, having forced the Irish leaders, journalists, etc., in Dublin to get into contact with us, which the *General Council* so far had been unable to achieve!

You have now a great field in America for working along the same lines. *Coalition of the German workers with the Irish workers* (and of course also with the English and American workers who will agree to join) is the greatest job you could start on nowadays. This must be done in the name of the International. The social significance of the Irish question must be made clear. . . .

MARX TO N. F. DANIELSON

London, February 19, 1881

. . . In *India* serious complications, if not a general outbreak, are in store for the British government. What the English take from them annually in the form of rent, dividends for railways useless to the Hindus; pensions for military and civil servicemen, for Afghanistan and other wars, etc., etc.—what they take from them *without any equivalent* and *quite apart* from what they appropriate to themselves annually *within* India,—speaking only of the *value of the commodities* the Indians have gratuitously and annually to *send over* to England—it amounts to *more than the total sum of income of the 60 millions of agricultural and industrial labourers of India!* This is a bleeding process with a vengeance! The famine years are pressing each other and *in dimensions* till now not yet suspected in Europe! There is an actual conspiracy going on wherein Hindus and Mussulmans co-operate; the British government is aware that something is "brewing", but these shallow people (I mean the governmental men), stultified by their own parliamentary ways of talking and thinking, do not even desire to see clear, to realize the whole extent of the imminent danger! To delude others and by deluding them to delude yourself—this is: *parliamentary wisdom* in a nutshell! Tant mieux!*. . .

* So much the better.—*Ed.*

ENGELS TO E. BERNSTEIN

London, August 9, 1882

. . . 4. It seems to me that in the Egyptian affair you are making too much of the so-called National Party. We know little about Arabi, but I am prepared to wager ten to one that he is an ordinary pasha who does not want to concede tax collecting to the financiers, because in the old Oriental fashion he prefers to put the taxes into his own pocket. It is again the eternal story of peasant countries. From Ireland to Russia, and from Asia Minor to Egypt—in a peasant country the peasant exists solely to be exploited. It has been so since the Assyrian and Persian state. The satrap, alias pasha, is the chief Oriental form of exploiter, just as the merchant and jurist represent the modern Western form. Repudiation of the khedive's debts is, of course, good, but the question is: what then? We West-Europeans should not be so easily led astray as the Egyptian fellahs or all the Romanic people. Strange. All the Romanic revolutionaries complain that all the revolutions they have made were always for the benefit of other people. This is easily explained: it is because they were always taken in by the word "revolution." And yet, no sooner a mutiny breaks out somewhere than the entire Romanic revolutionary world is in raptures over it uncritically. I think that we can well be on the side of the oppressed fellahs without sharing the illusions they nurture at the time (a peasant people just has to be hoodwinked for centuries before it becomes aware of it from experience), and to be against the English brutalities while by no means siding with their military adversaries of the moment. In all questions of international politics the sentimental party newspapers of the French and Italians are to be used with utmost mistrust, and we Germans are dutybound to preserve our theoretical superiority through criticism in this sphere as well. . . .

ENGELS TO K. KAUTSKY

London, September 12, 1882

...You ask me what the English workers think about colonial policy. Well, exactly the same as they think about politics in general: the same as the bourgeois think. There is no workers' party here, you see, there are only Conservatives and Liberal-Radicals, and the workers gaily share the feast of England's monopoly of the world market and the colonies. In my opinion the colonies proper, i.e., the countries occupied by a European population—Canada, the Cape, Australia—will all become independent; on the other hand, the countries inhabited by a native population, which are simply subjugated—India, Algeria, the Dutch, Portuguese and Spanish possessions—must be taken over for the time being by the proletariat and led as rapidly as possible towards independence. How this process will develop is difficult to say. India will perhaps, indeed very probably, make a revolution, and as a proletariat in process of self-emancipation cannot conduct any colonial wars, it would have to be allowed to run its course; it would not pass off without all sorts of destruction, of course, but that sort of thing is inseparable from all revolutions. The same might also take place elsewhere, *e.g.*, in Algeria and Egypt, and would certainly be the best thing *for us*. We shall have enough to do at home. Once Europe is reorganised, and North America, that will furnish such colossal power and such an example that the semi-civilised countries will of themselves follow in their wake; economic needs, if anything, will see to that. But as to what social and political phases these countries will then have to pass through before they likewise arrive at socialist organisation, I think we today can advance only rather idle hypotheses. One thing alone is certain: the victorious proletariat can force no blessings of any kind upon any foreign nation without undermining its own victory by so doing. Which of course by no means excludes defensive wars of various kinds....

ENGELS TO K. KAUTSKY

London, September 18, 1883

... I thought the article on colonisation very good. It is a pity that you make use chiefly of the German material, which is dull as usual and lacking the most vivid aspects of tropical colonisation, and its latest form; I mean colonisation in the interests of stock exchange swindles, such as is now being enacted in Tunisia and Tonkin by France openly and frankly. A new striking example here of the South Sea slave traffic: the attempted annexation of New Guinea, etc., through Queensland was designed directly for the slave trade. On the day when the annexation expedition departed for New Guinea, a Queensland ship, the *Fanny*, sailed for the same destination and for the islands east of it to kidnap labour, but returned without it and with wounded on board and other unpleasant signs of battle. The *Daily News* (the beginning of September) speaks of it and notes in an editorial that Englishmen can scarcely rebuke the French for practices of that kind until they do the same!...

ENGELS TO A. BEBEL

January 18, 1884

...If you wish an example of state socialism, take *Java*. On the basis of the old communistic village communities the Dutch Government has there organised all production in so "socialistic" a fashion, and has so nicely taken all sales of the products into its own hands, that aside from about 100 million marks in salaries for officials and the army it receives a net income of some 70 million marks a year to pay interest to the luckless states which are creditors of the Dutch. In comparison, Bismarck is an innocent child!...

ENGELS TO K. KAUTSKY

London, February 16, 1884

...It would be a good thing for somebody to take the pains of elucidating the state socialism now rampant by using the example of it in *Java* where its practice is in full bloom. All the material for that will be found in *Java, Or How to Manage a Golony*, by I. W. B. Money, Barrister at Law, London 1861, 2 vols. Here it will be seen how on the basis of the old community communism* the Dutch organised production under state control and secured for the people what they considered a quite comfortable existence. The result: the people are kept at the stage of primitive stupidity and 70 million marks (now surely more) are annually collected by the Dutch national treasury. This case is highly interesting and can easily be turned to practical use. Incidentally it is proof of how today primitive communism furnishes there as well as in India and Russia the finest and broadest basis of exploitation and despotism (so long as it is not aroused by some element of modern communism) and how in the conditions of modern society it turns out to be a crying anachronism (to be removed or further developed) as much as were the independent mark associations of the original cantons....

---

* Gemeindekommunismus.—*Ed.*

ENGELS TO N. F. DANIELSON

London, September 22, 1892

...Capitalist production, being a transitory economical phase, is full of internal contradictions which develop and become evident in proportion as it develops. This tendency to destroy its own market at the same time it creates it, is one of them. Another is the *безвыходное положение** to which it leads, and which is developed sooner in a country *without* a foreign market, like Russia, than in countries which more or less are capable of competing on the open world market. This situation without an apparent issue finds its issue, for the latter countries, in commercial revulsions, in the forcible opening of new markets. But even then the cul-de-sac stares one in the face. Look at England. The last new market which could bring on a temporary revival of prosperity by its being thrown open to English commerce, is China. Therefore English capital insists upon constructing Chinese railways. But Chinese railways mean the destruction of the whole basis of Chinese small agriculture and domestic industry, and, as there will not even be the counterpoise of a Chinese grande industrie, hundreds of millions of people will be placed in the impossibility of living. The consequence will be a wholesale emigration such as the world has not yet seen, a flooding of America, Asia and Europe by the hated Chinaman, a competition for work with the American, Australian and European workman on the basis of the Chinese standard of life, the lowest of all—and if the system of production has not been changed in Europe before that time, it will have to be changed then....

* Impasse.—*Ed.*

ENGELS TO K. KAUTSKY

London, September 23, 1894

...The war between China and Japan signifies the end of old China, the complete, if gradual, revolution of its entire economic foundation, including the abolition of the old bonds between agriculture and industry in the countryside by big industry, railways, etc., and thus also the mass exodus of Chinese coolies to Europe; consequently, a hastening for us of the débacle and the aggravation of antagonisms into a crisis. It is again the wonderful irony of history: China alone is still to be conquered for capitalist production, and in so doing at long last the latter makes its own existence at home impossible....

ENGELS TO F. A. SORGE

London, November 10, 1894

...The war in China has given the death blow to the old China. Isolation has become impossible; the introduction of railways, steam-engines, electricity, and modern large-scale industry has become a necessity, if only for reasons of military defence. But with it the old economic system of small peasant agriculture, where the family also made its industrial products itself, falls to pieces too, and with it the whole old social system which made relatively dense population possible. Millions will be turned out and forced to emigrate; and these millions will find their way even to Europe, and en masse. But as soon as Chinese competition sets in on a mass scale, it will rapidly bring things to a head in your country and over here, and thus the conquest of China by capitalism will at the same time furnish the impulse for the overthrow of capitalism in Europe and America....

NOTES

1 "Revolution in China and in Europe" was written by Karl Marx, like many other articles of this collection, for the *New-York Daily Tribune*, founded in 1841 by Horace Greeley, the well-known American journalist and politician. Until the mid-1850's it was a Left Wing paper and subsequently the organ of the Republican Party. In the forties and fifties it held progressive views and took a strong stand against slavery. A number of prominent American writers and journalists were associated with it. Charles Dana, who was strongly influenced by the ideas of utopian socialism, was one of its editors at the close of the 1840s. Marx's association with the newspaper began in August 1851 and continued for more than ten years until March 1862. Many articles for the *New-York Daily Tribune* were written by Engels at Marx's request. The articles Marx and Engels wrote treated the key issues of international and domestic policy, the working-class movement, the economic development of the European countries, colonial expansion, the national liberation movement in the oppressed and dependent countries, etc. During the period of reaction in Europe, Marx and Engels made use of the widely read American paper to expose with concrete materials the vices of capitalist society, its irreconcilable contradictions, and the limitations of bourgeois democracy.

In some cases the *New-York Daily Tribune* editors took considerable liberties with the articles contributed by Marx and Engels, publishing some of them unsigned in the form of editorials, or tampering with the text. Marx protested repeatedly against this. In the autumn of 1857, Marx was compelled to reduce the number of his articles in connection with the economic crisis in the United States, which affected the finances of the newspaper. Marx's association with the *New-York Daily Tribune* broke off entirely at the beginning of the American Civil War. This was largely due to the fact that advocates of a compromise with the slave-owning South had taken precedence in the newspaper and it departed from its former progressive positions. p. 19

2 Marx refers to Georg Wilhelm Friedrich Hegel (1770-1831), the outstanding German philosopher who developed idealist dialectics. p. 19

[3] In 1851, an anti-feudal liberation movement broke out in China, which grew into a powerful peasant war. It began in the South, in Kwangsi Province, from where it spread to the central provinces and to almost all of the lower and middle Yangtze. In the course of the fighting the insurgents formed the Celestial Empire (Taiping tan-ho), with its seat in Nanking, whence the name of the movement—the Taiping Rebellion. Its members massacred Manchu feudals who held sway in China, lifted taxes and abolished big feudal property. The rebellion assumed a religious character—the distinguishing feature of a peasant movement, especially in the East—thereby delivering a blow at the Buddhist clergy and monasteries, this bulwark of the Manchu dynasty. The Taiping Rebellion set off an extensive struggle of the Chinese people against the feudal system and foreign invaders, but proved unable to do away with the feudal mode of production in China. The Taiping state formed its own feudal top strata which made a deal with the ruling classes; this was one of the causes why the movement declined. The main blow at it was dealt by the armed intervention of England, the U.S.A., and France (originally these countries aided the Manchu dynasty under the cover of "neutrality"), whose troops joined the Chinese feudals and in 1864 put down the Taiping Rebellion. p. 19

[4] The reference is to the first Opium War of 1839-42, a predatory war waged by Britain against China, which started the conversion of China into a semi-colony. It was started over the destruction of foreign merchants' stocks of opium in Canton by the Chinese authorities. The British colonisers took advantage of the defeat suffered by backward feudal China and imposed the onerous Nanking treaty (August 29, 1842), which made China open to British commerce five of its ports—Canton, Amoy, Foochow, Ningpo, and Shanghai, cede the Island of Hong-Kong to Great Britain for "all time," and pay a big indemnity. In 1843 a supplementary treaty was signed, which granted foreigners extraterritoriality in China. p. 19

[5] Early in the 17th century China was menaced by the united Manchu tribes, which, along with the Turco-Mongol peoples, were known as Tartars (after a Mongol tribe inhabiting north-eastern Mongolia and Manchuria when Genghiz Khan formed his empire). Despite the stubborn resistance of the Chinese people which developed into an open armed struggle and continued until 1683, the invasion by the Manchus led to the rule of the Manchu Chin dynasty in the country (1644-1912). The subjugation of China was made easier by the crisis of the feudal state under the last emperors of the Ming dynasty and the coming over to the invaders' side of a part of the Chinese feudal lords who were alarmed by the peasant rebellions. p. 20

[6] *The British East India Company* was founded in 1600. Its agents established a number of factories in India. At the close of the 17th century the Company began to seize Indian territory. During the 18th and the first half of the 19th centuries it waged sanguinary wars of conquest in the Carnatic, Bengal, Scinde, Punjab, and other regions of India with the effect that by the mid-19th century almost all India was under the sway of the Company. By deceit, blackmail, vio-

lence, and outright plunder its businessmen laid their hands on colossal riches, which they transferred to England, thus making fabulous fortunes. The British Government granted the East India Company the right to monopoly trade with India and China and also the right to govern India and collect taxes from its population. The British Parliament periodically renewed the Charter of the East India Company, which defined its administrative and trading privileges.

The British industrialists who wanted to market their products in India and the British commercial bourgeoisie whose interests were harmed by the Company's privileges, waged a persistent struggle against the Company demanding the abolition of its monopoly rights. In 1813 the British Parliament stripped it of its monopoly on the trade in India. By an act in 1833 the Company was also deprived of the China trade monopoly, but its right to govern India was preserved. In 1858, by a special edict of Oueen Victoria, the East India Company was dissolved and its functions handed over to the Crown. p. 20

7 The reference is to the discovery of rich gold deposits in California in 1848 and in Australia in 1851, which strongly influenced the economic development of the European and American countries. p. 22

8 *The Economist*—a British weekly devoted to questions of economics and politics, founded in London in 1843 by the big industrial bourgeoisie. p. 23

9 This article is part of Marx's international review written for the *New-York Daily Tribune.* The full title of the review is "Affairs in Holland—Denmark—Conversion of the British Debt—India—Turkey and Russia." p. 27

10 *The Coalition, Coalition Cabinet*—the name of Aberdeen's Ministry which was in office in 1852-55 and consisted of Whigs, Free Traders, and Peelites (adherents of Robert Peel, the leader of the moderate Tories). p. 27

11 *The Observer*—a conservative British weekly established in London in 1791. p. 27

12 *Board (Court) of Directors*—governing body of the East India Company elected annually from among the most influential associates of the Company and members of the British Government in India owning company shares worth not less than £2,000. The Court of Directors had its seat in London and was elected by the general meeting of shareholders, at which only holders of not less than £1,000 in shares had the right to vote. The Court had extensive powers in India until 1853. It was dissolved in 1858 when the East India Company was abolished. p. 27

13 *The Board of Control* was set up in 1784; its six members were appointed by the Crown. The President of the Board of Control was a member of the Cabinet and, in effect, the Secretary of State for India and its supreme governor. The decisions of the Board of Control, whose seat was in London, were communicated to India through a Secret Committee comprising three Directors of the East

India Company. Thus, a double system of Indian government came into being—the Board of Control (British Government) and the Court of Directors (East India Company). The Board of Control was abolished in 1858. p. 28

14 *Downing Street*—a street in the centre of London where the official residence of the Government is situated.

Three Presidencies—according to the administrative division of British India, the name of the territories of Bengal, Bombay, and Madras governed by officials appointed by the East India Company. The Regulating Act of 1773 raised the Governor of Bengal to the rank of Governor-General of all Britain's Indian possessions. p. 28

15 *The Manchester School*—an economic school which reflected the interests of the industrial bourgeoisie. Its supporters, the Free Traders, advocated Free Trade and non-interference by the state in economic affairs. Their centre was in Manchester where the movement was headed by Cobden and Bright, two textile manufacturers, who formed an Anti-Corn-Law League in 1838. In the forties and fifties the Free Traders made up a separate political group which subsequently joined the British Liberal Party.

By the "*Indian Society*" is meant the East Indian Reform Association founded by Free Trader John Dickinson in March 1853. p. 28

16 This article is part of Marx's international review written for the *New-York Daily Tribune*. The full title of the review is "The Russian Humbug—Gladstone's Failure—Sir Charles Wood's East Indian Reforms." p. 30

17 *The Zemindari System* was introduced in Bengal and some other provinces by the 1793 Act on Permanent Zemindari issued by the British Governor-General in India. The law handed over the land, which belonged to the village communities from time immemorial, into the possession of the zemindars, or tax-collectors, thus establishing a new class of big landowners. As land proprietors the zemindars had to pay the East India Company a portion of the land taxes collected from the expropriated peasants by violence and torture.

The Ryotwari System was introduced by the British authorities in the Presidencies of Bombay and Madras in 1818. Under this system the Indian peasant, the ryot, formerly a member of the village community, was turned into a tenant of government land. The ryot was obliged to pay rent-tax for his holding to the East India Company. If the ryot could not pay this high rent he lost the right to the land. Gradually the ryots' land fell into the possession of profiteers and usurers. p. 31

18 *Religion of the Lingam*—the cult of the deity Siva; particularly widespread among the southern India sect of Lingayat (from the word "linga"—the emblem of Siva), a Hindu sect which does not recognise distinctions of caste and denies fasts, sacrifices, and pilgrimage.

Juggernaut (Jagannath)—depiction of one of the chief Hindu gods, Vishnu. The cult of Vishnu-Juggernaut was marked by pompous ritual and extreme religious fanaticism which manifested itself in the self-torture and suicide of believers. During the festivities some of the believers threw themselves under the wheels of the chariot bearing the image of Vishnu-Juggernaut. p. 36

19 *Moguls*—conquerors of Turkish descent who in the early 16th century invaded India from the east of Central Asia and founded in 1526 in northern India an empire of the Great Moguls (after the name of the ruling dynasty of the Empire). Contemporaries regarded the founders of the Mogul Empire as the direct descendants of the Mongol conquerors of Genghis Khan's time, hence the name "Moguls." The Moguls reached the zenith of their might in the mid-17th century by subjugating the greater part of India and part of Afghanistan. Later on, however, the Empire began to crumble due to peasant rebellions and the growing resistance by the Indian peoples to the Mohammedan conquerors and also due to the uninterrupted internal strife among the Moguls and the increasing separatist feudal tendencies. By the early half of the 18th century the Empire of the Great Mogul had practically ceased to exist.

Heptarchy—a term used by the English historians to designate the political system of England in the early Middle Ages when the country consisted of seven Anglo-Saxon kingdoms (6th-8th cent.). Marx uses this word by analogy to denote the feudal dismemberment of the Deccan (Central and Southern India) before its conquest by the Moslems. p. 36

20 *Brahmins*—one of the four ancient Indian castes originally comprising mainly privileged priests; subsequently it also embraced, like other Indian castes, people of various trades and social standing, including impoverished peasants and artisans. p. 36

21 The Island of Salsette, to the north of Bombay, was famous for its 109 Buddhist cave temples. p. 36

22 "*Laissez-faire, laissez-aller*" (grant freedom of action)—a slogan of bourgeois economists, adherents of Free Trade and the state's non-interference in economic affairs. p. 38

23 This article is part of Marx's international review written for the *New-York Daily Tribune*. The full title of the review is "English Prosperity—Strikes—The Turkish Question—India." p. 43

24 "Glorious" revolution—name given by English bourgeois historians to the *coup d'état* of 1688 which deposed the English king James II supported by the reactionary feudals and brought to power William III of Orange, who was associated with big landowners and the upper strata of the commercial bourgeoisie. The revolution extended the functions of Parliament which gradually came to hold supreme state power. p. 46

25 *The Seven Years' War* (1756-63)—a war between two European coalitions—the Anglo-Prussian and the Franco-Russo-Austrian. One of the chief causes of the war was colonial and commercial rivalry between England and France. Aside from naval battles, the war was

fought primarily in the American and Asian colonies of these states. The main theatre of operations in the East was India where the French and their puppets from among the local princes were opposed by the East India Company, which had substantially increased its armed forces and took advantage of the war to seize Indian territories. As a result of the war, France lost almost all her possessions in India (excepting five coastal towns whose fortifications she was compelled to demolish), while England considerably strengthened her colonial might. p. 46

26 *Anti-Jacobin War*—the war which England started against revolutionary France in 1793, when the Jacobins were in power in France, and which she continued against the Napoleonic Empire.

Reform Bill. The reference is to the Electoral Reform carried out by the British Parliament in June 1832. The Reform was aimed against the political monopoly of the landed and financial aristocracy and gave access to Parliament to representatives of the industrial bourgeoisie. The proletariat and the petty bourgeoisie, most prominent in the struggle for the Reform, were duped by the Liberal bourgeoisie and remained disfranchised. p. 48

27 Marx lists a number of wars of conquest which the East India Company waged in India with the purpose of seizing Indian territories and crushing its chief colonial rival—the French East India Company.

The War in the Carnatic lasted at intervals from 1746 to 1763. The warring sides—the British and French colonialists—sought to subjugate the Carnatic under guise of supporting different local pretenders to the principality. The English, who in January 1761 took possession of Pondicherry, the principal French bastion in the south of India, ultimately won out.

In 1756, in an effort to avert a British invasion the nabob of Bengal started a war, seizing Calcutta, the British base in northeastern India. But the armed forces of the British East India Company under Clive's command soon recaptured that city, demolished the French fortifications in Bengal and defeated the nabob at Plassey on June 23, 1757. The uprising that broke out in 1763 in Bengal, which had been turned into a vassal possession of the Company, was crushed by the English colonialists. Along with Bengal, the English took possession of Bihar, which was under the rule of the nabob of Bengal. In 1803, the English completed the conquest of Orissa, which embraced several local feudal principalities subjugated by the Company.

In 1790-92, and 1799 the East India Company waged war against Mysore, whose ruler Tippoo Sahib had taken part in previous Mysore campaigns against the English and who was an implacable enemy of British colonialism. In the first of these wars Mysore lost half of its dominions, seized by the Company and its allied feudal princes. The second war culminated in a total defeat for Mysore and the death of Tippoo. Mysore became a vassal principality.

Subsidiary system—or system of so-called subsidiary agreements —a method of turning the potentates of Indian principalities into vassals of the East India Company. Most widespread were agreements under which the princes had to maintain (subsidise) the Company's troops stationed on their territory and agreements which saddled the princes with loans on exorbitant terms. Failure to fulfil them led to the confiscation of their possessions. p. 49

28 The first Anglo-Afghan War of 1838-42, started by the British with the aim of seizing Afghanistan, ended in total failure for the British colonialists.

The British colonialists seized *Scinde* in 1843. During the Anglo-Afghan War of 1838-42 the East India Company resorted to threats and violence to obtain the consent of the feudal rulers of Scinde for the passage of British troops across their possessions. Taking advantage of this, the British demanded in 1843 that the local feudal princes proclaimed themselves to be vassals of the Company. After crushing the rebel Beluchi tribes the annexation of the entire region by British India was announced.

Punjab (northern India) was conquered in British campaigns against the Sikhs in 1845-46 and 1848-49.

In the 16th century, the Sikhs were a religious sect in Punjab. Their teaching of equality became the ideology of the peasant movement against the Indian feudals and Afghan invaders in the late 17th century. As time went on, a feudal group emerged from among the Sikhs whose representatives stood at the helm of the Sikh state. In the early 19th century the latter included all Punjab and a number of neighbouring regions. In 1845, the British colonialists enlisted the support of traitors among the Sikh gentry to provoke a conflict with the Sikhs and in 1846 succeeded in turning the Sikh state into a vassal principality. In 1848 the Sikhs revolted, but were totally subjugated in 1849. The conquest of Punjab turned all India into a British colony. p. 49

29 The conquest of Burma was begun by the British colonialists early in the 19th century. In the first Burmese War of 1824-26 the troops of the East India Company seized the Province of Assam bordering on Bengal and the coastal districts of Arakan and Tenasserim. The second Burmese War (1852) culminated in the seizure by the English of the Province of Pegu. A new campaign against Burma was expected in 1853, since no peace treaty had been signed at the close of the second Burmese War and the new Burmese king, who assumed power in February 1853, refused to recognise the seizure of Pegu. p. 53

30 See Note 15. p. 59

31 This article is part of Marx's international review written for the *New-York Daily Tribune.* The full title of the review is "The Turkish War Question—*The New-York Daily Tribune* in the House of Commons—the Government of India". p. 61

32 Suttee—the Indian practice of cremating the widow on the funeral pile of her deceased husband. p. 66

33 *Leadenhall Street*—a street in London where the East India Company had its seat, the East India House or the India House. p. 66

34 In this case reference is made to the President of the Board of

Control who was a member of the British Cabinet. The post of Secretary of State for India was instituted after the abolition of the East India Company in 1858. p. 68

35 This article is part of Marx's international review written for the *New-York Daily Tribune*. The full title of the review is "The Russo-Turkish Difficulty—Ducking and Dodging of the British Cabinet—Nesselrode's Last Note—The East India Question." p. 70

36 See Note 15. p. 70

37 *Change Alley*—a street in London where the South Sea Company had its board; a centre of all kinds of money operations. p. 71

38 *Nabobs and Rajahs*—titles of Indian princes; *Jagirdars*—representatives of the Moslem feudal gentry in the Great Mogul Empire who received in temporary use big estates (jagirs) for which they did military service and supplied contingents of troops. When the Empire disintegrated, the jagirdars became hereditary feudal owners. p. 72

39 *Babur* (1483-1530), the founder of the Great Mogul Empire, was a descendant of Tamerlane, who in his turn considered himself the successor of Genghis Khan. In the 18th century, after the disintegration of the Empire, the Mogul emperors were puppets of the governors of separate regions, Afghan conquerors, and big Indian feudals. After the seizure of Delhi in 1803 by the British they played the role of the men of straw of the East India Company and turned into its pensioners. In 1858 the British colonisers declared India a possession of the British Crown and eliminated the last formal vestiges of Mogul power. p. 73

40 This article is part of Marx's international review written for the *New-York Daily Tribune*. The full title of the review is "War in Burma—The Russian Question—Curious Diplomatic Correspondence." p. 75

41 See Note 29. p. 75

42 *Hampton Court*—a palace near London on the Thames; from the 16th to the 18th centuries it was the residence of English kings. p. 75

43 This article is part of Marx's international review written for the *New-York Daily Tribune*. The full title of the review is "The War Question—Doings of Parliament—India." p. 77

44 *The East India House*—the seat of the East India Company in London. p. 77

45 *Collector*—a British official in India who performed the duties of the governor of a region, its chief judge, and main tax-gatherer. p. 78

46 *Mahrattas*—an Indian people north-west of the Deccan. In the mid-17th century they started a campaign against the Mogul feudals thus delivering a serious blow at the Empire of the Great Moguls and adding to its decline. In the course of the struggle the Mahrattas formed

an independent state of their own whose feudal top stratum immediately embarked on the path of wars of conquest. At the close of the 17th century their state was weakened by internal feudal strife but early in the 18th century there was formed a powerful confederation of Mahratta principalities headed by a supreme governor, the peshwa. In 1761 the Mahratta feudals suffered a costly defeat at the hands of the Afghans in the struggle for hegemony in India. Weakened by the struggle for supremacy in India and by internal feudal strife, the Mahratta principalities fell prey to the East India Company and became subordinate to it as a result of the Anglo-Mahratta War of 1803-05. p. 81

47 *Jats*—a caste group in northern India whose bulk was made up of peasants; it also included military feudals. In the 17th century the Jat peasants repeatedly rose in revolt against the rule of the Mogul feudals.

For *Brahmins* see Note 20. p. 86

48 *The Temple of Juggernaut* in Orissa (eastern India)—the centre of the worship of Vishnu-Juggernaut, one of the chief Hindu deities. The priests of the temple who were under the protection of the East India Company reaped immense profits from mass pilgrimage while at the same time encouraging temple prostitution, and from pompous festivities which were accompanied by the suicide and self-torture of fanatic believers. p. 86

49 The reference is to the Anglo-Persian War of 1856-57. The pretext was afforded by an attempt of the Persian rulers to seize the Principality of Herat whose main city, of the same name, was an apple of discord between Persia and Afghanistan. The national liberation movement that began in 1857 forced the British Government to sign a hasty peace treaty with Persia. Under the peace treaty of March 1857 signed in Paris, Persia renounced her claims to Herat. In 1863 it was attached to the possessions of the Afghan emir. p. 88

50 The reference is to the Anglo-Chinese treaty of October 8, 1843, signed as a supplement to the Nanking treaty concluded between Britain and China on August 29, 1842. (See Note 4.)

The supplementary treaty of 1843 conceded new privileges to the British. It provided for the creation of special settlements for foreigners in open ports, granted the right of extraterritoriality, placing foreigners outside Chinese jurisdiction, and gave the British the "most favoured nation treatment". The reference here is to article 9 of this treaty under which Chinese associated with the British were removed from under the jurisdiction of the Chinese authorities. p. 91

51 At that time the British Plenipotentiary in China was John Bowring, the well-known Liberal and Free Trader. On his orders, on October 24, 1856, the British subjected Canton to a merciless bombardment. p. 92

52 After the first Opium War (1839-42) one of the demands persistently renewed by representatives of the British Government in China was the demand to allow British merchants to reside and trade in

Canton. In April 1846 the British succeeded in reaching an agreement with the Chinese authorities under which Canton was declared open to foreigners. But in view of the vigorous protests of the Canton population the question was not settled. In 1847, the British by using threats secured the promise to open the city two years later. In 1849, however, the British Governor of Hong-Kong, Bonham, fearing a popular uprising in Canton, was compelled to renounce the demand. p. 94

53 The reference is to the first Opium War of Britain against China, 1839-42. For details concerning the war see Note 4. p. 96

54 *Sunnites and Shiites*—adherents of the two sects in Islam which arose in the 7th century during the internecine struggle among the successors of Mohammed regarded as the founder of Islam. p. 98

55 After the death of Abbas Mirza, heir to the throne, in October 1833, his son, Mohammed Mirza, was nominated to succeed him and appointed Ruler of Azerbaijan. When his grandfather Feth Ali, Shah of Persia, died in October 1834, there were several pretenders to the throne. In a calculating attempt to make the new shah dependent on Britain, Campbell, a British envoy, helped Mohammed to succeed, having financed his expedition from Tabris to Teheran. Lindsy, an English officer, was in command of Shah Mohammed's troops. p. 99

56 The reference is to the first Anglo-Afghan War of 1838-42 precipitated by Britain with the aim of colonising and enslaving Afghanistan. In August 1839 Kabul was occupied by the British but as a result of the revolt that broke out there in November 1841, they had to abandon the city in January 1842 and began to retreat to India; their retreat, however, turned into a disorderly flight. Out of 4,500 British soldiers and 12,000 followers only one man reached the Indian frontier. p. 100

57 *The Friend of China* is an abbreviated title of the British official paper *The Overland Friend of China* published in Victoria (Hong-Kong) from 1842 to 1859. p. 103

58 This formula belongs to the British bourgeois sociologist Bentham, the theorist of utilitarianism—an individualistic ethics of a limited bourgeois nature. Utilitarianism is a teaching which regards "utility" and "profit" as the sole basis of morality and seeks to prove the possibility of universal "happiness" and "harmony" in capitalist society, torn though it is by class contradictions. p. 103

59 *The Peace Society*—a bourgeois pacifist organisation founded in London in 1816. It was actively supported by Free Traders, who believed that in peacetime Britain would with the help of Free Trade make fuller use of her industrial superiority and secure economic and political supremacy. p. 103

60 *Chief of Whitehall*—Palmerston.

Whitehall—a street in the centre of London where the Government House was situated. p. 106

61 *"Resurrectionists"*—people in England who secretly exhumed corpses and sold them to anatomical theatres. In the 1820's wide notoriety was earned by the case of William Burke, of Edinburgh, who invented a method of strangling people without visible signs of crime and sold dead bodies to anatomic l theatres. p. 107

62 *Punch*—an abbreviated title of the English bourgeois-Liberal humorous weekly, *Punch or the London Charivari*; has been appearing in London since 1841.

Grand Cophta—an imaginary name of an Egyptian priest, allegedly the head of a masonic "Egyptian lodge", invented by Caliostro, the well-known 18th-century charlatan. The latter affirmed that during his travels in Egypt he fathomed the secrets of Egyptian wisdom and in his activity was guided by the spirit of the all-powerful and omniscient Grand Cophta. p. 109

63 *Habeas Corpus Act* was enacted by British Parliament in 1679. By this act each writ has to be motivated and a detainee brought before a court within a short space of time, or freed. The act does not extend to high treason and can be suspended by Parliament.

With the words *"butchered the people at Manchester"* Marx alludes to the massacres by British troops on August 16, 1819, of unarmed people who participated in a mass meeting favouring electoral reform and repeal of the Corn Laws, which took place in Saint Petersfield, near Manchester.

Corn Laws—high grain tariffs adopted by British Parliament in 1815. The Laws prohibited the importation of grain if its price within the country was less than 80 shillings a quarter. An extremely heavy burden on the poor, the Corn Laws were a disadvantage also to the industrial bourgeoisie since they made labour power dearer, restricted the home market and hampered the development of foreign trade. For many years the industrial bourgeoisie fought the big landlords for the repeal of the Corn Laws. They formed, under the leadership of the two Manchester manufacturers and Free Traders, Bright and Cobden, an Anti-Corn-Law League which organised mass manifestations for the repeal of the Corn Laws.

The Corn Laws were repealed in 1846. p. 111

64 See Note 52. p. 114

65 The reference is to the Anglo-Persian War of 1856-57 and to Britain's second Opium War against China, 1856-58. p. 120

66 This and a number of later articles deal with the Indian revolt against British rule, which broke out in the spring of 1857. The sepoys constituted the military core of the revolt. It embraced large areas of Northern and Central India. Its driving force were the peasants and the poor rural artisans, but its leaders were feudals, with a few exceptions. Soon after the British authorities had declared that the possessions of the Indian princes, talukdars and others, would be returned to them (1858), the majority of the feudals who took part in the movement betrayed the rebels and went over to the British. The lack of united leadership and of a general plan of operations, to be explained largely by the caste system and feudal

dismemberment of the country, was also instrumental in the defeat of the revolt. At the close of 1858 and the beginning of 1859 the British put down the revolt and made short work of its participants. p. 130

67 For the conquest of Scinde and Punjab see Note 28. p. 130

68 In 1856 the British colonisers, in violation of existing treaties, deposed the governor of Oudh (principality in Northern India) and annexed his possessions to the territory administered by the East India Company. p. 130

69 *Rajputs*—a major caste and nationality of Central India.
Brahmins. See Note 20. p. 135

70 *Jagirdar*. See Note 38.
Enamdar—the holder of an enam, a landed estate which was not taxable.
Freeholders—a category of small landowners who originated from the mediaeval "freeholders." A freeholder paid the lord an insignificant cash rent for his plot of land which he could dispose of at will. p. 141

71 In the *Vendee* (a province in western France) the French royalists utilised the backward peasantry to engineer a counter-revolutionary revolt in 1793. It was crushed by the republican army, whose soldiers were known as the "Blues" (like all the supporters of the Convention).
The Spanish guerrillas. This refers to the national liberation movement of the Spanish people against the French invaders in 1808-14.
The Serbian and Croation detachments in the armies of Rajačič and Jelačič took part in crushing the revolutionary movement in Hungary and Austria during the revolution of 1848-49. The aristocracy of Hungary opposed the demands of Serbs and Croats for national independence. This gave the Austrian reactionaries a chance to use the Serbian and Croatian troops in their own interests to suppress the uprising in Budapest and Vienna.
The *Garde Mobile* was established by a French government decree of February 25, 1848, to suppress the revolutionary masses. Its detachments, chiefly composed of declassed elements, were used to quell the uprising of Paris workers in June 1848. General Cavaignac, being the Minister of War, personally commanded the massacre of the workers.
Decembrists—members of the secret Bonapartist society of December 10. They were active organisers of mass repressions of republicans and particularly of participants of the 1848 revolution. The repressions were organised after the election of Louis Bonaparte as President of the Republic and after his *coup d'état* of December 2, 1851. p. 152

72 *The Secretary of the Manchester Peace Society* was John Bowring, a Liberal, by whose orders Canton was subjected to a barbarous bombardment on October 24, 1856.
For the *Peace Society* see Note 59.
A French Marshal—Marshal Pélissier. During the suppression of an insurrection in Algeria in 1845 he ordered a thousand Arab

rebels hiding in mountain caves to be smoked to death by campfires at their entrances. p. 154

73 *Kouloughs or Kuluglis*—descendants of mixed marriages between Turks and Algerian women. p. 156

74 On April 30, 1827 a dispute arose between the Algerian Dey Hussein and the French Consul Deval in connection with the debt which the French Government owed and had not paid to Algerian citizens. In reply to the arrogant behaviour of Deval during the negotiations, the Dey Hussein struck him with a fly whisk. The incident provoked by the French Consul provided the pretext for the Government of Charles X to blockade Algeria for three years (1827-29). Later in 1830, the French colonisers began an armed invasion of Algeria. p. 158

75 The Algerian war of liberation against French colonisation was led by Abd el-Kader and lasted from 1832 to 1847. After the military victories, Abd el-Kader, who enjoyed the support of the wide strata of the Algerian population and had succeeded in uniting separate Arab tribes, in 1834 secured recognition of the independence of West Algeria with the exception of several sea ports. The French colonisers constantly violated the treaties concluded with Abd el-Kader and repeatedly invaded West Algeria. During 1839-44 the state of Abd el-Kader was occupied despite stubborn resistance and he had to retreat to Morocco. In 1845-47 Abd el-Kader again led the mass liberation movement in West Algeria; after it had been ruthlessly suppressed he continued guerrilla warfare against the French invaders from the Sahara oasis. In 1847 he was taken prisoner. But even after this, anti-colonial uprisings in West and East Algeria did not discontinue. p. 160

76 *Marabouts*—Mohammedan hermits, who took an active part in the war of liberation which the peoples of North Africa waged against European invaders. p. 161

77 *Bureaux arabes*—departments for affairs of the native population under the French administration of Algeria. They were established in each occupied region and were vested with dictatorial powers. p. 161

78 The reference is to the East India Company Charter approved by British Parliament in 1853, which restricted the monopoly rights of the Company. The Company Directors were deprived of the right to appoint officials in India; their number was reduced from 24 to 18. The President of the Board of Control was put on a par with the Secretary of State for India. The shareholders, however, were guaranteed a fixed dividend from the Indian taxes. p. 169

79 *The hero of Satory*—Louis Bonaparte (Napoleon III).

In autumn 1850, on the Satory parade-ground near Versailles there was a military parade which Louis Bonaparte tried to convert into a Bonapartist demonstration. p. 203

80 The reference is to unequal treaty of Tientsin which concluded the second Opium War of 1856-58. It was imposed by Britain and her ally, France, on China in June 1858. It was also signed by the

Russian Plenipotentiary. The treaty opened for foreign trade the Chinese ports on the Yangtze, in Manchuria, on the islands of Taiwan and Hainan, and also the port of Tientsin. Under this treaty diplomatic representatives of the foreign powers were to be allowed to reside in Peking; foreigners were to be permitted to travel freely throughout the country and to sail the inland waters; it also guaranteed protection to missionaries. A similar treaty was signed between the United States and China. p. 214

81 See Note 50. p. 222

82 In the 1850's the Ionian Islands, which were under British protectorate since 1815, were the scene of an increased national movement for union with Greece. In November 1858 Gladstone was sent to the islands on an extraordinary mission. Though the Legislative Assembly of Corfu (the chief Ionian island) unanimously declared for the union with Greece, the British Government managed to drag out the solution of the question for a number of years. It was only in 1864 that the Ionian Islands were turned over to Greece. p. 227

83 *The treaty of Vienna* was approved by the Vienna Congress, a congress of European monarchs and diplomats held from September 1814 to June 1815. p. 228

84 In 1798-99, the Russian squadron, under the command of Admiral Ushakov, liberated the Ionian Islands from the French. The islands received a Constitution which granted them self-government. In 1807, by the Tilsit Treaty, the islands were again surrendered to France and Napoleon I practically abolished the Constitution. In 1815, by decision of the Vienna Congress, the islands were transferred to Britain which established a protectorate over them and introduced a new Constitution endowing the British representative on the islands, the Lord High Commissioner, with unlimited powers. p. 230

85 *Printing-House Square*—a square in London where the main editorial office of *The Times* was situated. p. 231

86 The reference is to a war waged by England and France against China in 1859-60. It ended with the victory of the interventionists and the signing of a peace treaty under which the Chinese Government was obliged to pay a big indemnity to the victors, to open Tientsin to foreign merchants and to allow the exportation of coolies from China. p. 232

87 For the *treaty of Tientsin* see Note 80. p. 232

88 *Peelite colleagues—Peelites*—moderate Tories who supported the policy of collaborating with the Liberal bourgeoisie pursued by Robert Peel. p. 235

89 The reference is to the Civil War of 1861-65 between the northern states, which came out for the abolition of Negro slavery, and the slave-owners, the planters of the southern states of North America. As Marx put it, this was a struggle of "two social systems—the system of slavery and the system of free labour." The war ended

with the victory of the northern states and the abolition of slavery in North America. p. 250

90 Ireland, brought to utter impoverishment and ruin through British landlord rule, was struck by a famine following the potato disease of 1845-46. Over a million Irishmen died of hunger, and the cholera epidemic of 1849. In the ensuing years, several million Irishmen emigrated from the country, mainly to America. In an article in 1847, F. Engels described the position of Ireland as follows:

"...Famished Ireland is writhing in terrible convulsions. The workhouses are overpacked with beggars, the ruined proprietors refuse to pay the poor tax and crowds of starved people run into the thousands, plundering the barns and cattle-yards of the farmers and even of the Catholic priests whom they recently regarded but with reverence.

"It appears that this winter the Irish will not agree to die of starvation as submissively as last winter. Irish immigration to England is assuming increasingly alarming proportions from day to day. It has been calculated that at an average 50,000 Irishmen arrive in England annually; this year, however, there have been more than 220,000. In September, 345 Irishmen arrived there daily, in October, 511 arrive each day." p. 251

91 *Fenians*—members of an Irish revolutionary organisation which sought to liberate Ireland from British rule and form a republic in the country. In 1867, the Fenians organised a revolt which was suppressed by the British troops. Their leaders were thrown into prison. p. 253

92 *King Bomba*—nickname of Ferdinand II. p. 256

93 In 1869 a number of Irish deputies in British Parliament submitted a plea to Prime Minister Gladstone for granting an amnesty to the arrested Fenians. However, a condition for the amnesty to be granted was the prisoners' renunciation of their political convictions, which was tantamount to declining the amnesty. Soon after a movement for amnesty initiated by Karl Marx was taken up and headed by the First International and became very widespread. Marx tirelessly exposed the chauvinist stand of the trade union leaders and in November 1869 the General Council of the First International, at Karl Marx's insistence, adopted a special resolution which denounced Gladstone's policy towards the Irish prisoners. In January 1871, under pressure from the people, the British Government granted amnesty to the majority of imprisoned Fenians. p. 258

94 In 1800, British Parliament approved the Union Act under which Ireland was forcibly incorporated in Britain and the Irish Parliament was dissolved. The Union was made effective as of January 1, 1801. p. 262

95 In May 1882, in Phoenix Park, Dublin, Irish revolutionary terrorists assassinated the State Secretary for Ireland, Cavendish, and his assistant, Burke. p. 264

96 *The Brussels Congress* devoted to questions of Free Trade took place

at the end of 1847. Engels characterised the Congress as follows: "It was a strategic move in the Free Trade campaign then carried on by the English manufacturers. Victorious at home, by the repeal of the Corn Laws in 1846, they now invaded the Continent in order to demand, in return for the free admission of continental corn into England, the free admission of English manufactured goods to the continental markets."

Marx was supposed to speak at the Congress, but did not. He delivered his speech on Free Trade at a meeting of the Brussels Democratic Association on January 9, 1848. p. 268

97 *Malthusians*—adherents of the reactionary teaching of Thomas Robert Malthus (1766-1834), the well-known English economist. In his book *Essay on the Principle of Population*, he alleged that the growth of population outstrips, and will always outstrip, the growth in the quantity of means of consumption and that due to this "absolute law of population", the masses are inevitably doomed to poverty and starvation. Proceeding from this "law" invented by Malthus, his supporters asserted that wars, epidemics and natural calamities exert a "beneficial" influence on society since they reduce the population.

Karl Marx subjected to scathing criticism this reactionary teaching and showed that there is no "absolute law of population", that each socio-economic system has its inherent law of population, that mass poverty and hardships are products of the capitalist mode of production under which a tiny handful of exploiters appropriate the surplus labour of millions. He showed that the transition to communism will create such a high level of labour productivity and such an abundance of means of consumption as will make it possible for every man to fully satisfy his requirements. p. 281

98 The title of F. Engels's article is "Switzerland. Political Position of this Republic."

Tribune—the *New-York Daily Tribune.*

Marx refers to his article "The British Rule in India." p. 313

99 *Clearances or clearing of estates,* the forcible eviction of peasants from the land cultivated by them and their forefathers from time immemorial, the destruction of peasants' houses and villages by the English landlords, the owners of the land, with a view to turning it into fields and pastures. p. 317

100 In 1865 the Negro labourers and small peasants of Jamaica rose in revolt against the British planters who severely exploited them. British troops put down the revolt and committed dreadful atrocities against the Negro population. p. 322

101 *Federal soldiers*—soldiers of the northern states in the American Civil War of 1861-65. p. 322

102 The *Central Council* (later the General Council)—the leading body of the International Working Men's Association, the First International. p. 326

103 The *English* (Protestant) *Church* was an established church in Ireland

whose population was largely Catholic. The latter paid taxes to the English Church. p. 327

104 *Pale*—pointed piece of wood for fence; (Hist.) the (English) Pale, part of Ireland under English rule in the second half of the 12th century; it served as a bridge-head for British expeditions into the heart of the island and for colonising all of Ireland in the 15th century. p. 329

105 During the 17th-century English bourgeois revolution a rebellion broke out in Ireland which led to an almost complete severance of a large part of the island from England. The rebellion was suppressed in 1649-52 with unusual brutality, and ended in a mass expropriation of the land in favour of new English landlords. This strengthened the landlord-bourgeois elements in England and prepared the ground for the restoration of the monarchy in 1660. p. 331

106 *United Irishmen*—a secret revolutionary organisation that came into existence under the influence of the French Revolution and aimed at forming an independent Irish Republic. The *United Irishmen* were the organisers of the Irish uprising in 1798. p. 333

NAME INDEX

E

F

G

H

N

T

Y